How Far T[...]

Remembering the Georgia Battalion in Texas

Judith Austin Mills

Plain View Press
P.O. 42255
Austin, TX 78704

plainviewpress.net
pk@plainviewpress.net
512-441-2452

ISBN: 978-1-935514-96-1
Library of Congress Control Number: 2011934858

Cover art: *Misty Morning in Goliad State Park* by Karen Boudreaux
        Maps of Texas and Southern Region by Karen Boudreaux
Cover design by Pam Knight

Note: This book is a work of fiction. While people and events connected to the Texas Revolution were researched for reasonable accuracy, all characters are fleshed out according to the author's imagination. For authenticity, many names and dates included are those about which historians mostly agree. The author claims no special knowledge of any nineteenth-century individual's heart or everyday actions.

Acknowledgments

During research for this work of historical fiction, I developed a deep appreciation for the hours people across the country spend making history and original documents available to everyone through the internet. To all those in the Texas State Historical Association who have a part in keeping Texas History Online complete and accurate—thank you. Others involved in The Galileo Project deserve my gratitude, especially Georgia archivists responsible for putting pages of Macon's nineteenth century newspapers online.

Where characters read aloud from an 1835 article in the *True American* of New Orleans, brief excerpts are taken verbatim from their reprinted form in Macon's newspaper. Well-known last words from William B. Travis' final pleas at the Alamo are incorporated into characters' reading and dialogue as well. Also, a much quoted survivor's recollection of the Goliad massacre is woven into my telling of that Palm Sunday morning—"They're going to shoot us, boys. Let us die like men." The list of sources following the novel's text is my attempt to credit authors whose original research of Texas Revolution facts fueled my imagination and informed my telling of this story.

Lyrics about Lord Franklin's expedition are from a song not written until 1846, a date fairly close to their second use in the novel. An earlier allusion to "the fate of Franklin" is one of the few instances where time or any other fact was nudged for dramatic effect.

In the May 5, 1836 issue of the *Macon Georgia Telegraph*, the poem "Texas and Liberty" appeared on the front page. This issue came out exactly one week after the *Columbus Herald's* headline "Massacre of the Georgia Battalion." This poem, written by a Thomas Holly Shivers, M.D. first appeared in the *Augusta Sentinel*.

The last line of the first stanza became my working title, though I eventually used it instead to begin the novel's third and final section. During the months that I wrote, the line comforted me. I cannot picture the grieving families of Macon and other stricken towns without imagining that some people must have read and spoken the poetry line as one would say a prayer—

"The dove shall fly to thee."

In finishing this novel, I am so very thankful to both my parents for their keen interest in history and their perfect love of family. The members of Shoal Creek Writers will always have my gratitude for their friendship and encouragement. And I cannot thank my husband enough for the summer he spent reading the first version of my manuscript, and for the important changes he suggested.

Many thanks to my publisher Plain View Press, and the late Susan Bright in particular, for staying independent and open to unusual projects. I am certainly grateful to Pam Knight of this press for her willingness to carry the torch "onward."

To my grandfather Joseph Huddleston Hunt of Georgia
for remembering that "Papa had an uncle"
who went to Texas in the fall of 1835

and in memory of all those
who never came home from the revolution there,
especially our great-uncle First Sergeant Francis M. Hunt

James Warren Hunt ("Papa," born 1863 in rural Georgia) was my great-grandfather. His uncle—Francis M. Hunt—left hometown Macon in the fall of 1835 to help Texans fight for their liberty..

Contents

Acknowledgments 3

Gone to Texas 11

Map of Southern U.S. Region, 1835 12
Chapter 1 First Alarm 13
Chapter 2 In the Current 23
Chapter 3 Borders Without, Borders Within 33
Chapter 4 Drumbeats on the March 47
Chapter 5 Drumbeats from the Shore 59

Falling Stars 75

Map of Texas, 1836 76
Chapter 6 By Sea and Soggy Land 77
Chapter 7 Over Yonder 89
Chapter 8 There Art Thou Happy 105
Chapter 9 Give Us This Day 115
Chapter 10 Home, Over One's Shoulder 121
Chapter 11 For Love of Finnissee 139
Chapter 12 Within the Whirlwind 159
Chapter 13 A Banner for Believing 173
Chapter 14 Fair Are the Meadows 183
Chapter 15 Downpour 199

The Dove Shall Fly to Thee 217

Chapter 16 Sweet Pine Remembered 219
Chapter 17 Moving Heaven and Earth 241
Chapter 18 No Tongue Can Tell 259
Chapter 19 Belle-Mère 277

Afterword 291
Sources 293
About the Author 295

Truth in the Telling

American colonists moved into the northern territory of Mexico when its early 19th century laws offered self-governance as well as land. But when Santa Anna rose to power, the hospitality in Texas ended. In 1835 at a candlelight meeting in Macon, Georgia, officers called on patriotic sons to join Texan settlers in their fight against oppression.

Among the volunteers who traveled one thousand miles under the banner "Liberty or Death" was my grandfather's great-uncle. This is the story of the unsung Georgia Battalion, whose destiny led to a gray fortress in Goliad, Texas.

This is also a portrait of singular women, determined to cross borders and mindful of the banner's other claim—

"Where freedom abides, there is my home."

Gone to Texas

Map of Southern U.S. Region, 1835

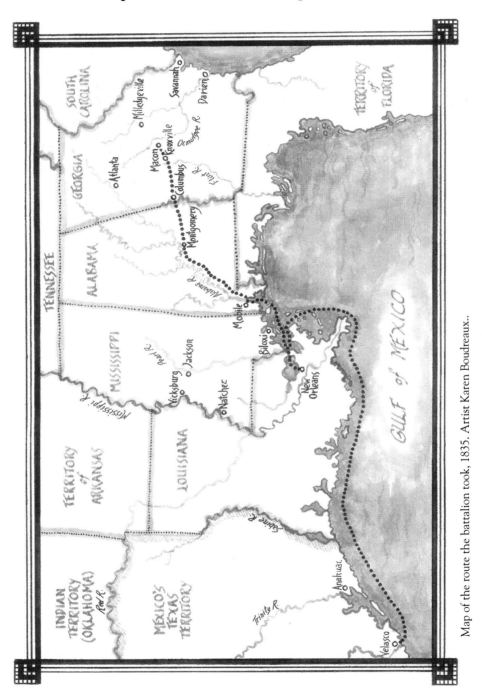

Map of the route the battalion took, 1835. Artist Karen Boudreaux..

Chapter 1   First Alarm

Awatery darkness in the kitchen let the white basin drift into view like an apparition. Adeline watched from the other room in the house. She was studying one spot, where just last year a two burner stove from Boston had been wedged in next to the rock hearth. She sensed Yarico's morning moves—barefoot steps to check the copper pail of water, fingers lifting the tricky latch on the firebox, one hand going into an apron pocket for the match tin. In the seconds it took Yarico to set a tiny blaze down in the kindling, her grave profile made the girl shudder. Then the metal door scraped as it was shut and the house plunged again into seas of gray.

Padding toward the threshold, Adeline felt the floor boards through a hole that had finally worn in one stocking. She knew not to wake her aunt, so she whispered into the kitchen toward Yarico's blankets.

"Is there gonna be shooting?"

"What kind of talk—"

"All those soldiers and wagons—what you and Aunt Maggie were talking about last night."

"Past time you should have been asleep."

"Did they quit shooting over in *Ana-wack?*"

"Child, you surely worry where there's no need." The woman reached out for Adeline and drew her down where she could put an arm around her. "That was back last June and all the way into Mexico. No such trouble any closer to us. I don't know why Miss Maggie takes news from Texas so hard."

"One of those men marching off to Milledgeville yesterday—when I waved a handkerchief at him—"

"When will you quit runnin' off to watch them pass—"

"That soldier was laughing—he said 'Pretty as a petticoat, but we don't heed no white flag afore we fire!'"

"His grammar wasn't much." Yarico thought before she went on. "Men folk forget some kindness on the march, I expect," she said. "Some, though—you need to stay clear of. Some never had the type mama could teach them what kindness is in the first place."

It had been five years since the child's mother was lost to lingering fevers, but there was more said just lately about what sort of individual

Delphine Harper had been. Adeline was close to an age now where talk among women included her.

When louder snoring came from the main room, the girl sprang up. She wanted to get her boots laced before her aunt perceived any need for mending. It was no pleasure nursing a blister on trips back and forth to the well, but her sunrise run up Sweet Pine Hill was ritual. Mixed in with poplars and oaks, a small clump of evergreens grew there. The scent drew her as much as the view.

Her aunt and Yarico had let her name the gradual incline that stretched behind their square, lapboard house, and the three of them sometimes forgot that no one else in the town of Macon, Georgia would have known which hill they spoke of.

"You'd best take your cloak," a soft voice from the kitchen reminded her. "We got our first cold snap takin' us by surprise."

"Shh—you'll wake the whole house."

Yarico shook her head about the noise the girl was making in the adjoining room. No one except her and Maggie and this headstrong twelve-year-old lived for a quarter mile in any direction. She knew thudding boots would wake the aunt. But who in any civilized land had the heart to correct an orphaned child about orders from grownups? Then Yarico laughed quietly and hugged her own arms to warm up. She also knew that no matter the season or year, 1835 or five autumns hence, no dark skinned person would be setting young Miss Harper straight about orders! When the back door off the bedroom opened and slammed shut, Yarico shook her head again.

Aunt Maggie had heard leather heels thump the wooden floor. She was brought out of deep sleep after a long night of tossing on her mattress. She needed to slide her travel satchel out from underneath the chiffarobe. But she couldn't start packing until she heard the kitchen door open and close, too. Before going out to the garden, Yarico would likely bring her a cup of sweetened coffee. Maggie considered what sewing implements and clothing to stuff into the satchel—only what she could carry. Gripped by dread, she thought her stomach might rebel against anything but a sip of water.

Adeline was already stepping blindly through vegetable rows behind the house, where bean clumps overtook furrows and squash tendrils sprawled. Once past the tilled patches, she broke into a trot along the sandy path. A town person might have speculated that she was part

Creek, but there was too much grief between settlers and Indians for any such jest.

When the girl made it to an edge of pines, she broke into an easy run, holding her layers of skirt and underskirt just to the tops of her boots. As wonderful as the pines smelled in humid springs and summers, when the air turned cool they were dizzying. She was careful not to dash like a fool in the half-light, and she tutored herself about reckless pride as her boots pounded. Breathless, Adeline arrived at her hilltop spot in time. An orange sliver cut through blackness on the rise beyond the Gideon plantation. Glorious cold snap!

The Harper lot backed up against their neighbor's farthest acreage, planted this season in tobacco. Broad, veined leaves broke the monotony of cotton from the rise where she stood. Sunlight spilled over the horizon, and the foliage turned from dark copper to gold. Something about these leaves was worth studying. Aunt Maggie, recalling her years in Kentucky, said the north never would be beaten for getting the finicky crop to grow full at the right time, between bugs and frost.

Recently, a wagon would roll along the edge of the swelling field and come to a stop wherever a man on horseback pointed. This morning Adeline could hear the creaking before she made out wheels. The rhythmic creak grew loud and stopped.

Figures the same shade as their gray clothing climbed down from the wagon to the soft ground. Today they were not shouldering the familiar open bags used for picking cotton. Pouches, folded like slings, hung from several men who walked down the rows behind the overseer. He had hitched his horse loosely to the wagon brake.

As Adeline hopped in place to keep warm, she saw it was not the usual, stockier man, but another one, even younger, wearing a broad hat. Holding up one specimen and then another to the brightening sky, he spoke with a small group of workers looking on.

Two women who had stayed briefly in the wagon were helping each other out when the scene convulsed in panic. Before one was even halfway to the ground, the woman with a squirming baby wrapped in her shawl tried to climb down without further assistance. When she began to lose her balance, she let one leg take the worst of the scrape. She dangled from the top board, with the child slipping from its cloth cradle and her outstretched arms onto the shadowy dirt.

"Help!" shouted Adeline. "The baby!" The women also cried out, and men twenty paces down a tobacco row came running, first to secure the victim, whose leg seemed to be caught in a wagon lashing. The infant crawled several feet away from the commotion, before it began to wail.

Field workers were tending the mother's leg and foot, when the slender overseer went over and did something that struck Adeline into silent breathing. He picked up the baby and held it to his side. The small crowd around the woman grew quieter in their dark clothing. In the still, cool morning, the only sounds were the whimpering of the baby and the voice of the young man in charge.

"Don't you go fallin' on your head, Ishmael." He gave a little jiggle, and sobs from the tiny boy subsided. "Were you trying to race your mama to a hard day's work? I don't know a soul in Georgia so eager to start up a morning of toil."

Then the ⎽ man did one more startling thing.

"He's all right!" he called up to Adeline. "You can come on down and see for yourself!"

She could only wave and run away. But she heard soft, good-natured laughing as she fled back down the hill as far as a narrow side path, where she ducked in and stole along the thicket trail back up to the ledge. Hidden there, she looked down on the Gideon property in the growing light.

The young overseer was handing the baby back to the recovered mother, just as another man on horseback came trotting along the crop's perimeter. He sat especially upright in his saddle, and even though he was heavier than the one already out among the workers, he took on a lean look. He seemed to Adeline, disinclined to coddle babies.

"Francis Marion!" She could hear his crisp voice as his horse drew alongside the wagon. "I finished with the signatures faster than we thought." The first man, mounting up again and heading in the opposite direction, seemed to know what the stern rider meant.

"I see the duty gave you a flair for using *my* full name, as well." A likeness in their voices and fair hair suggested they were brothers. The two let their horses amble to just down the rise from Adeline. "Tobacco's looking fine, Thomas," the slender one went on. "That's what we were thinking from these first three rows—"

"*We?*"

"You know Samuel— he grew up in Virginia, so he's seen a lot of—"

"So you don't mean...you were consulting the baby."

"Not about tobacco, at least. I was asking little Ishmael if he thought it was going to be a beautiful fall day." Adeline couldn't tell whether the two were about to laugh or break into a fistfight.

"You ought to ride on back and pen a dandy poem about those sentiments."

"If I need chastising," the younger man said mildly, "I'm sure Papa will find himself up to the task—Thomas Gideon, sir." He handed his brother the broad rimmed hat.

"The account sheets are out, so he can use you."

"Fields are all yours." Francis was already leaning forward in his saddle and moving away from the man now in command. The quiet gray figures clumped together, awaiting an order.

"Thanks for bringing them out," Thomas thought to say.

"See you at dinner!"

How men either got along or argued was a mystery to Adeline, who'd grown up only around women. She was still trying to sort out what she had heard.

The unsettling exchange made her determined to find some distraction she could take back to Yarico. October was thought to be her birthday month, but the woman had no certificate to prove her age. Family stories had passed down. When Adeline's own mother was just learning to read, the barely weaned Yarico came to her Savannah home as part of a Pagnol family inheritance. In these circumstances, adults merely guessed at the slave child's age, but the two girls grew inseparable. Twenty-five years later, even Yarico said it was providence that handed Adeline into her care. No one in this odd Macon family missed the company of Pagnol relatives or Harpers still living in Savannah.

The light was good enough now for the girl to see what lay around her feet just under the soft pine-needle mat. It didn't take long to find the sharp point of an arrowhead in the ancient lookout, but there was something else in the dirt—a longer chiseled rock with a tiny hole in one end. A rock needle would make Yarico stop in her work to wonder at the sewing instrument. Only one person could do more magic with stitching than Maggie or Adeline herself.

When the girl raced down the hill, her confidante was already picking sage for cornbread dressing. Delphine had always insisted on having an herb garden off the back porch. The daughter now nurtured memories of her mother in the sunny patch, speaking French on the sly with Yarico.

"*Belle-Mère!*" Adeline couldn't keep from calling out. "Look!"

"Hush!" She was smiling. "What *chérie* cautioned me not thirty minutes ago about waking the house? Another vegetable scraper?"

"It's a needle! For their moccasins or putting tent flaps together—"

"Well, look at that—"

"I could try some stitches with twine, soon as I get my stocking darned."

"Don't go planning your leisure on the porch, Miss Adeline." She stopped because she didn't know how to put what she needed to say, and the child's hazel eyes were fixed on her before she could find the words. "Your aunt…seems to be not quite herself this morning."

"Aunt Maggie?"

"Don't you worry. Her forehead's as cool as a water jar. She just ate something yesterday that didn't quite agree, I expect. I wasn't so sure those field peas got rinsed like they should. Then, too much talk last night— "

"She hasn't got a fever?" Yarico couldn't bear to see fear working its power.

"You can go touch her, after she sits up."

"No chills?"

"Cool like a water jug…not a pond in January, she's just—"

"What?" Now Yarico appeared gripped by sudden emotion. "A fear's taken hold, hasn't it, if it's fever—"

"No, it's not about that—" Adeline spun in the direction where the woman nodded soberly. A single horse was pulling an open cart down the path that led to their house. The gangly fellow in the seat let his horse trot at will.

"You go on in the house and tell Aunt Maggie there's a person coming. Don't make her get up. Just tell her. Get ready to go to the door."

Adeline put the chiseled rocks in her dress pocket and ran. Maggie was already sitting up on her mattress and putting hairpins in a wild strand of gray. She had heard wheels rolling fast and thought her heart might give out. But her eyesight was keen and when she saw it was no stranger coming, she had found time to shove the travel bag out of sight and flee back to her bed.

"Slide your trundle on under here, Addy."

"I can tell him you're feeling poorly."

"I can go ahead and—" Her aunt fell back and made a soft moan.

"It's Mr. Humphries again, looks like. I can go talk to him."

Yarico was busy dragging her blankets out from the kitchen. As a habit, the woman kept her bedding on the open back porch, made more private by the thick mesh of scuppernong vines that ran up a trellis and onto the roof. The chilly night had brought her inside, but the gentleman might come on in, too, and she saw no need to offer any insight as to how the Harpers made themselves a family.

Mr. Humprhies, Macon's original pharmacist, owned the drug emporium on First Street. He did a brisk business even though three more shops opened in the last few years. As a bachelor, he had lived comfortably in the room over his store, but since last Christmas he was married. Now, he and his wife wanted garden space, something close enough to town that he could come home for a noon meal with his wife and the baby they expected soon. A busy carpenter was already sketching plans to double the size of the Harper house.

The druggist had been out twice since late spring, when his wife first determined her condition, and he'd hinted to Adeline's aunt at a purchase offer. He suggested the women share a location in town with the widow Bedeford, who struggled handling her house but was reluctant to take in roomers she didn't know. With funds available, Adeline could start her formal schooling at the academy. So far, all Mr. Humphries' appeals brought no more than a shrug from the Sweet Pine women.

He stopped his small rig, and just as he was tethering the mare to a sturdy mulberry, the Harper girl came out back and around the side.

"Miss Adeline, how are you this morning?"

"Waking up. You, sir?"

"Fixin' to be too busy to budge from the store, else I wouldn't be out here before you had a chance to even start your day." He was all right, in Adeline's opinion, but his elbows bobbed when he talked to her. She thought he might be too nervous to be someone's papa.

"Heard there's a new drug store going in on Cherry Street."

"That's right, that's the truth. I don't dare stay away long." He smoothed his narrow tie. "Your Aunt Margaret finish her coffee yet? Is she in a mind for chat?"

"Not until she feels better."

"Ailing?" The girl couldn't help tugging at one of her dark braids.

"Something she ate, Yarico says...."

"Well, I know it's nothing more than that, but I'm sorry to hear it. I was wantin' to speak in clear numbers about your property here."

"She doesn't like town the way I do," Adeline warned. "Besides, I do take regular to my morning runs up the hill."

"Don't know how you ladies manage. Say," Mr. Humphries was moving up closer. "Can I talk to your help? Yarico, is it? Is she around back or in the house lookin' after your aunt?" He took off his hat and examined its rim.

Yarico was in the house by one of the front windows, where both she and Adeline's aunt could hear the conversation.

"Go on out," Maggie said. "He's tame as a lap dog, even if he is odd. Can't say I have a powerful inclination to sell my sister's house, but just go on out and let him speak his mind."

Yarico dreaded conversation with anyone but her people, men especially, and she came out the front door stiffly when the girl spoke to her again from the steps.

"Mr. Humphries wishes to converse."

"Yessir?" She stepped down to his level, but she knew better than to lift her gaze.

"I wonder could you ask Miss Margaret to let Adeline come in to town with me. I'll send her back with my clerk and some tonic for that poor stomach. I know the child's aunt likes to ride in herself early on a Thursday for the paper, sewing notions, and what not. But young Miss Harper is growin' up before our eyes. I'll bet you all could send her with a list. Then the weekly news and my elixir would work wonders."

Adeline scurried back up the steps. She was trying to temper her enthusiasm for a ride into town with her worries over Maggie's illness. She disappeared into the house, and Yarico followed calmly as if she hadn't just been stranded with a town gentleman.

"I'll go see what Miss Margaret says."

"Tell her it'll be best to stock up!" The man kept on talking from the sandy clearing in front. "There's a swarm of folks headed to Texas before the cold sets in, and soldiers probably blazing off that way too. Seen such as this when I was a boy no older than your Adeline—when the British come at us again near twenty-five years ago! Miss Margaret can read about it all. Those goin' might clean Macon out of thread and every other blessed thing if you don't get your list filled!"

20

Yarico and Maggie agreed without much talking that they could both be down with poor digestion for days if they didn't let the animated girl go on to town. The list they made was long, and Mr. Humphries was pacing nervously around his cart by the time Adeline came out the door. She wore a fresh apron over her dress, a cloak, and a bonnet neatly tied. The pharmacist let her handle the reins as far down the grassy lane as the main road.

"You know he's just putting you in position to thank him," Yarico said watching the mare trot away. "I don't doubt he'll name a good price, but my meaning is— he won't let up about your selling. He aims to press you." Only bad premonition made her talk so much.

"I know." The plump woman sitting up in bed made an effort to steady her cup of coffee, but the saucer wouldn't hold still. "I also know it wasn't any garden dirt that pained my stomach this morning."

Yarico was trying to remember when the two adults had been in the house for a long stretch without Adeline. On some occasion when the girl was playing up on the hill, she thought. But, Yarico herself was almost always out working in the garden or in the kitchen, and the three of them sewed together in the afternoons or by lamplight. She didn't understand the look on Miss Maggie's face, and she didn't like not being able to guess what white folks were about to say.

"About your stomach?"

"About a letter I got in the post last Thursday when I went in. It was from Savannah, and I could see it was from Addy's great-uncle, his writing and seal."

"Him?" Yarico was sorry she too had indulged in hot coffee for breakfast. She swallowed, and there was a sour taste. "Five years his nephew's wife is gone..."

"I couldn't muster courage to read it until last night..."

"What—he want the house now? Never before paid one note to Delphine's side of the family—what's he want now— Adeline?" She couldn't ask if the letter might be about use of the family slave.

"Town's bursting at the seams. There's money even in little houses these days—"

"Don't you give him—" Yarico was afraid she might say something dangerous, and she let her thinking turn. "Maybe you could sell, after all—you could—take Mr. Humphries' nice offer. You got rights to the place, and then Mr. Harper won't come poking around—"

"Yarico."

"Miss Maggie, I'm sorry. I know you can figure out what your little sister would want, I just—"

"Listen Yarico—"

"I didn't mean to sound—"

"Yarico, no—it's something else." The older woman swung her legs around and settled her feet on the floor. She needed to steady the saucer on her knees to keep the cup from shaking. "Yarico, it's just…I am not—not really Adeline's aunt." A breeze rattled the scuppernongs and swept a chill through the house. "I'm sick I didn't tell our Addy or you sooner. It was never meant for anything except to help—poor Delphine in her last days and me just passing by one day—nearly on the run, and on a search for seamstress tasks." She saw that Yarico was hugging herself, and wore a lonely look as if the feeling would never subside. Maggie wanted to say the rest, while she had some control over her own trembling. "So I'm thinking now… I'd best not be too sick to pack up from Macon, before Mr. Harper takes a steamboat out here and pays us a call. I possess no rights at all, Yarico dear. That's what I'm trying to tell you."

Chapter 2   In the Current

Macon weather in the last two weeks had been bad for picking cotton. White tufts still in the field went limp and dripping in intermittent showers. The bottom of a bag dragged by even the most experienced picker would have grown too heavy too fast, would have mashed the cotton balls into a moldering mat.

"Your papa is more than smart," the dealer set up at Pioneer Steamboat Line said. Slow work at the gin had nudged him toward the wharf, and he was glad for two wagonloads of hulls that Thursday afternoon. The young man he addressed was stepping down to look over the mounds.

"We wouldn't bother to ship it any farther than half way to Darien, but we've got some kin there figuring to add it to winter feed for his milk cows. Anyway, it's the last sweep for us—scooped it up ten days ago—had it in the barn—"

"Mr. Gideon had the big bulk picked, ginned, and down river before then!"

"He's lucky like that—"

"Smart enough to get the seed in early and get the crop in bales early, I'd say."

The stuffing and weighing of odd bags would take some time, and the dealer went to fetch his crew waiting down in the thick grass of the Ocmulgee riverbank. Francis Gideon, as a favor to his father, had brought the one wagonload into the wharf area. His rarely occupied cousin drove the other. Now there was little for either to do, except in the mind of Francis to stay out of his father's and older brother's way for the rest of the day.

"Now, Francis, answer me one question." The young man addressed was busy setting the wagon brakes, but he was smiling.

"In one word, the answer is *no*."

"Don't be tellin' me that now—I haven't even asked—"

"Are you going to ask if we can slip on board the brand new *David Crockett* and stowaway on its two-engine power to Savannah?" The question was put pleasantly, but Malacai responded with an exaggerated frown.

"If that's the way you're going to be then. Well. I have no idea why any of the merry women in my Irish family fell in with the Gideon clan—"

"We haul our cotton in early."

"You're gettin' to be as sober-sides as Thomas!"

Francis told his cousin about the curt treatment he'd received earlier in the day for "familiar deportment" out in the tobacco fields. Malacai Mulholland was kin only through an uncle's adoption, but he was sympathetic underneath any playful criticism, as Francis thought family ought to be. Now Malacai was laughing too hard to feign injured feelings.

"I wouldn't even know how to pick up a baby, Lord love me!"

"The sky was half dark. The child could have crawled over into the next furrow—"

"When that face of your brother's goes to twitching—"

The second Gideon son didn't feel comfortable making too much light about it all. His father had kept the same kind of patience he always had with both sons.

"Thomas is just a natural for giving orders—perfect fit for Papa's shoes one day, and I won't argue with that."

"Did you get a dressing down, then, for showing a woman's tenderness in front of the field labor?"

"The lesson to me is—if they see tenderness once—"

"They'll just expect it next time. Oh yes," Malacai was laughing less. "My first dad had a softhearted quarry foreman in Cork when he was a lad. But never so tender as to let the children stop shy of the twelve hour bell, bleedin' fingers or not."

Neither man cared to look farther down the wharf where occasionally small groups of plantation slaves were sold when an owner died without a will. In town, the air of free prospects was palpable, and a thousand ready-made shop articles were on display —everything from gold watches to varnished trays, from peach brandy to pianofortes, gentlemen's boots, crystal glasses, riding whips, dyed silk, and German scissors made for trimming a mustache. Life bubbled between First and Fourth Streets, Walnut and Cherry. Except for the sight of steam-powered barges, the wharf held little fascination for young men reared around cotton dealing.

"Well, having recollected fingers, I'm put in mind of new gloves. You can stay here if you want, but your father puts trust in Mr. Dougherty."

"He's fair with the scales—"

"Ah—the *fair*—those I hope my style impresses." Malacai was already walking away from the Gideon wagons. "And if a lady carries a stout purse, maybe not as fair as all that." His cousin only waved at Mr. Dougherty before the two young men took off for an end street toward the din of Macon business. "But for pity's sake, Francis, don't go reaching out for some baby. You don't want any female claiming that it's yours!"

In an hour they were coming out of Ell's Mercantile several blocks away, where Malacai found a pair of kid gloves to his liking. He turned to admire a set of seal skin trunks in the window, when a man with a full gray beard rode up, as out of breath as if he had done the trotting.

"You Mr. Gideon?"

Malacai pointed to the next storefront. Francis was looking at leather-bound books arranged on a walkway table. The man slid down and took time to throw the reins over a railing and tug at his belt.

"Mr. Gideon? Sir?"

"—Sorry," Francis said, closing a book and brushing his tan hair from his eyes. He took the man to be someone his father knew. "—drawings of Hispaniola...fantastic islands—"

"We can't waste any load on books." The bearded man took a deep breath. "Me and my wife and sons, we're off to Texas with another four families. Headed down to Mobile together—then west. It was only yesterday we decided, but they tell me at both liveries there's not a single wagon unspoke for. With the end of cotton baling for some, they said, why not go see if there's one at the wharf to be bought—"

"You want to buy my wagon?"

"Just the one, whichever you think won't break down on me."

"It's not that." Francis was trying to envision a family traveling in one of his cotton wagons. "Did you see how they're worn in the bed? One's newer than the other, but I don't see how it would give shelter—"

"They've got a cover worked out —canvas with whalebone inserts— it'll give a little shade and makes do to repel water. Will you take sixty dollars for the one you think best?" Francis was sure neither was worth that amount.

"We're mostly done with them this year—-we can order a new one before we have any use. But if my father—"

"Sixty-five then—it's all I've got to bargain with."

"You can have the newer for forty," Francis said.

"He'll surprise people that way," broke in Malacai, tipping his hat. "He's as easy as a baby to bargain with."

"I'd shake your hand, but I've got it worn raw from packing."

"I wouldn't set out on a long trek until you're good again," Francis advised.

"Can't wait. We roll out on Saturday. Anyway, I've got to get the awnings lashed to the sideboards. Will you write a bill of sale so Dougherty knows I'm no thief?"

"Try on my cousin's gloves, why don't you, while I go in and ask Mr. Ell for a sales page."

Malacai stood for a moment as if he suddenly had trouble with his ears. His dark gloves went so well, he thought, with his black felt hat and the wool coat he had just taken from a storage box that morning. But he looked at the hands of the bearded man and thought the new pair might fit. The frantic fellow scratched his gray whiskers. His eyes conveyed such gratitude for the wagon deal that Malacai couldn't help handing over his new purchase.

"They're just right," the man said, flexing the leather gloves. "How much?"

Malacai gestured that it was part of the bargain, but then thought to ask if the single horse hitched nearby was expected to pull a wagonload from Macon to Mobile.

"That horse…and another one even stronger." The first hint of doubt crept into the traveler's voice. "Have to sell the horses at the coast, but they promise you can secure your wagon on a sizable schooner. Word is, not even two horses get a wagon rolling in Texas."

"I've heard some tales."

"It's the roads, such as they call them. Even worse than here when it's rainy, if you can believe it."

"Surely I can't."

"Clay that buckles in the heat or wet. Can't nothing but oxen pull a wagon through that hell—beg pardon."

"Then why the—beg pardon—are you so fired to go?"

This question made the man laugh, and when Francis came out of the mercantile store he found his cousin and the breathless man slapping each other on the shoulder like long-time neighbors. Malacai's curls shook.

"Many thanks," the man said taking the receipt for the wagon. "I was fixin' to tell your friend here. About the land they keep near giving away in Texas. Perfect as a painting once you get off the trails. Not by the acre but the league if you can put some to livestock."

"You're not worried about the ruckus—with Mexico on and off its taste for newcomers?"

"We reckon to get only as far as Harrisburg for the winter. Right off the coast. All the trouble's way over west. And by spring—reports say—any overstepping patrols from Matamoros will be marched right back across the Rio Grande."

"Don't know who'd want to match threats with America's most stubborn," Francis added thoughtfully.

"Plenty Mexican settlers don't want under Santa Anna's thumb either, not by a long shot!"

There was a final handshake on the deal, and the two cousins watched the man pull himself back into the saddle and trot off toward the Ocmulgee wharves. The whirlwind exchange left them feeling aimless and a little envious. While Malacai fended off the appearance of purpose, he would have welcomed a plan, one that would result in land, or land scrip that he could trade for a livelier enterprise—gentleman's clothing or interest in a steamboat—not a poor ambition for a twenty-year-old.

Francis Marion Gideon ambled over to the new books again, but he couldn't regain interest in drawings of faraway islands. Over the last years, he had felt a restlessness building, maybe since his thirteenth birthday when people began to ask what work he would take up in manhood. He was good with numbers, and a sharp accountant in the family was an advantage for any cotton grower. His well-known gift was why Mr. Dougherty had only waved back as the two young men headed to town. Dougherty was honest, but none that weren't would have tried to cheat young Gideon. The boy—grown man now— could judge the weight of any wagonload by eyesight. He was always apprised of the latest fair price, and he could even explain how changes in the textile factories of England influenced those latest figures.

No one would have doubted the young man fit to merge his talents with his older brother's in the cotton business.

But, other dreams and other self-doubts pestered him. His name, Francis Marion, bothered him whenever another elderly hero of 1776 was laid to rest at the capital nearby in Milledgeville. Just three Octobers ago, James Gideon had taken time to ride with both sons for such an occasion, to witness services for Captain John Clarke. The local hero's first brave act had been to join up against the Tories at age fourteen. Tributes paid him by the throng of Milledgeville citizens brimmed with superlatives. Certain words struck Francis especially—"the ardent courage which prompted him to encounter the dangers of battle..." Also affecting Francis were the words addressed to him in particular, as one stranger and then another in the assembly became acquainted.

"We know you're proud to be christened Francis Marion," people had said.

"Hope you know what all the Swamp Fox did for the Revolution!"

"Bless him you're named after and all the brave souls!"

Francis thought himself as proud an American patriot as could be found in 1835. But as his brother Thomas had joked earlier in the day, the younger man's powerful beliefs about nature or liberty were more likely to be to put to a page than to any physical contest. He liked to see numbers on a clean piece of paper, but he liked even better the balance of resonant words. Luckily, his parents were not the kind to insist on paths contrary to a child's nature. Whenever his name came up, there was kindly head shaking. An innocent error had been made on the day of his baptism. Maybe the first son could have handled life as a Swamp Fox namesake, but Homer or Wordsworth would have been more fitting for the second boy.

"We'd better get a paper before they're sold off," Francis said. Malacai had gone back in to Ell's and come out empty handed.

"Well thank you kindly, cousin. They have to order me another pair. And they don't get a new shipment until the first of November. I hope you're happy."

"I'll buy you a newspaper, if any are left. More people in town than usual— the *Telegraph* can sell its entire run on a day like this."

"Since we're down to one wagon, you can drive, too. I'll read to you on the way home."

From another direction, just off Poplar Street, Mr. Humphries' clerk Will was losing enthusiasm for the task of taking Adeline Harper from shop to shop. She had dispensed with half the afternoon, he felt, at Bartlett's Dry Goods selecting cloth, thread and a packet of needles. And that was after spending a large part of the morning examining ready-made calico dresses at two different locations. Before that he'd had to stand by the drug store register at opening hours while Mr. Humphries packed up a nice box for the girl's aunt— herbal teas, digestion tonic, headache powders, lemon syrup, as well as cocoa and licorice. He didn't like parading around with a talkative twelve-year-old, though he wasn't too put out by the prospect of driving the quick rolling cart out to the Harper house and back.

If he could only hasten her along in the direction of Mulberry, they could pick up a newspaper and he would get to the end of the work day. Will was struggling to carry two boxes from the grocer as well as a quarter bolt of cloth covered with stiff paper. He wished they'd walked back to the drug store and driven Mr. Humphries' rig to the printing office, but a shouting boy made him hasten his footsteps.

"*Georgia Telegraph!* Last *Telegraphs* going fast!"

"C'mon, young lady—" In a town the size of Macon, most young men had some sense about patience with a girl who might turn out comely.

"I'll be needing that new surgeon if my blister gets any worse."

"Just another block, Miss Adeline."

"Call to him, why don't you—"

"Paper! I'll take two!" Will set down the packages and ran.

When he returned with the newspapers, the girl was picking at her boot laces as if she next intended to go barefoot. The clerk didn't know but what she'd insist on a piggy back ride if the hurt was worse without shoe leather. A rough bench was nearby in front of a tin-ware shop, so he positioned her there with the boxes and told her to wait.

Adeline wasn't sorry to shake loose of his company either. At the moment it suited her to sit on Second Street and imagine living in the pale house right across the way, where Mrs. Bedeford's full length porch extended to brick steps. Yellow flowers bunched at the railings. The girl had not forgotten her aunt's illness, so she was relieved about the *Telegraph* purchase. Aunt Maggie would read nearly every word aloud and cure the doldrums at least. Then Adeline could read again by candlelight while Yarico pinned a length of dark blue calico.

Suddenly, the girl leaned forward and looked down the street to see whose voices were intruding. A man wearing a stylish black hat was speaking to the newspaper boy and then peering up the lane in her direction. After the boy pointed and shrugged, the man began hastening along the sandy thoroughfare toward the tin-ware shop where Adeline sat. She had heard German in town earlier and at first she thought the man was pronouncing something other than English.

"Is it you has two papers, then, miss?"

"Pardon?" She liked how his curly hair fell over his ears when he took off his hat.

"I'm breathin' hard as a plow horse." He made a nod and put his hat back on. "My cousin will fall into a fit, a spectacle, if he doesn't get his Thursday paper."

"We just bought two—"

"That's what the *Telegraph* lad tells me. Could we purchase one from you then? Share the last two copies?"

"One's for my aunt. She'll get sicker than she is already without the newspaper."

"Eight cents for the other—cost and a nickel for your trouble."

"You have to ask the clerk that Mr. Humphries—"

"I get all my pharmacy from the dear man—surely he'll—"

"Know what?—"Adeline interrupted, "He was telling me what all a *telegraph* will do one day—more than ship signals—like calling out the news, where they can hear you all the way to Darien!"

"Just give the inventor sorts another five years or so—"

"Here comes Will now—" The man turned to see the clerk driving a rig toward them, but he also turned to shout down Second Street at the printer's corner.

"Francis! Up here! We've got one!"

Humphries' assistant secured the rig and then jumped down to get the loading done in a hurry. Adeline watched the Irish gentleman follow him back and forth to the little storage ledge behind the seat. At last, the man took four coins out of a pouch. He was muttering something when he held his hand out to Adeline for a newspaper.

"Francis Marion?"

"No, that's me cousin."

"Is Francis your cousin?

"You know him then?" The girl's intensity was winning his attention.

"Doesn't he have some tobacco this year, planted in the far west corner?"

"Bless me. Small world."

"I saw him pick up a small boy— a baby really—at first light this morning."

This information sent the man into a laughing dance, and he had to call in the direction of both the departing cart and the more reserved young man standing at ease at the end of the street.

"Francis! Here's a witness!" He pointed at the girl, who was moments later waving to the younger Gideon son as Will hurried them on past the corner.

On their own way home, Malacai couldn't let his cousin alone about it. Francis regretted selling the one wagon, if for no other reason than had all eight wheels been clambering in the direction of the family plantation, he wouldn't have heard such teasing.

"Ah, the tender care for babes and little children—I wonder you don't take on the name *Saint Francis!*" Francis gave the newspaper in his cousin's hand a swat with the reins.

"Find the foreign page and start reading. I need a topic or two that will turn my father's attention away from how much went to the Texas cause out of his own balance sheets today."

Malacai read a little about the protests in Ireland, but the article depressed him, and he went on to make light of a prince in Berlin whose new Prussian bride was more than twenty years younger. There was an attempt on the life of the King of France and some English troops threatening Spain. But it was the news from Texas that Malacai understood his cousin to be sorely interested in. As he read, the racket of turning wheels seemed to diminish. The lead horses and the spare two tied in back clopped along softly, and Francis was attentive to every word.

"It's by way of *The American* in New Orleans, the *News from Texas* is." Malacai adjusted a fold in the second page. "This is from September 15—"

By the arrival of the Schooner Lady Madison...Captain Dunford from Velasco...we are put in late intelligence from Texas...now at the eve of... a revolution—

"What?"

"I'm reading—"

It is stated that all the states of Mexico, except Texas, have given their assent to centralism and the dominion of Santa Anna...This system is doubtless the proper one for the Mexican people, but it will not do for the Americans.

"Doesn't sound like a good time to take a wagonload of family—"

"Hush, Francis—listen to this—"

Santa Anna is concentrating a large force near Saltillo. If he moves one step towards Texas, it will amount to a declaration of war.

Francis had pulled up on the reins and his father's cotton wagon rolled to a stop. He lifted the newspaper from Malacai's hands and began to read where his cousin pointed.

In fact, we believe that at the first signal, thousands of hardy sons of the West will cross the boundary to join their former fellow citizens in maintaining the principles of '76.

"Well, well," was all Malacai could say.

"But crossing into another country…"

"I know one step-brother of mine who's sure already buying shot and powder."

"You think Joseph will muster for Texas?"

"He won't need a militia, that one. Probably already cooked up a plan to chase off a thousand enemy regiments single-handedly." The damp October air settled around them.

"How will your mother take it?" the man with the reins asked. He was ignoring the exaggeration and soberly considering what a decision to join the fight would really mean.

"Why, Francis Marion—" Malacai was next going to call his cousin *Swamp Fox,* but he could see the moment for any merriment had passed. "Is it Joseph's mother and mine you're thinking of then, when parting day comes? Or are you wondering how you'd leave your own?"

His cousin seemed not to hear him. The young man in charge was so intent on reading the article again that his lips were moving, though there was no sound except the restless stomping of the reined-in horses.

"Francis?" Whatever the man with the newspaper was mulling over, Malacai was not really sure he was ready to know.

Chapter 3   Borders Without, Borders Within

If the season any child reaches maturity is memorable, the month that Adeline Harper lived in Macon proved so remarkable as to be indelible for a lifetime. She could not have explained how swiftly her guardians changed their minds about selling Sweet Pine.

Yarico told the girl in private that Miss Maggie insisted on having the cash "for Addy's academy tuition." The two women had taught her "all the schooling" they could on their own. Maggie, on the other hand, reasoned that walking in town would benefit her health more than weekly cart rides. Both made the case against any of them continuing to haul water buckets from a well, when Mrs. Bedeford had a pipe that ran straight from a source in back of her house and right into her large kitchen basin. "All you have to do is pump!"

Mr. Humphries, who set out to have similar water delivery ready for his wife on their new property, continued to help the three "Harper women." He accompanied Adeline to check in at the Macon Academy for Young Ladies, since he volunteered on the board that helped oversee finances. Aunt Maggie was still shy about much town conversation and usually took her walks before the jingling of doorbells on Mulberry.

The battery of tests that Headmistress Stovall, administered—to justify admission of a girl more than a year under the guideline age—did not take up as much of her Monday morning as she thought it would.

"So, I suppose you are literate in other languages besides English?"

"Only French." The teacher's raised eyebrows alerted Adeline to her own *faux pas*. "I probably remember just a few words, from my mother."

"Of course, yes."

"If I start over, I could learn it proper."

"Madame LaSalle will instruct by the book."

Though Adeline was thinking that Yarico knew enough to write a book in French, there was little risk of her blurting that out. Before removal from Sweet Pine, the two women engaged in long talks with the girl about what could and what could not safely be alluded to in town. Yarico's learning was among the unmentionables. But Adeline's protection of her mother's memory was instinctive. Delphine Pagnol and her childhood companion Yarico had studied everything together— literature in French as well as English, modern and ancient history, mathematics. Adeline skirted the issue of who had given her instruction in what. There was no need to have Macon talking about the domestic servant who read with better comprehension than some Milledgeville statesmen.

It was, after all, against laws in the South to allow slaves literacy in any tongue.

What Aunt Maggie added to the list of forbidden topics in town brought Adeline to an equal sense of willingness, but much less immediate understanding.

She was not to discuss the day Margaret showed up unexpectedly at the little house just south of town. Or go into details about how surprising the news of her arrival was, since Adeline had not been aware previously that her mother ever had a much older sister. The sudden aunt was introduced as "long thought lost."

In fact Adeline ought not to muse on, not even refer to, how swiftly Maggie settled in as part of their family, caring for the weak and feverish Delphine, there with the surviving child through the burial and adjustment to the young mother's absence, there for good.

Mrs. Bedeford, who was fond of endless chat, was a constant test for Adeline's promise to stay reserved on the subject of her Aunt Maggie.

"Where did you say your aunt was living before she came to Georgia?"

"North."

"And she'd lost her husband long before that..."

"Long before."

"But your mama and daddy, they had met and married in Savannah—"

"Yes'm." There was a friendliness underlying the lady's questions.

"So now it's just you and your aunt...and your help?"

At this level inquiry Adeline knew to just shrug, even though she understood mere wiggling to be a child's response. Both her guardians were insistent—had made Adeline promise with her hand raised—to refuse any talk about the great-uncle they all knew to be living in Savannah. It was one thing to attend real school in Macon for the first time and get used to polished boots, polite nods, the folding of napkins in one's lap, and the proper holding of a pen over an inkwell.

To travel on a steamboat to the coast and shake hands with her grandfather's estranged brother, to register at a boarding academy for

34

eleven months out of the year, to be away perhaps forever from Aunt Maggie and Yarico—unthinkable.

The shrug was easy.

Mrs. Bedeford, they found, was as generous as she had been lonely. She insisted on walking Adeline directly to Wilkins Mercantile to buy enough light blue silk for making the girl a Sunday frock, a thirteenth birthday present even though that would not occur until after Valentine's. The Harpers adhered to the tradition of Sunday repose, just like the rest of Georgia, but there had been only Bible reading at home until now. Adeline was not sure how still she could sit for sermons and singing at the Methodist meeting place down on First. But as Yarico began to measure for a silk dress, the girl's incentive grew. And there was talk of hiring brick layers in the future, for a fine new chapel.

With the promise of a stylish arrival into adulthood, Adeline considered the struggle of moving from country to town as a labor of the past. She looked, even in these volatile times, on trading solitary sprints for public promenades as a costly purchase one would make once in life.

Rounding up belongings from the two-room house had been exhausting— chairs and bedding, trundle frame and marble top tables, basins and tin tubs, hatboxes, letter boxes, aprons and capes wrapped in blankets, the harmonica and the autoharp, the thirty books that had been brought from Savannah right after the Pagnol-Harper wedding— everything but the Boston bought stove, which Mrs. Humphries had her heart set on. Before signing over the two-burner beauty, the Harpers labored to put the rest of the scuppernongs into preserves, and make corn relish to put some sunshine into winter dinners. At night, they shelled any more peas ready to dry.

After the move, settling in held rich pleasure.

Adeline walked herself to the academy each morning. To begin each day, she had recently been trotting like a child to the top of a secret forest lookout. With her aunt recovered, she now concentrated on French and penmanship without distracting worries. All three women helped piece together and hem the dark calico that Adeline wore underneath a heavy cape. As she made her way down the block on one such trip, a muslin curtain in Mrs. Bedeford's parlor was held to the side for better viewing.

"You going to tell her, Miss Margaret?" Yarico spoke almost in a whisper, even though Mrs. Bedeford had gone upstairs and out of earshot to finish dressing and arrange her hair. Maggie seemed lost in her own thoughts.

"It's been three weeks since the sale was posted in the paper."

"She'll turn thirteen by spring."

"Old enough to be told—"

"Might help her set her sights with schooling," Yarico broke in. "When you know you're on your own—you listen more to the inside voice."

Margaret Linder—not Margaret Pagnol Linder, after all—was quiet for a while. Who knew what either one was trying to say? The changes that the older females in the family had gone through, were not yet in Adeline's hemisphere of imaginings. Their island of communication just outside town had left them free from constraints within the city limits of Macon.

Here, a child was obliged to consider a guardian aunt's directives about the future—unless that aunt proved an imposter. Within the boundaries of town, a servant held no sway in the plans a child might contemplate, unless that individual had forever been as beloved as family. "Aunt Maggie" found herself swallowing before speech inside the pleasant house with yellow flowers. There was so much apologizing due to Yarico that she couldn't find the right words to say. Yet she wanted to sound hopeful.

"I've just about quit worrying—since three weeks is more than enough time for any newspaper to reach the coast—"

"And with the house already signed to Mr. Humphries—"

"In a declaration of purpose I filed with Mr. Gibbs, I put in a sentence about the cost of Addy's tuition."

"Most likely we won't hear from any Harpers again," Yarico said. Maggie was nodding, but an abdominal twinge made her hug herself.

"—unless he's the type my husband was—unmerciful."

"So you decided—took your maiden name and ran off on your own?" The escape story had held the younger woman transfixed.

"I took the money that was my part and ran for the first boat away from Louisville."

"And if he never came after you, I expect Adeline's old uncle will lose interest too."

Yarico repositioned the curtain, since the girl had made it down the block and out of sight.

"Just in case, I have a travel bag packed," Maggie said, almost too low for the woman at the window to hear. "And a coach ticket, but I won't say which way." There was a noise upstairs, and Mrs. Bedeford was calling the aunt to help with a hair comb if she didn't mind. "Even if someone was to take a switch to you, you just really won't know."

Margaret smiled with some relief, however, when she folded a section of Mrs. Bedeford's silver hair over a comb so that it held. She had said "coach" in Yarico's presence. Milledgeville or part way to Darien would be suspected. But there was no certain stage line at all in the direction she intended to flee if ever there was word of an investigation heading to Macon from Savannah.

Maggie believed she could set out immediately southwest toward Mobile, or she could leave in the direction of Montgomery before making her way to the gulf. There were two common beginnings on the route to Texas, and should there ever be another scare like the one she had survived five years before, in getting away from her harsh and mercenary husband, she would not take another chance at escape to a far edge within United States borders. As true as it was that she was not Adeline's aunt—that the child's mother had begged her to stay the day she'd only knocked on the door as a passerby looking for seamstress work—as true as it was she had no blood ties to Addy, it was just as true that she did have a nephew in Texas.

The "Gone to Texas" signs popping up at first sporadically and then more regularly over the last three years, had always given Miss Margaret a fleeting urge to run one more time. Should the need ever arise, she would fall in quietly with any number of people committed to crossing the line into Texas. She had a true nephew in a little place called Gonzales. If Matthew Linder could adjust to new life in a foreign country, she could start over once more as well.

It was the second week of November, and when Maggie started out for her early town walk, she was possessed of an idea that the town's population had read her thoughts, and knew about her contingency plans. The word *Texas* showed up in shop windows that were usually still dark. Speeches were to be made at a gathering in front of the courthouse that evening by candlelight.

Doors were jingling well before the Tuesday morning opening hour, and Maggie hoped she wouldn't be spoken to when she stepped across the threshold of   Joshua Gibbs' office, the attorney who had managed the legalities of the Sweet Pine transfer. Back when Delphine had wanted legal papers giving Margaret guardianship of Adeline, he hadn't suspected any ruse. He'd been as sympathetic as he was professional, so the "aunt" hurrying along Mulberry considered the man a family friend. He was talking vigorously with a gentleman she did not know, however, and she thought she might faint if she heard the word *fraud* or the name *Mr. Simon Harper* as she went by.

"Mr. McLeod's son, Hugh," the man she didn't know was saying.

"Back from West Point, isn't that right? A lieutenant now you say?"

"I heard him deliver a few words not long ago, up at the capital," he nodded. "I'll tell you one thing, he can give a rousing talk."

"We've been giving out handbills all along here the last few days—should be a good crowd."

"They'll come to see Captain Eckley, for sure. Cavalry's always a fine sight."

Mr. Gibbs had reached into his vest pocket and was checking his time piece.

"I've got a half hour before opening. Believe I'll get some biscuits and sausage from the hotel. No point in going home this evening. I figure to eat a bite here after closing and just watch it all form up right across the street."

"Well, fix a couple more bills to your window there, Joshua. Somebody'll tell somebody, and you never know how many will take the cause all the way to Texas!"

"Terrible shame what our people are facing over there—"

"And Captain Ward, too—he'll rouse any that hear, I mean to tell you!"

When Adeline came home that afternoon, she had to be shushed by Mrs. Bedeford. The child was not to talk so much, especially about agitating subjects, at the dinner table.

"I'm just telling what we had our lessons on today," she protested.

"Now, Addy. We know all about the candlelight meeting."

"Who told you?" Maggie was trying not to make eye contact with the widow, because she didn't want to read an expression that meant, *You let this child sass her elders!*

"I became completely apprised on my early walk and had enough sense not to get you riled before you set out to school."

"Well, everybody there was already riled," the girl grumbled. Hoping to catch a sympathetic eye, she looked over to Yarico, who was maintaining her position at the doorway of Mrs. Bedeford's dining room, ready to dart into the kitchen if necessary. A lot of the talk from even Madame LaSalle at the academy had been about the liberty God hands out, and Adeline felt surely Yarico must understand the importance of the Texas gathering that evening. But Yarico seemed to have her eyes fixed on a spot even farther away from Macon than Texas. She was there, but not there, in the room with the rest of the Harper women. In town of course, Yarico was no longer allowed to speak up, and that understood household rule had been building up in Adeline's mind as an intolerable shift from the way life had been at Sweet Pine.

"Now then," the silver-haired widow said. "We ladies are going to discuss pleasant dinner topics."

"That's right," said Maggie, who felt she couldn't eat another bite of black-eyed peas and greens if the word *Texas* were spoken.

"Let's talk about silk Sunday dresses." She was not a silly woman, though, and Adeline pondered long afterward the next thing Louisa Bedeford had said. "Let's talk about our superior student here going one day to Macon's newly chartered Female College."

For the rest of the afternoon, shorter now that the sunsets rushed in, Adeline was glad she had been shushed about world affairs. She could say she had understood only that she was not to discuss the candlelight meeting at the dining table. She could claim that no one had ever told her she could absolutely not walk two blocks to the spot on Mulberry where so many people would be gathered in the early evening.

Mrs. Bedeford retired up to the sitting room that adjoined her bedroom chamber early. She was a sound sleeper, and Adeline was rather sure any cheers from the center of town would not be enough to wake her from comfortable sleep. And Aunt Maggie had looked especially tired, though not chilled or feverish. Since Yarico's quarters were now behind the main house in a vegetable shed, slightly enhanced for her privacy and comfort, the girl was sure she could slip out at dusk and behold the important gathering. Carolers, come Christmas eve, would gather there, but the candlelight speeches of Tuesday, November 10, 1835 would surely go down as an event to make all who had attended proud.

Even Yarico slumped by six o'clock that evening, and she went off to her embellished shed without any special reminders to the girl about securing her braids or taking off her stockings before climbing into bed.

Adeline worried as she turned the crystal doorknob in the widow Bedeford's foyer. So many times, she had run before daylight up Sweet Pine Hill to the sunrise lookout. She was still running up that hill in her dreams. But Macon was far from assimilated nature to her yet, and she now admitted to herself a gnawing dread that Second Street would be too dark for her by early evening. She had enough imagination to picture herself making several wrong turns, losing her direction, and falling down slippery banks into the Ocmulgee.

But an eerie beacon appeared the moment she stepped silently out onto the wide porch. From the direction of Mulberry came an inviting glow. However many people gathered in front of the courthouse, their candlelight cast a quivering spell all the way down any lesser arteries. Adeline could even make out the façade of the tin shop across the way where she had sat only weeks earlier, daydreaming of dwelling in the Bedeford house.

Her walk down toward the center of Macon, toward the soft but rising murmur of random discourse, was dreamlike and without danger.

Though the timid women watching over her had discouraged talk of the *men's meeting* and had certainly suggested that ladies would be nowhere in sight of soldier speeches, that was not the case. Adeline saw Madame LaSalle immediately on an edge of a large assembly. There were families as well as individual young men, some in uniform and some looking as if they had lingered in town after a day of driving wagons to the wharf. Madame's two wards, young ladies wearing autumn bonnets and about to finish the academy, stood alongside her, their candleholders cradled in gray gloves.

Adeline stood up perfectly straight, as they were doing, and only nodded when her presence caught their attention. They nodded back, as did the tin-shop keeper, Mr. Mosely, and Aunt Maggie's attorney friend Mr. Gibbs, and the Littlefields, who knew all the Harper women from their seamstress purchases. There were dozens of people Adeline was sure she had never seen before, but there was also a stocky young man looking as solemn as he had the day he scolded his brother for rocking a baby in the Gideon tobacco fields.

Nobody approached Adeline to ask why she was there without a chaperone. She had always felt so at home in the dark in the company only of the first gray streaks of sun. This evening was the first time she had felt kinship with so many human beings at once. Regular lessons in the academy that day had been set aside, and all the pens kept busy listing *inalienable rights* defended in the American Revolution. Adeline had read Madame LaSalle's copy in French of *The Rights of Man* and was gripped as children seldom are, by the influence of her own country's ideals on the revolution in France that came not long after 1776.

She had felt thirteen. Her seeming acceptance by any who noticed her infiltration of the meeting made her stand even more erect and comprehend this Macon meeting as marking her entrance into adulthood.

An officer in dark blue rode majestically to the forefront of the crowd before dismounting. He went to a makeshift podium, and the humming of voices among those holding candles fell away suddenly when he began to speak.

What Captain Eckley said was stirring by itself, and his introduction of several other speakers, including Lieutenant McLeod, drew greater and greater applause from the congregation in front of the courthouse. American born settlers, stranded now in Texas, they all said, had immigrated in good faith according to Mexico's constitution of 1824. It guaranteed the colonists self-governance in exchange for helping newly independent Mexico tame and secure their vast stretches of Texas wilderness. Now, settled families were being threatened by the Napoleon like rule of the country's latest high power. Red-blooded American patriots could not stand by and allow their brothers and sisters to be stripped of their hard-worked farms and ranches as retribution for insisting on rights they had been promised.

The mistreatment of the colonists, and their threatened dispersal—or worse—was an outrage that none safe in America should abide.

And those were the sentiments expressed before Captain William Ward of Macon rose to address the crowd. Those were the words spoken even before his stirring call to arms was delivered.

Other brilliant words spoken at other urgent gatherings would live in a similar way, Adeline Harper sensed even then. How many times an inspired claim, such as "Give me liberty, or give me death!" can be quoted, carved into granite, repeated in equal sincerity, and yet fall short of the galvanizing effect the words had on those who first heard them spoken. Nothing, for instance, could duplicate the shiver of gratitude experienced by those who chose to risk an ocean's distance between themselves and persecution, and who saw at last the signs of a new continent in the west. Nothing could measure up to the engulfing spasm of relief and pride in those first hearing of a British surrender and the birth of a new country.

So it was that Captain Ward's speech struck all in attendance as the unbridled expression of their new country's idealism. If the very same threat— the threat of an imperious central power pointing its elite sword at common people who shaped wilderness into vibrant community—if the same threat our forefathers rose up against in 1776 was now menacing Texian colonists with extermination, there was but one course of action to take.

Adeline had only been to three of the Methodist meetings, but she would later describe the scene of one young man and then another stepping forward as very much like those rising from their benches in church and coming forward to promise their souls to the service of God. Some stepping forward were already officers, but most were young men who had just laid down an account book or set a door to its hinges.

She hadn't realized she was crying until the Gideon man worked his way forward through the dwindling candlelight. It was not the stocky, solemn brother, but the younger one, whom she had not seen at the beginning of the speeches. He did not notice her, but she was close enough to read in his eyes a gentleness that she had assumed since that morning in the tobacco fields. And yet there was a determination that spoke of unwavering commitment. He still looked like the same young man, mild enough to be holding, right then, a baby to his side as he stepped forward to sign at the table where Lieutenant McLeod stood. There was a fearlessness too in young Gideon's expression, however, a look that convinced Adeline he might be capable of handing over a baby, only to pick up a rifle and charge in the dark toward any lethal opposition.

She had been saying his name softly when Captain Ward read it out. But when the crowd applauded and broke out in respectful cheering, she had not sensed that she was moving toward the podium herself until a hand came out from the crowd and pulled her gently by the shoulder to the side.

"Adeline Harper?"

"…Sir?" It was the attorney, Mr. Gibbs, and he seemed not to be angry in the least about her presence there.

"Your aunt here in the back somewhere?"

"She was thinking about it, but she's home in bed now," she answered evasively.

"Well, this is something to remember."

"Yessir."

"But I thought when I saw you that your aunt might be here to take a message."

"A message?"

"I don't know if she got notice, too—if she picked up anything at the post— but I want you to tell her not to worry." The meeting in front of the courthouse was adjourning, and the people moving with their last flickering candles past Mr. Gibbs and the girl made it almost impossible to hear until they had dispersed.

"She doesn't like to worry."

"And I don't want her too. With female inheritance rights being upheld these days," he went on, "I don't see how Mr. Harper can count on the old laws working in his favor." He was patting Adeline, though the girl had no idea what he was talking about. "And anyway, I'm a sworn witness to your mother's signing over guardianship and ownership to your Aunt Margaret. Leastways until you're of legal age, and I'll swear to it in any court, right across the street or in Savannah if it comes to that."

"So tell Aunt Maggie not to worry?"

"Tell her Mr. Harper's advocate isn't headed here until the first of December—that'll give me plenty of time to get my documents in order. Just tell her I don't see how he has any case, and anyway, the transaction from last month has already gone through the public declarations."

"I'll tell her."

"He just doesn't have a case—tell her not to worry."

Adeline found herself trotting home in the darkness much more like a child than a lady. She didn't know whether it was excitement or fear propelling her more, but it was not the message from Mr. Gibbs that sent her recklessly down Second Street. She had wanted to hug each of the young men moving forward to shake the hand of Captain William Ward. Now overwhelming her was an urgent need to cling to someone. She had only a slight hope that Yarico was still awake to fling her arms around, and when she tripped not far from the steps to the long front porch, she just brushed the sandy grit from her palms before running up the steps and lumbering into Mrs. Bedeford's darkened parlor.

"Addy? What in the world?"

"Aunt Maggie!" The woman in the unlit room was sitting in one of Mrs. Bedeford's dining chairs, and the girl ran up to put an arm around her shoulders.

"I thought you were in bed by now, you dear girl."

"I thought you were asleep!"

"I couldn't stay asleep," Maggie said, smoothing Adeline's hair. "And now I see you've been out—to the meeting, I suppose—I see now I should never have gone up in the first place."

"You should have been there—"

"Tell me all about it, then. It'll be my lullaby."

No light filtered into the dining room where Maggie was sitting, so Adeline could not have noticed when her aunt's expression changed. Only the woman's pat on her arm gave the girl a sense of her effect. At least, she was not angry, though it was never like Maggie or Yarico to demonstrate poor temper. She could tell, anyway, that her account of the candles and the fine words spoken by the soldiers and the applause of the inspired onlookers had meant almost as much to her aunt secondhand as it had to her. When Adeline told her about the young Gideon son stepping forward, Maggie had tightened her grip on the girl's wrist. And in the dark, the two were breathless together with wonder and admiration—until the message from Mr. Gibbs was recalled.

There was no light. And then the room went darker. The perspiration Adeline had worked up from her sprint home, the sting from her fall, and the dizziness from retelling of events were beginning to subside, and the cool air was starting to give her a chill. But the chill of her aunt's sudden recoiling was sharper. Maggie withdrew from the girl as if she had touched a corpse. Only long moments later could she struggle enough to speak, and then as if her own voice were coming from inside a coffin, where leaden and lifeless words were all that could be formed.

"I must tell you something, Adeline," she said at last. "I fear—you will never forgive me."

A tablecloth had been left folded on a sideboard during the day, and as her aunt spoke the girl felt for it and wrapped it around herself like an extra shawl. She was listening to the woman her mother had introduced as kin, but she was thinking oddly of the beautiful penmanship she had produced at school earlier in the day. She was hearing the words "Aunt Maggie" said, but she was listening inside to a soldier's exhortation and to the applause of strangers. Adeline heard her guardian beg for forgiveness, but it was she who felt sorry. Why had she not thought more deeply about one of the few story books in her mother's library?

Had she really thought a doting aunt could suddenly appear just as she was to lose her adored mother? Were children really so silly as to believe in magical comforts brought around by Father Christmas?

On some level, Adeline knew she would have to grieve anew for her mother, but she could only step woodenly in Maggie's direction again and repeat the final gist of Mr. Gibb's message.

"Don't worry, Aunt Maggie. It'll be all right."

"You're the dearest girl—"

"Everything will be all right."

"If I leave, yes. It will be," Margaret Linder said.

"What do you mean?"

"If I leave for…leave you and Yarico—"

"Leave?"

"Your house is gone, but your estate is in the bank, Adeline. Mr. Gibbs—"

"Leave for where?"

"I've done it before—I won't stay and taint your whole inheritance, I—"

"Aunt Maggie?" Adeline could feel the woman's shoulders shaking. She was a round woman, a strong woman well upwards of forty, but some underlying fragility was taking hold and the girl felt called on, like a soldier to a cause, to charge at any more fevers, real or imagined, and beat them back. "Aunt Maggie—you and Yarico and I are staying together. We belong to each other and you're not going anywhere without us!"

"You'll wake up the whole house, Addy," her aunt whimpered.

"You go on to bed. We'll talk about it tomorrow."

Some document had been signed in Adeline's mind, and no witness was necessary. Her hands were stinging again, and her sense of being alone in the world was stinging as never before. And yet there was an accompanying spirit, freer than she had imagined she could know, free but responsible. There was only one person she wanted to hug before collapsing into her bed upstairs.

Yarico was often awake long after turning in, and Adeline hoped to find her tossing on her bedding out in the shed off the back porch. It was impossible good luck, she thought, when she saw faint light coming from the crack in the structure's loosely nailed door. She knew Yarico to read often by candlelight out on the Sweet Pine porch or kitchen, and she was glad to think how quickly in their new circumstances her confidante was returning to her cheerful habits. The move to town had proved somewhat cruel to her, Adeline knew, but there was so much for everyone to adjust to.

As she padded down the back steps, she fended off the impulse to tell the solitary woman tonight that they were all likely to pack up and steal away before the month was over. She would just get a goodnight hug and talk to her and Maggie both in the morning.

Adeline cautioned herself not to disturb Yarico in her reading. She approached the door slats and peeked in before she knocked. She winced seeing *Belle-Mère* about to slip under a rough blanket. The thick cape Adeline had worn all evening was beginning to soak up cold, and she was ashamed that she hadn't checked on the adequacy of Yarico's bedclothes before. By candlelight, the woman was arranging two books in a hole scooped into the dirt floor. Even though Addy knew the literacy secret well, she was intent on preserving dignity that night, and she stayed noiseless at the door until a discreet cover had been made of an apron and one boot.

Then Yarico reached into the other boot and took out an envelope. She slid her candle down to the end of her pallet where she intended to lay her head and stretched out with the envelope in her hand. The writing inside, on the yellow piece of paper, she might have been reading. The open page, however, looked as if it had been folded and unfolded many times. She could have been reciting its contents.

Both Maggie and Yarico—close as they were to Adeline— had withheld some secret from her, the Harper girl now was forced to understand. She took her hand from the door and turned back toward Mrs. Bedeford's house. The evening was deepening without a moon. There was nothing to see but stars flung out to whatever borders the night sky knew. It was odd to Adeline to feel less curiosity about Yarico's envelope than she would have a season ago, or even a week ago. She cared less now where the three of them were to steal away to for seclusion, than she had cared just a month ago about the move into Macon.

What Adeline went to bed trying to read was the rolling script in her own mind, the figment document she had signed this evening about growing up. Where the overlooks and borders were in the adult world, she could not say.

Chapter 4   Drumbeats on the March

Francis Gideon's mother looked as if she had been the one tripped up by a wagon lashing in the tobacco field. She wore a stricken expression, as that field worker might have, had she sat in mounting fear on the ground, and heard only at the end of a nightmare search that the baby had crawled off in an unknown direction and could not be found.

Lily Gideon was in fact young enough to be holding her own baby, her seventh and last in all probability. And her oldest son Thomas was already married and the father of a little, red-headed infant. As unwarranted as it was to grieve long in those days for just one child lost—fevers and field accidents being more common than longevity—it was not possible for her to set aside worries about losing her second born to a venture so fraught with uncertainty from the start.

"I don't claim knowing all about the law," she started up quietly, "but won't the states take you as outside legal action, if you muster against another country?"

The men were sitting at the dining table set specially, while she and Thomas's wife Mary Beth worried over the morning meal and rocked the babies. Extra kitchen help had been brought in, but there was none of the usual utensil clinking coming from the room with the stove.

"Mama, I know how our treaty lies—the officers from Milledgeville made sure we all know—" The look on his mother's face made Francis search for words.

"No doubt I would have stepped to the signing too, Papa," Thomas was saying. An unaccustomed level of emotion was straining his voice, and both women had to look away to the cradle blankets when he went on. "If it weren't for Mary Beth and our William, so young—I would be going to the—"

"Nice of you to think of the spring planting, which I'd be left to do on my own," James Gideon said, trying to lighten the farewell scene.

"For three months officially, that's what we're going to muster for," Francis reminded them all. "—once we land in Texas. That way we won't be flouting our treaty with Mexico. Absolutely to the letter of the law, is what Lieutenant McLeod said, and he's straight from officer training. When we get there, we'll be private citizens signing up to help Texas show some supported force—"

"As seldom as you take up a rifle, brother, I must admit being astounded by your aim when occasion calls for it."

"A man can aim without having to shoot," Francis said. "Though the panthers there have been known to sniff out saddle bags—" He waved away the remark to reassure the women.

"You won't work up any sores on your trigger finger, I wouldn't wager!" Thomas went on. "You'll be back in time to get your blisters from lashing plows to horses, that's what I'll put my money on."

"Speaking of funds—" It was their father again. "I surely am heartened they're sending you off with near to four thousand dollars taken up last week alone and—did you hear, Lily?— with Captain Ward's family laying down some of their own fortune for the travel costs. And borrowing some new Georgia firearms, too, some kind of breech loading rifle, if you can picture it." The older man worked steadiness into his voice. "We have to say we're proud of the way all of Macon has come to be part of this mission. The cause of Methodism, the cause of the country—that's two we Gideons don't back away from—isn't that right, Mama?"

The young men's mother was nodding, and they knew she had said about all she dared. But she had looked up and out the dining room window where the morning sun was coming in, crisp as it finally does in southern Novembers. The fields in her view were shades of reddish-brown and tawny where cotton had been picked clean but the grooves in the earth still rose and fell regularly, and the intervals formed arcs within arcs of soil now barren for a season.

Something about one of the young men riding counter to those grooves and coming closer into view reminded her of her older brother, whom she last had seen in Ireland. It was true that Malacai was kin by adoption, but he was either of the same jovial nature as her brother Terence, or he had prospered so well in closeness to his step-father that he might as well be related by blood. Lily would have been the one to welcome him into their home from across the ocean when he'd lost both parents, but her sister Gwen had only the one stepson Joseph, and the two dark-haired boys looked to be brothers as they grew up, as different as Thomas and Francis were from each other, but just as devoted.

She was anticipating Malacai's uplifting company, thinking that surely he would come by for a cup of coffee this morning to see his favorite cousin off, but she had not expected to see her sister's other son Joseph riding in, too. The fiery young man was not long back from galloping in the direction of the Floridas to help discourage any Creeks from making raids in the newer settlements. She had not expected to see the near brothers, just a year younger each than her Francis, riding in together as if they'd both had all the coffee they'd need for a fortnight. Their energy level must have been sustained by some new height of decisiveness, such as the raw instinct it took to pound a fist.

Lily Gideon sat quiet so long watching the two young men approach on horseback, that her youngest son of riding age, Hiram, came to watch their stalwart approach. And then Thomas and Francis drew up slowly to the window, where their father was putting a kind hand on his wife's.

There would be no consoling Aunt Gwendolyn Tidwell in the days and weeks ahead, they all knew. No comfort would soon be gained in taking a carriage out to their smaller farm farther down along the river. Maybe she would appreciate holding one of the babies some time around Christmas. Only when the plows and wagons began to roll out into the fields of spring would Lily's sister begin to speak of Irish hope again.

"We'll cut the rest of the ham and wrap some more biscuits. It looks like you'll be needing a dinner packed for three."

In town, not far from the banks of the Ocmulgee, three drummers and a fife player from Milledgeville brought a faster pulse to Wednesday morning, November 18. From six blocks away, Yarico could feel the reverberating *thrum-thrum-thrum*, a drumbeat taking hold inside her own breast and bones.

She knew since the day Mr. Humphries took Adeline into town that life would never be the same. It was a different *never the same* from what any field hands knew in her part of Georgia alone. The groaning, singing laborers who belonged like the plow horses and squeaking wagons to plantation owners were most often worked as families. But one could never count on any stretch of belonging. *Never the same* could rise up again like an angry storm cloud, any day an auction block appealed to those in possession.

That Yarico as a child had lived like a sister to Delphine Pagnol was an anomaly of the starkest kind. The two learned and played together within the private confines of home. The lovely dark girl and the light skinned older child disavowed any servant-mistress construct assumed by the world outside, their sisterly affection surviving into adulthood. During the restrictive month within Macon, a raw apprehension wrenched Yarico. She felt she had taken on years.

"Is that you?" she asked her reflection. Only a small, little-used looking glass was counted among the Harper possessions. What stared back from the handsome, beveled mirror in Mrs. Bedeford's upstairs sitting room shocked her. "Stay, and likely the old Harper uncle comes. He'll fetch a handsome price for your fine feet that don't know the word *tired*. Those arms, Yarico—still strong enough to carry more than somebody's water, maybe chamber pots in Savannah for a family of fourteen."

"Yarico?" Maggie's voice from the base of the stairs surprised her.

"I found the bottle, I think—" It was smelling salts she had come up to fetch. "I'll come down immediately!" Running off to a new country would have made Delphine laugh. "C'est la vie!" she told herself. "If it's a place as big as they say, maybe there I can breathe again."

"It's all right! She's coming around!" Adeline called up.

"Go with Delphine's sweet child, Yarico." *Ratta-tuh-thrum.* "Who is it loves her, but you?" She could not keep her pulse from speeding, and she shook her head one more time at her own image. She went on down saying to herself, "Who else in the wide world loves *you?*"

The widow Bedeford never did come around well enough to see the travelers any farther than the porch. The Harper women had stationed a wagon with a canvas canopy in front of her house nearly a week ago, and the horse they'd brought from Sweet Pine seemed to get along well with the companion they'd harnessed to pull equal weight.

Even though they had dispensed with furniture, they packed extra quilts and blankets, and containers that might be used for who-knows-what besides hauling water or cooking over makeshift fires. Pillows and a straw-filled mattress lay in the floor of the wagon, so that they could take turns sitting in something softer than the wooden seat directly behind the reins. In a trunk, a similarly stuffed pillow sham cradled glass jars of jelly and relish. Rolled up linens and a bag of dried peas were mashed between to keep the jostling stockpile from breaking. Another trunk held their seamstress implements in careful arrangement, including layers of silk partly cut for a dress, partly hemmed off for a banner that Adeline worked obsessively. Lashed to the outside of the wagon were their hoe and shovel. Mrs. Bedeford insisted they take her late husband's axe and musket.

All Aunt Margaret understood of their finances, she had discussed with Adeline as well as Yarico. They were leaving a reasonable sum from the house sale in the Macon bank, for Mr. Gibbs to draw on whenever his services were needed. If he thought it prudent, there was enough to hand over a compensatory amount to any Harpers of Savannah that felt they'd been deprived of property rightfully theirs. The rest was Texas seed money.

Joshua Gibbs thought they were being more than fair, and he was still unconvinced that removing themselves to as far away as Texas was advisable. On the other hand, he understood Mrs. Linder wanting her niece and nephew to grow together as family. There was certainly no denying the auspicious timing of their departure to Gonzales. ~~from Macon to Montgomery and then to Mobile in the company of armed soldiers would amount to a very small risk of Indian attack~~ Traveling from Macon to Montgomery and then to Mobile in the company of armed soldiers would amount to a very small risk of Indian attack. From New Orelans, the Harper women could make their own way.

Yarico wanted to stay inside the wagon, under the cover of the canopy on their way to the edge of town. Though Adeline rarely gave her an order, her voice had been insistent about taking that spot for herself. She was frantic to make progress on the sky blue banner, and she knew that the roads in town were far smoother than what they would soon encounter beyond the limits of Macon proper.

"I want at least to get the letters pinned and basted."

"What are you aiming to have it say?" Yarico asked.

"*Texas, Free and Proud—*"

"I see."

"And a star in the upper left corner on the other side—you like it?"

The woman looking in on her nodded.

"The words aren't going to be easy," the girl admitted.

Yarico let the flap to the inner canopy fall, and a new *ratta-tuh-thrum* left her trembling as she turned to get a better feel for the reins. Maggie and she had talked about the safer way for them to leave town. Even though Adeline's older guardian hadn't suffered a stomach flare-up in days and would gladly have handled the horses, they both felt it would look better to have Yarico taking on visible work.

She was more nervous than the other two around such powerful animals, but she was relieved to have the team to fix her eyes on as they rolled away from Mrs. Bedeford's. They took a left at the tin-shop to head away from town down the length of Second. Maggie was wearing a dark rose dress and her gray coat. Her bonnet featured both colors, and Yarico felt sure that Mrs. Linder, as several townspeople knew her, would draw any special attention.

Yarico's dull brown coat fell over a faded apron. She had one other dress, but she wore the one more resembling an outdoor laborer's nondescript attire. She kept her mind from drifting to the message on Adeline's banner.

She went past Poplar and Plum, all the way to Pine Street before she took a right turn so that they could come back toward the edge of town on First. The *thrum-thrum-thrum* had faded away but was gradually building again, and she shuddered to think what the horses might do if the drumming had the same effect on their bodies as it had on hers. What her heart did when the wagon came within view of the Methodist Episcopal Church on the corner of Mulberry, she was not sure her body would tolerate. When the Harper wagon pulled up alongside the church, she was sure her pulse had stopped altogether. A special group of church members gathered there for a farewell blessing. The pastor, Yarico believed, was the solemn and confidant man in black, standing in front of people with clasped hands.

The wagon in which Yarico and Maggie sat did not resemble a military procurement. But the town knew that anyone on the move that morning was headed into danger, was part of a cause approved by higher powers. It was the group behind the pastor's congregation that made Yarico's head pound. A multitude of respectfully folded hands were brown. These individuals, their expressions, struck her like a thousand muted drums. In the middle of Mulberry, at the urging of a louder *ratta-tatta-Tuh-thrum*, soldiers in civilian dress hoisted their knapsacks for the march out of town. But the smart rows were not where these church people directed their gaze. Yarico, pausing in the Harper wagon, wanted to concentrate on the leather straps in her hands and the twitching manes of the horses in front of her. She found she could not keep from turning to meet the eyes of those observing her.

Since the candlelight gathering, she had heard in the rapid-fire discussions so many statements, some cautionary and some full of hyperbole. There was so much talk that she could not say whether one particular declaration was true. In Texas, if what was said about the latest rule in Mexico could be believed, slavery had been abolished. Yarico made the faintest nod in the direction of well wishers at the church.

Not quite believing that she or any of the accompanying travelers would really make it to the foreign territory, she certainly could not then have sworn on a Bible which cause would merit her prayers for victory.

Suddenly the entire town of Macon precipitated itself into a rhythmic euphoria— *ratta-Tuh-thrum-thrum-thrum!* The waving of handkerchiefs was a motion inseparable from the flurry of drumsticks. The lurching of wagon wheels and leaning of officers in leather saddles seemed one coordinated movement. Though none of the foot-soldiers were in uniform, their polished shoes and boots caught the cadence as if the proud men were decorated already for glory. The roar went from spectators to marchers, from militia to townspeople, from the far end of Mulberry to the steeple end, where Yarico's team leaned in the harness hard enough to move on. At last they were moving out, north at first, toward the banks of the Ocmulgee.

Who could bear to look back? *Thrum-thrum-thrum!* They were on the way, now, to a world none had ever seen. Only a few knew from experience where the winding Georgia road soon cut southwest, where the town of Knoxville was first on the path to Columbus at the far edge of the state.

With precision unraveling five miles from town, the parade paused for a few minutes. The volunteer soldiers dashed off into the brush and poplars to relieve themselves of their coffee intake, and the ladies present took care of the same needs in the privacy of their covered wagon. Some of the men—who had ridden into Macon and let brothers or neighbors take their mounts back home—were discovering the damage that sock wrinkles do to ankles, and the discomfort a rifle strap could cause if not properly hoisted over the shoulder. But Captain Ward, in command of the formation, and the other military regulars knew not to extend the marching respite. There had been no training period before the morning of departure, and time on the march provided rare opportunity to exercise as a unit.

"I have three letters basted in," Adeline said, before the order to move came again. Edges of the sky-blue silk were neatly tacked down. The handkerchiefs Mrs. Bedeford donated from her husband's effects were a fine quality for script. Stitching around the sharply turned letters, though, was next to impossible in a rocking wagon.

"Don't be in a hurry," Maggie reminded her. "When we stop for an evening, you can make sure progress. Why don't you come up here with Yarico and let your ole auntie settle into a cushion for a while?"

The next fifteen miles went by faster, even though the drums and the clamber made conversation untenable. What could anyone say? All one had ever known, all left behind—words were inadequate. Yarico and the girl directed their attention to frequent ruts in the sandy path, to remnant geese moving southward, and to intermittent chants from the lead marchers setting and resetting the pace. Adeline searched the front of the marching line regularly for the Gideon man, since she knew him to be among the first volunteers.

It was past noon and well into dinner time. The fast gait and the bright November sun had brought the growing battalion to a state of sweaty fatigue. Three stern men on horseback came to ride alongside the procession just before Knoxville's buildings sprang into view. In town, the entire group flung themselves down under what awnings and tree shade the village provided. While nourishment was unpacked from sacks and saddlebags, men and boys came out to the road and moved in close. More joined the volunteers, some on foot with their rifles and day packs hanging from their shoulders, some ready to hand over the reins of their horses to a relative staying behind.

Lively talk broke out in the autumn air about the energizing send-off from the town of Macon, the thoughtful welcome in front of the inn there in Knoxville. The innkeeper carried a hot meal out to Captain Ward and more seasoned soldiers riding up front—two men by the name of Bulloch and one with the familiar name Lamar.

Adeline, Maggie, and Yarico devoured their biscuits and jelly, shared a thick slice of pork from the previous evening, and passed around a jar of cool tea. Knowing the chance to stretch would be brief, Maggie took Adeline's arm afterward and they walked the length of the town. They were winding their way back through pockets of young men, when the girl pulled sharply on the older woman's elbow. A fellow with wavy brown hair had taken off his hat and his gesturing made the others seated around him laugh. The soldiers wiped their mouths with their sleeves or kerchiefs.

"Don't fret over your blisters this side of the border. When we get to Texas they'll grow as big as puddles —everything's grander there, they say—" When his comrades shook their heads, he smiled and looked in the direction of the two women. His expression went through quick changes as he tired to place the younger one.

"We let you buy a newspaper," Adeline said shyly.

"For heaven's sake," he laughed, jumping up. "They said there were ladies following along behind—we had no idea it was you. Francis? Look here—"

Adeline liked how they both came over and put their hats on again, only so they could take them off and shake hands. They were pleasant, but even the one named Malacai ceased his joking, as if such jesting were for men sworn to dark tasks and not for bystanders. Francis asked how far the Harper wagon expected to go and where in Texas they eventually hoped to connect with settled relatives. No one made the usual extended inquiries into family, since the Gideon man and his cousins—all the others finishing their midday meal—functioned in a state of rapture mixed with disbelief. How could they listen to talk of kin? Mulberry Street felt a million worlds away. The most any could conclude was to be trudging, mile by mile, away from all the family they'd ever held close.

The two she knew, and the third young man Joseph, were still on their feet, when Adeline sensed it was time for ladies to head back to their wagon. But the girl fought an urge to speak of her sewing project. If only she possessed the finished flag just then. She wanted to say, *Before you go back to marching, I have something you may want to carry with you into the charge!*

She was a little dizzy, suddenly, and she thought for a moment that she had slid into a barrel, where she was able to hear the echo of her own thoughts. A flurry of excitement broke out in front of the Troutman Inn. Captain Ward sat tall on his rust colored horse there, though he didn't look to be on the verge yet of resuming the march. Instead, he waved a piece of shimmering white cloth. A dark haired woman, a girl not too much older than Adeline, stood blushing and smiling on the steps of the inn. The captain made another flourish with the banner.

"Before you fall into ranks! I have something here that you all must see—that we will carry proudly into Texas and into the struggle for freedom there!" Her parents eased up behind the girl, the mother smiling as bashfully as her daughter, and the innkeeper needing to take an apron edge to his eyes to keep his manly composure.

"Where freedom abides—there is my home!" Captain Ward held up one side of the banner where the Latin version had been beautifully stitched. The azure letters were inscribed smoothly as if some hand superior to mortal action had guided the needle and thread. When the other side was shown to the soldiers, now all on their feet to see better, a cheer went up that might have been heard all the way back to Macon. The azure star at the center of white silk boasted *independence!* Three simple words brought to all the sense of urgency that had made them join up.

"LIBERTY or DEATH!"

Maggie was pulling on Adeline's coat sleeve. No one in the throng would resume sitting or chatting. The captain, as they passed by the front of the inn, had dismounted only to kiss the hand of Joanna Troutman in a most gentlemanly way. He was assuring the girl and her parents that the flag would be presented to McLeod in Columbus, where the lieutenant had gone ahead to engage more recruits.

As Maggie and Adeline came upon the cluster of wagons at the back of the procession, they found Yarico patting the horses.

"Make friends with fear," she said, alluding to her warinees of horses. She saw Addy's expression and cast a questioning look to the woman headed first under the canopy.

"A different banner for the soldiers was already finished," Maggie said, shrugging. Yarico studied the girl.

"Let disappointment's stay be brief…"

The woman who had come into the family as an aunt still needed rest on the straw bedding, but she didn't mind that the girl wanted to put her head down, too. Adeline fought a compulsion to inform someone that Captain Ward's glimmering banner was cut from petticoat material—like the gathered white slip visible when Miss Troutman had lifted her skirts to curtsey. *My banner was being made, not from petticoats, but from a Sunday dress!*

But the Harper girl was ashamed suddenly of her desire to protest. Before crossing any thresholds into adulthood, she might have sulked after such an affront. Inside the lurching wagon, Adeline could not remain listless long. Too much discomfort was being endured by others. The *thrum-thrum-thrum* brought her out to the seat where Yarico managed the reins. At least now, the girl didn't have to press herself. The blue banner would have its own moment. Eventually, she could give it to Francis Gideon or the man named Malacai. Or she could make handkerchiefs. The other one, Joseph Tidwell didn't look much like he'd doff his hat in acceptance of a gift from a lady of any age.

"I love it," was the first thing Adeline said, after settling in next to Yarico. "I love it out in the open, where you can see the geese fly."

"You all right, *ma petite?*" The sound of horse hooves and trudging feet, the thrumming came without interruption. Direction, if not destiny, was certain. A ragged strand of birds flew overhead, and the odds of their making it safely to wintering grounds struck Adeline as deeply poignant. Her own door to Sweet Pine was shut forever. Some new appreciation welled up, for comfort of a more sustaining kind.

56

"I love—*you*, Belle-mère," Adeline said. It was not the sort of thing one spoke out loud, and Yarico looked from the road to the girl hugging her arm. It had seemed like the right thing to say, under the vast sky with the skimpy thread of geese calling plaintively. Adeline considered her flag, *free and proud*, and she listened to the sound of men marching away from their mothers and wives. There had seemed only one reasonable thing to say.

By the third day, they made it to Columbus, where another fifty men increased the roll of the Georgia volunteers to well over a hundred. There, Lieutenant McLeod, needing to take on his commission at Fort Jessup, after all, said his farewells. A different captain, Wadsworth, and the troops from Columbus gave a farewell cheer as they strode beyond the last Georgia town. McLeod and they were headed to different sections of Louisiana, and the volunteers were sorry that they might not see the lieutenant again for some time. But Captain Ward had proven his own powers of oratory. And his connections in Milledgeville had been instrumental in procuring artillery. As the regiment left its home boundary, wagons followed carrying Georgia's new breech loading rifles, a battery of small canons, as well as grape and powder for their eventual lethal use.

Little opportunity arose for the steadiness Adeline Harper needed to finish stitches on washed blue silk. Less time for jotting down words came Francis Gideon's way. Phrases nested in his mind as the formation marched through the territory of Alabama toward Montgomery. A recognizable path was engraved into the sandy earth from wanderers and traders, settlers as well as Indian nomads. Ruts certified the route as that taken by the sporadic coaches making westerly treks from the bustling Georgia towns left behind. What fed the imagination of Francis, though, were the deep, impenetrable forests alongside the narrow trail.

"I know what you're thinking." It was Malacai—like all the others, growing more fit daily, and better at catching his breath after a week on the march.

"Grateful the snow this time of year is all up north—"

"Snow? Good Lord forbid!" Malacai was laughing. Joseph and the men closest by began chuckling or swearing.

"As long as we're headed south," Francis said mildly, "this one coat will do."

"And if it were to snow, you wouldn't be asking for another coat—not you!" Malacai could make light of them all. "More like a box of water colors, or a fine quill pen!"

"Well, I don't need a pen to remember how cheerful our direction makes me. I'll say it again—I'm grateful as long as Texas territory is south from this point on a map." The woods had captured his attention again. "As beautiful as November is—"

Francis fell again into silent marching, because the drummer at the front of the ranks had just been directed to bring the men to pace—*ratta-Tuh-thrum-thrum-thrum*. With a sense of urgency, Francis reminded himself that he and his cousins had now passed well into the bounds of Alabama! They would be in Alabama until the wide ocean pressed in from all sides. He fell silent because he was inscribing a line in his memory.

Deeper still the forests grow, swelling ranks of stately trees,
On our way through densest pines, may our cause a clearing be.

Chapter 5   Drumbeats from the Shore

The first one hundred miles of marching toughened the men under Captain William Ward's unofficial command. They were all fit to begin with, the way young men of their times had to be to rise early and ride on horseback to the fields or to town. They took to walking as naturally as creatures of the meadows or woods. But the next one hundred miles put blisters on their blisters and built in their shoulders a durability they had not needed before—for carrying loads by strap, and armaments. Their lungs responded to endurance breathing. The muscles in their legs tingled at night and ached in the morning at first drum roll. Stamina broke through to foreign heights.

Occasionally, a scouting party of Chickasaw or Choctaw was glimpsed at the edge of the Alabama woods. They came close enough to measure the scene, before slipping back into the thicket of pines. The march from Macon to Montgomery was making the Georgia men a tough body of warriors indeed.

Without the promise of travel by river upon reaching Montgomery, however, the final fifty miles might have altogether wrecked every soldier's resilience.

By the last day, Yarico, Maggie, and Adeline had all squeezed together on the seat behind the team. Inside their wagon, six or seven men at a time took turns resting from the grueling march. Most immediately eased off their footwear. Shoes that held up in stirrups or in striding from field to wharf appeared scavenged after a stampede. Boots stretched out in the heel or toe looked to be lopsided castoffs. When the procession paused, a first year physician took up the opportunity, and Adeline turned to watch him open a small brown case of cutting instruments and needles before offering to treat the worst blisters.

As soon as Adeline saw a thin pliers and a thick curving needle, she asked if she could examine one of the men's shoes. She was able to match up the spot inside the soldier's left shoe with the severe blister on his foot. From her sewing bag, she took out the silk banner and quickly separated the half with basted letters from the star side. Once the letters were plucked off, there was plenty of material from which to make miniature panels, the size of blisters. With the physician's needle, she picked up the edge of the material. The pliers helped her work the threading through the softer, inside leather. She used the same whip stitch she would have chosen for appliqué. The small silk patch, especially after the doctor minimized the blister and dabbed it with spirits, served to ease the worst drag of leather over wound. For other cases, she matched up panels inside and outside a sock.

She and Maggie had completed a dozen more patches by the time the battalion neared Montgomery. Then another twenty men walked back to their wagon and asked if the Harper women—once river travel commenced— could take a look at the size of their blisters and examine their shoes. Some with boots decided against taking them off for fear of not being able to put their swollen feet back in.

Montgomery, once they arrived, drank in all their attention and numbed their senses to anything but the wharf activity. Six miles downstream from where the Coosa River flowed into the Tallapoosa, business throbbed. Beans, rice, coffee, sugar, cornmeal, salt pork, and flour were loaded onto steamboats and small-engine barges where the wide flow of water became the Alabama. Within the first two days there dozens of young men responded to Captain Ward's stirring appeal, to go *where there was most danger and most honor to be won.* Forty-eight hours later, the volunteer battalion boarded the river boat *Benjamin Franklin* and two barges, and they all braced for late November travel down the winding waterway to Mobile.

The respite from marching did not quite feel like calm after a storm. Chugging from one lazy river bend to the next worried even the most optimistic under Ward's command as the deceptively soothing prelude to frightful strains in Texas. Before leaving Mobile the last time, the barge captain steering the Harper's wagon and the battalion's food supplies had been pumped with information.

"New Orleans is all heaved up about the situation—I can tell you that!" He was talking to a Dr. Judkins and two other men with medical expertise, as well as Adeline Harper and her aunt. A handful of soldiers, being quarantined and treated in a rudimentary way for coughs or exhaustion, lay close enough to hear. The tents secured on deck, ordinarily sheltering cotton bales, provided the recovering men snug protection from the cool autumn air.

"You expect another round of men will join up even there?"

"It depends on what part of town Captain Ward sets up his speaking podium."

"What do you mean?" the doctor wanted to know.

"If you read the *True American*, you've already heard from the side that will be cheering you men on." The barge chugged up to another sharp bend, and the pole workers looked to their captain for maneuvering signals. "Mobile gets most of its news from that bold paper, so you'll pick up some enthusiastic fighters there too, I'll bet this river on it!"

"But, there are others?"

"It's not like up here—not like Alabama and Georgia—not all the way through to New Orleans. A big part of that city, don't ask me why, keeps some heart in the ways of France, and the Spanish."

"I don't understand." Dr. Judkins sounded as if he had been looking at a case of fainting that would not respond to salts.

"Well sir, even our own folks up in Washington have their agreements set with other countries, don't forget. Let's just say there's a big part of Louisiana that's mighty slow to go against foreign decisions—as long as they ain't going hostile against us—specially not if they've got some kin mixed in with Mexico's mighty—there's a hodgepodge of sentiments is what I'm saying."

"You're not saying some are ready to fight us right there in New Orleans, are you?" Margaret Linder asked. Both men shook their heads, in a natural response to concerns expressed by women.

"No, ma'am. You all, I imagine, are just going to stick pretty much to the side of town happiest to stock your schooners and see you off. They've nearly got the whole city partitioned, so as to keep peace between all the hot-headed views. Anyway, I won't be going any farther than Mobile."

"Not by poles, anyway—." They all chuckled nervously at Adeline's implication. Wooden sticks were no match against ocean crosscurrents in even the short distance from Mobile to New Orleans.

"Ward'll know where to set up his speech platform," the barge captain went on. "Don't know when I've heard such blazing glory talk!"

"All Milledgeville got mighty worked up by the reports from Stephen Austin." Uriah Bulloch spoke from one of the covered sick bays. The military man was resting with a bad cold, and trying to recover before coming down with anything worse.

"Some folks I trust in Mobile know him as *Estevan*," the captain said.

"As proper as he's been, acting a Mexican subject—Hell, Mr. Austin called himself *Estevan!*" Bulloch apologized to the ladies before going on. "But not after wasting away inside a prison in Matamoros for a year." Margaret Linder had seen the name Stephen F. Austin in her nephew's letters, as the first leader of an English-speaking colony in Texas.

"What'd he do?" She wanted to know.

"Not a thing God wouldn't call honorable," Bulloch said. "Santa Anna never did formalize a charge." He coughed into a handkerchief before speaking once more. "We thought when they released him this past summer it'd be an end to the overbearing wrongs. Now, Austin himself has thrown down the gauntlet, and even went to Washington to ask for American help. I met him once. If that upright gentleman has banished hope of fair treatment—there's nothing to do but stand to and start carrying rifles and—"

"Now, sir," Dr. Judkins broke in. "You let Captain Ward do the fiery speech. We're all with the cause on board this barge! You need to get well—"

"That's right, Mr. Bulloch—now let us bring you some lemon water," Margaret said. She didn't much like to hear about the founder's imprisonment, not with her nephew at a colony so close to where Austin had set up.

Dusk was settling onto the surface of the water, and from the thick woods either side of the winding riverbanks an occasional beating of drums could be heard. The people from Milledgeville, Macon, and Columbus couldn't any more tell what rapid events lay ahead in Texas than they could interpret the thumping messages from one Indian camp or the next.

Yarico had been settling into a kind of mental dusk since the change in transportation at Montgomery. Just as she had begun feeling in charge of the Harper wagon, friendly at last with the steady horses, the push and pull of authority had shifted again, and she knew to stay as quiet as she had in the Bedeford household. Even talk with Adeline had to be short and tempered of emotion. Before Montgomery, she had let Margaret take the reins briefly late in the last afternoon of the march, in order to take a turn with the mending of socks and shoe linings. The men had been grateful and respectful. When the Gideon neighbor that Addy seemed to know, and the two with him, fell to the rear and inquired politely about getting in on the Harper shoe treatment, she recognized their general kindness. She felt herself to be among good Georgia people.

In Alabama, she was already experiencing the disorientation of crossing into a foreign country. A wagon train that had pulled in at a cautious distance from the Montgomery wharf held her in a state of silent turmoil. They rolled in near the busy district in the late afternoon to acquire supplies before withdrawing to the outer edge of town. Inside her own wagon, away from unwelcome scrutiny, Yarico had been able to see and hear the conversation between two wharf dealers and soldiers.

"Choctaws, from outside Mobile," one man in a blue federal uniform was saying.

"Been new trouble down there?"

"One kind or another."

"How many you got?"

"Near sixty."

"Look about as hungry as the Georgia volunteers poured in just yesterday."

"Headed to Texas, I reckon. Wish I was goin'."

"Well, can't say it looks like you'll get any mischief out of these you got this month."

"Still, I aim to ration out the provisions you're loading up for us." The soldier stopped to look back at the wagons. Yarico had been looking too. There were mothers, infants, and children old enough only to cling. Elderly men and women leaned against one another. Mixed in, a young man or a boy almost grown sat in a cramped stupor. They weren't in chains, but they were defeated in other ways, that was clear.

"You aiming for Vicksburg eventually, like before?"

"Yessir. Hand 'em over at that point. That's as far as I take them on their way to the Oklahoma territory. Say—" He had just remembered something. "You seen a copy of that Cherokee newspaper? Come out from somewhere up here or over into Georgia, I guess."

"What are you tellin' me?"

"Some chief fella got them an alphabet, and the next thing you know, they're printing up their own newspaper!"

"You don't say!"

"I meant to bring a copy along—it's something hard to believe."

"A newspaper—well!"

"Still, there's always bound to be trouble if we don't get people a ways out of the mix—"

"It's for the best," a wharf man said, shaking his head. "I'll be glad when we get all this done and over—"

"Just wish I was goin' to Texas."

Yarico had never seen Indians of any kind as close up as those sitting in the wagons just forty feet away. She was glad she was under the cover of the Harper wagon, because she thought her expression might be interpreted as more dangerous than any of those she had witnessed among the Choctaw families.

When another group of people came through the dock area an hour later, she thought she was going to get sick in Adeline's sewing bag. There were a dozen men and women from "Guinea," she heard the seller say. It was not a country that came to Yarico's mind from the geography she and Delphine Pagnol had studied. The man in charge was in no sympathetic mood the way the soldier and wharf man had seemed. He was angry that he couldn't get any of the shackled workers to follow directions— "not a one can understand the first simple word of English. Not one word!"

Yarico had to dig into Maggie's purse and find the tonic for stomach twinges. Then, and days later as the Alabama River wound back and forth upon itself, she began to feel as if the Sweet Pine existence had been just a winding dream. She began to sense that her mind was going to need new poultices, frequently, like the soldiers' blisters needed attending to. She was not sorry to have missed some chances already for fleeing into the deep woods at night and risking the horrors of a slave hunt. The daughter of Delphine Pagnol was hers to love, as she had been from the joyous moment of her birth. Now Addy was her own to raise, her own child in spirit, in every way except by law. But she was still glad her plain leather boots fit well enough to run in, even with the envelope stuffed down at her ankle.

Yarico was thankful that the Georgia Battalion kept moving and moving. The ceaseless motion kept her mind off the predicaments of others, and the hopelessness she'd recognized in their eyes. She didn't see how Texas could be any worse.

News articles throughout the region heralded the American volunteers heading for Mexico's northern territory. So much enthusiasm pervaded the coast of Alabama that a public dinner was planned for the traveling soldiers. In Mobile, Captain Ward spoke as eloquently, as vehemently as ever. After their leader prevailed upon the crowd, another fifty men stepped up to sign for service. By the time their ships approached New Orleans, the militia under the supervision of Georgia officers was almost two hundred strong.

Francis Gideon, Malacai Mulholland, and Joseph Tidwell had stayed in the same cabin or deck spot on the steamboat trip down the Alabama, and they stuck close together among the swelling ranks under Captain

Ward. The convoy of steam-powered boats skimmed coastal edges westward up into the nation's fastest growing port.

"They say New Orleans docks are busier than New York these days," Malacai marveled. "Two ship workers in Mobile swore it to be the case."

They were turning a corner in the bay where the canal route was suddenly visible. As well-traveled as the waterway had been since leaving the mouth of the Alabama, the sight awaiting them as they chugged into New Orleans left them speechless. All those from western Georgia and north Alabama—the landlocked hundred and fifty aboard who thought of busy waters as two riverboats angling for the clearest side of a freshwater stream—could not at first believe the line of waiting vessels at the New Orleans docks, six ships deep in some places.

"If all those were Santa Anna's," Joseph observed solemnly, "I'd need to double powder my rifle."

The burst of laughter over his deadpan observation rose up fast, but died away just as quickly. The Georgia Battalion had certainly never imagined a scene as overwhelming as such vigorous port dealings. No wonder it was known as *the jewel city* of the gulf. They knew not to carry the joke any further about what all the Mexican supreme commander might have in store—sights that would leave them without adequate words.

The men had heard of Canal Street and the French sector of town, but their ship steered inland quickly, toward the northern wharf area, where some had been told there were zealous enthusiasts for their mission. There, they could rest, as well as practice formation, while their final supplies were gathered up.

They knew they were not to be sworn in and officially mustered as soldiers for the Texas cause until they reached a town off the coast there. But it was unanimous without being spoken that William Ward would lead them by whatever officer commission he was offered. Wadsworth and Uriah Bulloch, recovered from his cough, were understood to have won equal respect among those who had been on the march from the start. As volunteers, they would be allowed to elect their own leaders, yet they knew without being given orders that their days in New Orleans would not be spent in any of the dissolution for which certain addresses in both the American district and the Vieux Carré were known.

There was very little interest in the kind of gambling that men from cotton fields and small town shops sometimes found tempting. They had wagered their signatures, all of them, in the last few days or weeks, and there was no contest of interest except the one to be taken up on the Texas plains. Rather than scattering out among the hundreds of private inns in the American district, Ward marched them in toward a large brick building in the heart of the thriving city.

North of Esplanade, an astonishing number of structures, they learned, had been built in just the last three years. They passed by one majestic façade after another, all with marvelous exterior grillwork they could previously have imagined only in Savannah. Through tall, bright windows they glimpsed chandeliers, paintings in golden frames. While carriages of exquisite crafting ran along the streets, multi-story verandas and tile rooftops rose up from the side avenues. Whatever the residents of Milledgeville or its surroundings knew of style from their country ballrooms, they found the fashions paraded on New Orleans walkways humbling.

William Ward understood that the stopover in New Orleans was no time to succumb to any of the city's charms. He kept the Georgia Battalion close to their quarters and restricted them all to marching in formation near La Fayette Square, resting only on Sundays, when the Louisiana Legions in companies of varied ethnic loyalties, and uniforms of widely ranging colors, drilled in the avenues all day.

"Good Lord," Malacai said to Francis." If we end up that motley an army, the blasted Mexican troops might go to fleein' across the Rio Grande from confusion."

"I expect Captain Ward to hang onto his federal blues."

"Well, what colors do you think the Texas government means to issue us?" Francis and his two cousins were looking at one company of Louisiana soldiers in bright blue, marching smartly, but standing in sharp contrast to the next unit headed down the street from near Georgia's temporary garrison. Especially expert in handling their rifles as they stepped, the advancing company seemed just as proud to be in red.

"I don't care what we're issued for trousers and jackets," Joseph said spitting. "I want to get my hands on fresh powder bags. Any made water proof, that's what I want." His companions gave him the space to speak his mind fully. "I can't say I'm not nervous about getting used to these yagers we're bringin' along."

"What you do with your own rifle in eighteen seconds could well beat an upstart with a new breech loader—"

"Still—" Sundays in a city weren't where Joseph fit in. He couldn't get comfortable without a firearm across his chest. "I'll be glad to get where we can see how the damn things handle." Malacai smiled. He was proud of his brother, but used to turning a conversation away from awkward dead-ends.

"Francis, they were asking you about the number of men and provisions—"

"Bulloch and young Lamar." He was thinking as he half answered, and he nodded slowly. "I was doing some figuring this morning about all of it—arms of either kind, and what they need for hard use. I don't think enough will come our way before Velasco, but just as important are the corn meal, flour, and beans, coffee and sugar for the long stretch."

"You do have the reputation at home for numbers and portions, cousin."

"They wanted me to figure—for any waiting time inland, in case we stand our ground for a while without new supplies—"

"Well—here, it's all day for rest." Malacai was fishing into his coat pocket. "We'll be watching Louisiana march until the sun goes down. Who wants a beignet before we're relegated to stale biscuits and cold coffee for the rest of winter?" He left Joseph and Francis for the side street bakery.

"You think they can get the *Pennsylvania* loaded up by the end of next week?"

"I have two worries, Joseph, both struggling to get the upper-hand."

"Powder and —"

"I've been accounting for all the known necessities." The other young man settled into quiet and gave Francis time to think. "Then I feel just as hard pressed to imagine what provisions we might use in the heat of it—what unlikely things, taken for granted here— could make a difference in some scrape we don't imagine."

Malacai's step-brother was watching yet another Louisiana company march briskly by. This one, in distinctive gray, proceeded toward the square. Joseph was only a year younger than the man who was talking, but Francis was one of the few people he had the patience to listen to. He watched the family worrier rub at his temple before penciling the word *twine* on the corner of a paper.

"One overriding requirement," Francis went on, "no matter what we load on deck—is that we get there in all haste. It's hard to idle here, even to ponder supplies. With the Texas force begging for help, our numbers alone can shape the outcome. With or without the provisions we want—what's sure is that they're counting on us."

The two volunteer soldiers sat near the steps of the brick building where all Ward's men were stationed for the week. Noise in the paved avenues—from the legion companies drilling, the subdued Sunday vendors, the carriage wheels, the traffic of polished slippers and boots— was the kind of hum that could allow a man to listen a while to his private thoughts, without seeming aloof for not engaging in conversation.

Malacai, their lighthearted cousin, could keep up a dialogue with himself or any stranger. He was probably chatting away with a pastry chef, Francis and Joseph both thought, maybe asking what kind of specialties they would serve come Christmas day in a fortnight, or for the new year.

Not in any hurry for beignets, however, the other two from Macon farmland were contemplating the harsh contrast ahead. They had marched harder than any of them thought possible. They had traveled farther by steamboat than ordinary Ocmulgee dwellers ever envisioned. They had seen sights to rival any brilliant structure in New York. Though Malacai had often recalled his lonely trip as a boy crossing the Atlantic from Ireland, none of the three had been on a ship headed into the pitch of war.

All Ward's men had been encouraged to take advantage of the bath house and to enjoy the expert barbers near the street of their lodgings, but they had been somewhat reluctant to clean off completely the physical grit they had acquired. What they were headed for would take sand of a kind they hoped they could sustain, and they would have been happy to remain tense and sweating until the Texas victory was won.

From across the city, from south of where Malacai watched six beignets sliding into a paper pouch, the strains of violins and guitars wafted over lovely houses and inns in the French sector. The lilting Sunday afternoon music could not completely drown out the drums of drilling Louisiana legions near the Georgia Battalion quarters. But the melodic strumming was all the Harper women could hear from their airy room overlooking a green courtyard at the Auberge Avignon.

Adeline could not quit marveling at the mildness of the New Orleans weather, even more inviting in temperature and pleasantly humid in December than Sweet Pine Hill would be with its deep, shady recesses.

"It's almost two weeks 'til Christmas, and I don't even need a coat, not even out on the balcony!"

"The housekeeper downstairs says wait until January," Yarico warned. "And then, she said, don't put any cloaks under the bed, because February comes along and it's the coldest."

"By then we'll be in Texas."

Maggie was both relieved and sad to hear the girl mention Texas. They had all been so happy to get rooming to themselves, just the three of them, that they hadn't wanted to speak of their final destination for the last few days. It flitted through Maggie's mind that maybe New Orleans was a place so big one could stay lost. A hundred and forty thousand people, if you counted travelers—transients like the Harper women—created a sense of anonymity. But how could you live wondering if one of those thousands was a tracker hired by an irate Savannah man to hunt you down.

"I'm glad we'll be here through a bit of January," she joined in. "But wait until we get to Texas—where we're going, I wouldn't be surprised to see they build town squares right around the seamstresses and tailors."

"They do not." Addy was trying hard these days to appear an informed lady.

"She's right about there not being much store bought yet." Yarico had layered blankets for herself in the dormer floor just above Maggie's and Adeline's bed chamber, easily accessible by a grillwork staircase. Life was feeling more like good old Sweet Pine than it had in weeks. "Madame Genet, the housekeeper, she says anyone with stitches like ours can make a living. She said that's for sure—C'est certain!"

"I'm finished!" Adeline was holding up the light blue silk she had been hemming. There was just enough of the material left from the half-done banner to make a gentleman's handkerchief. One side was plain, with a double edging, and the other side had a shooting star in the upper left, with points perfectly appliquéd.

"Extraordinaire, chérie."

There had been an immediate easing up about Yarico's knowledge of French. This city, the Harper women felt, was freer about who was permitted to speak to whom. At least in this part of town, Madame Genet, who was a tall black woman with the posture and blithe air of a dancer, bid the hotel guests *Bonjour* regardless of appearance or luggage style. She was more cheerful than most of the free people of color Yarico had known to work in the livery or docks at Macon. The housekeeper was quite at home in the Auberge Avignon and spoke as merrily as if all New Orleans knew her by name.

She was the person Yarico asked the following Sunday about arranging for a carriage in the morning to take them to the wharves north of Esplanade. Word had spread that the Georgia Battalion, the volunteers heading for glory in Texas, were to assemble there and embark.

"Gaston will be in front of the inn here tomorrow morning after café—Ça vous plaît?"

"Bien sûr, merci Madame." From the balcony, Adeline listened to make sure her own French was holding up.

"When I'm grown, I'm going to bring Yarico back here from time to time—she looks so pretty when she smiles—"

"So do you," Maggie said. "You need to let me brush out your braids and put a twist in your hair one day."

"Let's put all this— the vines in the courtyard and our balcony—let's put it all in our memories, like a poem."

"It's been a nice rest...I don't see how we could forget."

"But people do forget," Adeline said. She was looking more and more to Maggie like a young lady, who would be graceful and serious with her hair up. "People forget even the nicest things."

"I expect more people have a care to forget than to recall—what brought them most sorrow."

"I just want to put all this in a picture or a locket." Adeline was promising herself to read more of her mother's French literature books, once they really settled in Texas and put up some shelves. "I wish I had a sonnet to give the Georgia boys tomorrow."

The next morning, after croissants and café au lait, Gaston brought his shiny carriage down the street and was waiting in front of the old inn where the Harper women had checked in. Adeline had seen him passing the time in conversation with Madame Genet, and she knew him to call out *Bonjour* to the other carriage drivers, so she was surprised that his mood had turned distant and cool.

She thought maybe he had gone without coffee, or that the trip up to the northern sector of the city was a farther drive than he and his horses liked to go. But she'd overheard him encouraging other hotel guests to let him take them on a tour all the way around the Vieux Carré. She thought that the French sector must be at least as far from one end to the other as it was to the docks where the *Pennsylvania* and three other schooners were prepared to make their six day voyage to Velasco, Texas.

Apparently, New Orleans was talking of nothing else, and chances were Gaston's fare would have been to the American District, no matter who had reserved the carriage first. Well past Canal Street, and on their way to the intersection that marked the newer part of town, the carriage driver spoke up.

"So, you are bidding farewell to the pirates—they are your friends?" He was addressing Margaret, as the woman of an age to be in charge, but she suddenly began to shuffle through her hand bag.

"Pirates?" Adeline repeated.

"It is not for me to say," Gaston went on, "But since you ask—are they not, what you call *pirates*? Going without American uniform...to make some war in another country?"

"Pirates jump on friendly boats and steal gold—they make people walk the plank, and use their swords to—"

"I beg you do not mistake my meaning—the good Creoles of New Orleans sent many thousands of dollars to the cause against Santa Anna only this October. But does it not provoke—"

"No Macon volunteer is a pirate!"

"It is clear they are your friends, Mademoiselle, so I will speak no more."

Adeline was thoroughly irritated with the fool that Madame Genet engaged as their driver. She thought of telling Yarico to pass along her displeasure, to tell the housekeeper what an unsatisfactory choice he was. She had overheard some conversations, though, and it had slowly sunk in how divided opinion was on intervention from the American side of the Sabine. Some felt outside opposition to Santa Anna would only make matters worse. The Harper women, however, were all in agreement that the mere sight of the determined Georgia volunteers would dent any despot's ambition. Along with all those who had joined Ward in Alabama and right there in New Orleans, the Texians would surely hold their ground.

Gaston, when they arrived three blocks from the crowded boat docks, told the ladies he would be back in two hours, if that was enough time—"to bid the friends adieu."

The women might have had a hard time finding the exact location of the fleet's departure, but the movement of the throng was in the correct direction. Companies from the Louisiana Legions had sent their drummers and fife players, so there was a rhythmic undercurrent to the roar of those gathered. It seemed that, no matter what view was held on the proper amount of American assistance in Texas, New Orleans residents wanted to say they had seen Ward's battalion off. There were so many people nudging one another to get within sight of the Georgia men and their comrades, that only Adeline was petite enough to thread her way through to the front, pulling Maggie and Yarico behind her like a slow embroidery knot.

The long plank to the deck of the *Pennsylvania* still touched the canal wharf. Boxes and trunks and crates were being rolled on platform carts up to the first deck for storage. Though it would have been harder to distinguish individuals from among a battalion fitted out in uniforms, Adeline began to despair of being able to spot the plainly clothed Gideon man or his kin. Then she spied Malacai, from the gestures he was making, and saw immediately that Francis and Joseph were close by helping to load bags of rice and peppers donated from the local markets. They were absorbed in their efforts, but a sense of urgency, of finality, was overriding any shyness on Adeline's part.

"Mr. Gideon!" Even she knew not to call out first names in a crowd of soldiers.

He and his cousins turned and set their crates down. The girl was terribly relieved to see they still knew how to smile.

"Hello, ladies," Francis said. All three took off their hats for what they knew would be a hasty exchange.

"We came to see you off!"

"You and half the world," said Malacai, looking around the wharf.

"We've been thinking about you—we wish you godspeed," Margaret said. She refrained from the motherly hug she wanted to give.

"We appreciate your thoughts." It was Joseph, who to Adeline's knowledge, would not have spoken in such a conversation just a few weeks ago. Maybe this journey had already brought out boldness untapped at the outset.

"Your nephew will be expecting you by spring?"

"Yessir," the girl's aunt was telling Francis. "But we're staying the winter in Harrisburg, so you fine soldiers can clear the way...for us to settle—"

"I have something," Adeline broke in. She didn't know what she would do if Aunt Maggie started to cry, as she'd been likely to do at the thought of her nephew already deep in Texas. "I should have made three, but after all the patches—and what I need to save for my Sunday dress—"

The men were close to laughing.

"Sweet Mrs. Bedeford—if I ever do get to another hometown where the women go properly to church—"

"Well whatever it is that you don't have enough of—I want one," joked Malacai.

"It's just the one I have. It's for Mr. Gideon."

"Nothing for me? That's a find send-off, then—"

"It's because he was my neighbor," Adeline rushed to explain. She could feel her cheeks burning. "Here, it's just a handkerchief. From one Georgia neighbor to another—you don't know about the hill—but—"

"Thank you, Miss Adeline." Francis took the time to look at the stitching. "It's fine work. It'll be my own little flag."

"Well, give us all a kiss, at least," Malacai shrugged. Maggie and Adeline gave each man a sisterly peck on the cheek, and it was Yarico who suddenly found she could not keep tears from welling.

"Oh, I forgot!" They had been about to pick up their crates again, but something came suddenly to Francis. "Can you get these to the post—there's no hurry—if you're staying in New Orleans until after the new year."

"Of course, of course we will."

"It's just some letters to Macon. I don't know why I thought I could get them sent myself."

"We shall post them tomorrow," Maggie assured him.

"Just a few letters home."

They went on up the angled plank, and the women lost track of them in the mix of young men on board the impressive schooner *Pennsylvania*. At the docks, a fife player from the residual New Orleans Greys—a contingent already gone to Texas— picked up a strident tune, and drummers from other various companies joined together in the cadence. *Tatta-Tuh-thrum-thrum-thrum!*

Deafening cheers rose up as the convoy ships pulled away from the docks one by one. Adeline was suddenly gripped by the difference from Macon's send-off. Four fine vessels under Captain Ward's command were on their way down the Gulf of Mexico. But people in this crowd were strangers. Would any truly miss the men heading out of sight? For a moment the girl thought she could see her neighbor waving a blue handkerchief from along the ship's railings.

"Come to Gonzales in the spring!" she shouted, but she knew no one could hear. "Come to our town in the spring and we'll give you all a parade!"

An hour went by before the four schooners under Captain William Ward's command disappeared around the inlet coastline. Though the middle of December always made blooms feel far away, Adeline strained to distinguish the blank strip of jutting land where the last ship had vanished, and she could not quite imagine lush vegetation in the place called Texas, much less a heartening reunion with the friendly Macon cousins.

Falling Stars

Map of Texas, 1836

Map of Texas, much as it appeared just before and just after its independence from Mexico in 1836. Artist Karen Boudreaux.

Chapter 6   By Sea and Soggy Land

"What I wouldn't give for a raft on the Ocmulgee."

"Dr. Judkins is passing these out." Francis gave Malacai a folded packet of powdery salts and his water flask.

"It was like this across the Atlantic. Nothing will help."

"About half the men are down. Joseph too—you're not alone."

"If I could sleep," said Malacai. A harsh wind had kicked up in the gulf in their second day out from New Orleans. They needed a strong headwind, of course, but the sudden gales and swells were powerful enough to send an untested sea traveler overboard. No one but the crew was permitted topside.

Francis was more worried about his cousin than he could let on.

"You stole on up to the deck last night," he said. "If I'd been an officer, I would have had to report you."

"It was clear last night—never mind the wind. I'd have stayed longer, but I was afraid my damned coat would go to ice. I wanted to see if there was any sign yet of the shooting stars."

His cousin waited for him to take another sip of water.

"I learned it in Cork, when I was a boy, every year about this time."

"When to look for falling stars?"

"If it wasn't too cold to be out after midnight—starting about now in December," Malacai said, pausing to swallow and hold his stomach while the schooner rocked. "Even more of a sure thing right after the new year."

"I've only seen one or two."

"Well, you'd remember these."

The *Pennsylvania* lurched suddenly at a dramatic angle and then nosed down a broad wall of seawater. Francis managed to keep his balance.

"It'll be all right once we get back on land. Warmer too, I don't doubt."

"Only marching will get the rubber out of these legs—"

Joseph Tidwell appeared to be asleep, but he was really making an effort to keep his eyes shut tight. He found that if he didn't look at the faces of the other ill men around him, and if he didn't witness the jiggling and sliding of satchels and water flasks as the ship rose and fell, he could calm the upheaval inside his lower body.

He liked to hear Francis and Malacai talking. He couldn't know that the girl Adeline had recently pegged him as reluctant in speech, though his own mother had cautioned him more often for being somewhat short on temper. He didn't want to open his eyes, but he found it soothing to picture his cousins as they spoke quietly to each other.

Malacai would be wincing, he thought. Regardless of his step-brother's circumstances, there was always something cheering about his countenance. He had a high forehead, but round cheeks, and his eyes always crinkled in the corners, usually from jest or laughter. But now Joseph imagined the same lines forming at the corner of the Malacai's dark eyes as a measure of endurance. His curly brown hair seemed to him the only appropriate crown God could assign to such a friendly, goodhearted disposition.

For some reason, Francis—the most educated and contemplative of the three—looked the way Joseph thought he should, as well. He'd known of plenty dark-haired scholars, but it pleased him to think—should he open his eyes—that the almost blond hair and the mostly blue eyes bespoke a clarity of thinking he had always credited to Francis. There was no correlation, he was enlightened enough to know, between physical looks and character. But there on the ship, it gave him comfort, to think of the clear-eyed Gideon cousin as alert and well—still feeling like himself, still thinking like himself, no matter how many men around him fell victim to the sickening rise and fall of the ocean.

Joseph wondered if people thought his own dark, drooping mustache as fitting a man so disinclined to converse. Or if his premature flecks of gray struck observers as brought on by his militia experience, by what he'd already learned firsthand of the steel it took to fire back at an attacking party of Creeks. He knew that his cousin and brother were yet to grasp what battle meant, what it took to wait until a man was close enough to fix in the sights of a rifle. Joseph knew what it was to pull the trigger, drop down in a sweat to count off the reloading steps, and then point without flinching to the next man coming at you with deadly intent. Counting his own rifle as a vital organ, he was loath to swap it for one of the breech loaders Ward borrowed from Milledgeville.

This sea sickness was nothing compared to the other feeling that stuck in one's gut. He could wait until the *Pennsylvania* pulled into the harbor near Velasco. Joseph Tidwell came to do what he had done before, but he didn't mind keeping his eyes closed for a few days, listening to the low talk among soldiers.

On the sixth day, there was great activity among the schooner's crew, and even those who had not been well enough to eat more than a meal a day began to stir in the lower levels of the ship and sense that solid ground was close by. The expectation of relief from seasickness gave most of the men the strength to pick themselves off the wooden floors. They began strapping their belongings to their backs and shoulders.

About to step out into a foreign country with the other plainclothes volunteers from America, Francis made a mental note of the date—December 20, 1835. Only fleetingly did he think of that Sunday's proximity to Christmas. There was nothing about the mild, almost balmy air greeting them or the nondescript and rocky shoreline to put holiday chill or festivity in mind. Messages passed back to those who were the last to withdraw from bunking quarters. The schooner carrying Wadsworth's group from Columbus had already arrived. And, at that very moment, the newly appointed Colonel Fannin and Stephen F. Austin, too, were on the wharf waiting to greet Ward's Georgia Battalion in person.

"I don't see a single cactus plant," Malacai observed.

"There," Joseph said. "That's either Fannin or Santa Anna himself." Joseph had nudged Francis and was nodding in the direction of the bow. Below, on the loading dock Captain Ward was being greeted by a tall, lean man with especially long limbs. His dark blue uniform had gold epaulettes, and buttons of the same sheen embellished his coat front. He was shaking Ward's hand, and he gave a wave of greeting and a victory gesture to the soldiers converging on the schooner's deck. Some of Wadsworth's men were ready on the shore to help, and word was that Fannin's Lafayette Battalion was greatly cheered by the arrival, at last, of so many new enlistees. What a proud and energizing moment after the draining voyage from New Orleans! The rush of air and quivering of the docked ship made them lightheaded.

"Is that other one Austin? You think that's Stephen Austin?" A more reserved gentleman stood next to Fannin. The individual in question was not in military dress. The volunteers learned that in the last few weeks Austin had, in fact, relinquished his command as general of the Texas forces. Conceding that position to Sam Houston, he was now committed to trying again for American support in Washington D.C.

"I don't think they expected him to be here," Francis said. "He's on his way to New Orleans and up to the capital."

"He looks too tired to have started up San Felipe by himself." A Macon man moving toward the ramp spoke. "He's in charge of three hundred families there?"

"If that's what a year in prison does to a man—"

"Well, I'll say it," Malacai broke in, "I'm glad we're only signed up for three months."

"There—he's smiling, even if he is tired." Walking toward Texas soil fully awakened Joseph. He felt the effect of adrenalin, of pride from being greeted by the man who had braved so much already on behalf of the colonies. And, he was ready to follow this new commander in the siege—a Georgia man as well! Only a year ago, Fannin had moved his own family from Columbus to Velasco, a port securely under settler control.

"We'll check into quarters, I expect, and then unload the ship." Francis was already piecing together the process. "It doesn't quite look like the 'Boston of the Texas coast,' as some were calling the place."

Joseph didn't care to spend much time in Velasco, he admitted to himself, whether it had looked like Savannah or a village on the Alabama River. He wanted to get on to Matamoros—if he understood the rumored plan of attack correctly. He wanted to march down the coast to Matamoros and stifle this Santa Anna despot once and for all.

The town was not much more than a fort and barn for stockpiling supplies, two dozen clay buildings, a few log cabins, and a shipping office. Sometime the year before, cholera had swept through the place, reducing the population by half, either directly from the epidemic or from grim apprehension that makes one move on.

It was no matter. A lively township with choirs or laughing children could not have drawn the attention of these soldiers to December's customary holidays. What was scheduled for their second day at Velasco was all that the men were primed to anticipate. The election of officers had been on the minds of every volunteer between Macon and New Orleans. If this call to duty was, after all, about the preservation of freedom, what more serious exercise of liberty could such individuals demonstrate than the selection of their most honored to lead them into battle.

Whatever reservations they had felt while briefly in New Orleans about washing up and shaving, trying to fit in somewhat with the smartly dressed population there, the men in arms at this military town felt an odd obligation to look their best for the occasion of choosing their officers.

The weather their first days in the harbor was uncommonly mild, and they took advantage of the opportunity to haul extra buckets of water from the two wells. The early evening dinner allowed them time to wait for kettles to heat, towels to soak, shaving blades to sharpen again between scrapings. All the men had recovered from the effects of seasickness, and most felt enough enthusiasm on the rebound to wash out their undershirts. If they could not reach for any ready dress shirt, they at least rinsed the arms of the one they'd worn and hung it by stick to dry in the morning breeze.

It was to be an evening for rededication to the cause.

In the late afternoon, they assembled in the fort, a modest building of split log beams and homemade stucco. Used as a mess hall when Mexican troops and earlier Spanish had held it, the fort contained numerous long tables of rough wood and benches providing more comfort than most young men had experienced on the rocking voyage from Louisiana.

A far more reserved atmosphere reigned than at the public dinner last held for them all in Mobile, but now they were on foreign soil. Soldiers gravitated to the tables where they saw their closest comrades sitting. Men from Macon and its surrounding plantations drew as near as they could get to the table where William Ward and Uriah Bulloch were seated. Columbus men were squeezing in at the long benches where William Wadsworth had stationed himself, and James Winn drew another table of volunteers toward his side of the room.

What many anticipated was coming to pass—a ratification, where most respect had been earned and where worthiest experience lay.

Certainly, no one doubted the wisdom of selecting William Ward to command the battalion's three companies. A cheer went up when the new major stood, and it was just as well to be gathering by candlelight instead of by stark day. Eyes glittered when Ward presented to Fannin the white and azure flag crafted by Miss Joanna Troutman of Knoxville, Georgia. It was better to cheer proudly in the relative dark, than acknowledge what allusions to home could do to grown men just now officially signing on for battle. It may have been Ward's wish or Fannin's command, but it was decided to let the soldiers eat well before electing captains and other officers.

Francis Gideon had relinquished his seat to a fellow whose blisters were still being treated by Dr. Judkins. But he found a stool by the wall, and just behind Malacai. It suited him to lean back, keeping in touch with his own thoughts.

"I can hear just fine," he told his cousin. "And if I stand, I can see Ward just as easily as I can Joseph over there." Malacai's step-brother was across the table, but without any new discussion among themselves, they knew what man besides Ward had won over their complete confidence and trust. Their primary vote would be for Bulloch as captain.

"Whoever is letting us eat before anything else—I'm voting for him twice."

"Smells as good as home cooking," Francis agreed. "Looks like our supplies have been put through some savory workmanship."

"Unloaded and uncorked—they've got brandy out, unless that's only for the officers."

Sitting with Fannin at the head table was a slight woman with her hair pulled up in a white cap. Her dress was as modest, a pleasant doe color, as her husband's formal dress shirt was showy, though the colonel had removed his officer jacket and was doing his best to make the occasion a welcome to every rank. His little daughters, apparently, were also at his side, but only until the cooks and kitchen help began to bring in dishes of rice and peppered beef. Then the two children eagerly brought plates of something new to those from Georgia.

"Flat bread, is it?" Joseph asked one of Fannin's daughters.

"It's tortillas," the girl answered before skipping back to get more.

"A week ago I would have made a jest about flattened biscuits," said Malacai. "I'm so hungry after torture on the high seas, I don't care if everything is cooked as flat as—"

"As flat as Texas!" A man spoke with his mouth full. "Did you survey the horizon as we sailed in?"

"There are hills somewhere, they say."

"Bless us all, if this is as bad as the food gets, we shouldn't complain."

"The peppers from New Orleans help!"

"We hope the 'Greys' have more than pepper to recommend themselves!"

"You Macon boys'll see what we have—most of us can drop a squirrel from a Spanish oak at near three hundred yards—"

"If it comes down to that," Malacai broke in, "whether Mexicans or Americans pile up more pelts—I'll keep the tally!"

The dinner was excellent, if not precisely what the men had thought of longingly in their more homesick moments. No one complained about the flatbread. When dipped in the beef sauce or wrapped around the stewed peppers that Colonel Fannin's personal cooks made especially for the event, the tortillas were appraised as delicious.

The more the soldiers ate, though, the more conversation began to subside. The entire regiment, men who had come from Georgia, from Alabama, Mississippi, Louisiana, and some in the Lafayette Battalion from as far away as Tennessee and Kentucky, all savored the meal. Down the line—maybe soon—there would be no such noteworthy taste or tenderness to their rations.

When Colonel Fannin rose, the gathering responded in profound silence.

"Gentlemen, I have served with the brave fellows of Gonzales. As you know, this last October they were able on their own to turn back the threat of dictatorial authority. The first step of Texas independence was firmly begun. At Concepcion, we watched the enemy flee. Now, comes the news that our forces just two weeks ago brought General Cos to a surrender at the Alamo. Our hold there is firm. As your commander, I call on this regiment to add its own victory. May our march take us to Matamoros, where the affrighted ranks of Mexico and their despot general will not dare face soldiers sworn to the ideals of freedom!"

His words generated unrestrained applause, but again all sound dropped away when William Ward took his turn to address the men.

"Honored volunteers, all you here for the cause of Texas liberty," Major Ward addressed the gathering. "It is now time for the three companies of the Georgia Battalion assembled to elect their officers and pledge their sacred honors to the duties our commander Colonel Fannin orders on the Texians' behalf."

There was no surprise in seeing William Wadsworth chosen as captain of the First Company, comprised mostly of those men he had helped gather in Columbus. Then, his sergeants and orderly received rounds of applause.

Francis was on his feet, leaning against the wall when the Second Company nominated Uriah Bulloch, whose selflessness and military knowledge had won his men over from early in the march. The entire company rose to attention for the vote. His election by the Georgians, as well as a contingent of Alabama and Mississippi men, was immediate. Basil Lamar was chosen for one sergeant and Alexander Patton received the same unanimous vote after nomination. The duty list for Company Orderly was read out loud again as a formality, and Malacai turned around to his cousin.

"You've got the penmanship for it—" he whispered, and Francis glowered, signaling it was not a moment for making light.

"Francis Marion Gideon!" Joseph called out, rising to his feet and speaking as no one had known him to do in public. "For his serious nature, his talent at accounting, his general care in deportment, and for his courage in being among the first in Macon to step forward to Major Ward's call, I nominate Francis Marion Gideon as Orderly of the Second Company!"

Vigorous applause followed his election, the same response that all the others had won. And the same sustained cheers rose up after James Winn won captain's honors over the Third Company and the right to lead those remaining from Georgia and other southern states.

The date marked the end of some lightheartedness Malacai had always enjoyed with his cousin. He would sequester his most jovial comments from the hearing of any other enlisted men. Francis did not need to ask him. As soon as Malacai turned to the new orderly of Bulloch's Company, he could see the deepening of his cousin's serious intent. If he was to account for the supplies coming in and going out, if he was to pen messages sent from one sergeant to another, he was going to fulfill those duties with the same intensity he would employ in keen rifle aim when the time came.

By Christmas, the regiment had encamped two miles away from the fort near the banks of the Brazos. The weather grew fickle. While one day could produce sunny skies but a temperature not climbing above the fifties, the next day there could be nothing but leaden gray overhead, with an atmosphere as muggy and warm as one could expect in a Georgia September. The next day could produce mists with a plummeting cold that caused the guards to check at the river's edge for ice. Regardless, the canvas tents—provided discreetly from one of America's states— convinced the mustered men that there were indeed sorrier quarters than a rocking schooner. They dared no longer recall the brick barracks of New Orleans, much less the snug comforts of home.

While drilling that filled their month at Velasco brought no joy, close marching in any direction kept them occupied and thawed, if not warm. The exertion gave the men a sense of thanksgiving at sundown, and a chance to rub feet and stab threaded needles into the holes they'd worn in socks. Only the worst mud was worth cleaning from shoes. The meals had surely diminished in appeal, but each man's daily portion of beef with cold rice was swiftly consumed. Whatever manner of bread accompanied morning coffee was of little concern.

"Request permission to speak," Malacai said, approaching his cousin late one evening while on guard duty. Had his coat been more easily buttoned, he wouldn't have minded night watch during the quiet hours when most slept.

"Speak, Private Mulholland." The practice of formality, where no one else could hear, was understood as an expression of affection.

"Is your arse half as frozen as mine, Officer Gideon?"

"Half or more."

"Sir, might I ask what you are doing about at this hour then?"

"I couldn't sleep. I was looking for your stars."

"I pointed my rifle their way earlier in the evening—now they're afraid to come out."

"Truly, cousin. How are you holding up?" There was a pause before any answer.

"Well, I never thought I'd say I'd be glad to board a ship again—"

"It shouldn't take more than a long day or so to sail to Copano," Francis said. "Will your shoes hold up on the march from there to Refugio?"

"They'd better last that far."

"There's some baling twine packed—in case any soles separate in this mud."

"I rather talk about stars, sir—than *souls*, if you don't mind."

Major Ward and his lieutenants were still up at the late hour, it seemed, as intense discussion came from his tent nearby. Ward had been back only recently from a two-week trip up the Brazos to San Felipe for official commissions from the acting governor. Word of the major's return had at least warmed the spirits of those camped on the cold prairie. The two cousins nodded toward the officer tent, in tacit understanding that no matter who was promoted to what, the man who had spoken so powerfully in Macon, and tendered some of his own riches to equip the Georgia volunteers, still commanded their highest allegiance.

The exchange between guard and orderly was over, and Francis headed to his covers to attempt rest again. He was more worried than he would let Malacai know about the level of supplies. While they had stocked the schooners at New Orleans for two months of provisions, they had not counted on another battalion being in need at Velasco when they arrived. Their month long encampment on the banks of the Brazos had nearly depleted what the Georgia fleet brought along. They were to sail the relatively short distance to Copano within a week, and Francis kept asking about the expected arrival of food—and boots, they were told, donated from somewhere in the states!

When he heard footsteps approaching his tent, he thought there could be news about such a resupply. He would have loved to find Malacai later, still on patrol, and ask him his foot size, tell him to throw away the muddy shoes that could hardly be tied. But when the flap of his tent was raised, he saw that it was Basil Lamar. He assumed Bulloch's first officers to be in on any discussion at Ward's tent. But he did not like Lamar's expression, and he wondered if he should grab his rifle before even jumping to his feet.

"Not that," the sergeant said.

"What's happened?"

"The doctor was just in Bulloch's tent— it's the measles."

A gloom settled in before the *Columbus* was loaded up for its sojourn to Copano. Even Major Ward had a hard time boosting spirits of the Second Company, though he was unflagging in his optimism that their captain would recover in time to join them in a week or two. In the meantime, he secured permission to promote both Patton and Lamar—whose uncle was already a known figure in Texas—to the station of Lieutenant.

Francis Marion Gideon was made First Sergeant.

The increased sense of duty did not make Francis sleep any better before the movement of volunteers to the docks of Velasco. Some of the Lafayette Battalion was staying behind to keep the port secure, and possibly to receive later shipments of provisions, which could then make their way to the front companies in the regiment. The *Columbus* pulled away from the fortified town, and the balance sheet of food and soldiers replayed itself in the mind of First Sergeant Gideon. He would have felt more secure about the numbers, if he had been asked to account for the stars.

As if to provide apt backdrop to their worries, a storm brewed up off the coast that tossed the vessel for nearly as many days as it had taken to make the trip from New Orleans. Worse, the cold rain did not subside when the soldiers disembarked at last less than a hundred miles southward down the Texas coast. They were then thirty miles from their destination, the inland mission at Refugio.

Joseph Tidwell was in a front row of the company's marching formation when the men set out westward from the lesser port. By the time the docked *Columbus* was out of sight, there was little evidence of the drilling practice that had been the mainstay of their month on the Brazos. In the heavy rain, the regiment's companies were reduced to clumps of staggering individuals, not uniform in dress and hardly able to command their own feet. Ahead, even Colonel Fannin had to let his horse stray where it wanted, to avoid the riskiest puddles. The oxen, muscular as they were, had no easy time pulling the wagons of artillery and commissary supplies. Ward rode up and down the amorphous bands of volunteers, trying to make sure that none were too off course in the soupy fields and wandering in a direction that would get them lost in the downpour.

Malacai Mulholland hummed the tune "Irish Washerwoman," at the outset, but his innate sense of merriment was wrung from him by the end of the first mile. He stayed to his own thoughts and spoke to himself of the need for stamina, and the possibilities of endurance. Only when Sergeant Gideon came marching alongside to check a clump of men, before going on to another wavering line, did the cousin try to sound cheerful.

"This brings to mind what me own dad used to have to go through in Cork, in the quarry," he called to Francis and anyone else who could hear. "Nothing to it at all. There's bound to be a clanging bell—at the end of twelve hours or so!"

Francis had been counting steps made in the cold mud and looking at his pocket watch. As soon as he put back his watch, he took off his hat and shook it. Then he took out the blue handkerchief the Macon girl had given him. This he rolled into a band and tied around his forehead before setting his hat back on firmly. He had been looking at the solid gray sky from which pelting rain fell as far as he could see in the direction they were headed. He was multiplying the slow pace and the number of miles to Refugio in his mind, and it seemed to him—without any breakdown of wagon wheels or men whose shoes had come thoroughly undone—that twelve more hours of this march might be a merciful accomplishment.

Chapter 7   Over Yonder

In front of the Auberge Avignon, after the first of January, Madame Genet had a nice present for her friends—Yarico Harper, and the girl Adeline with her aunt Margaret Linder. They were especially *sympathique*, even though most women traveling alone gravitated somewhat to the hotel's housekeeper. Ladies often showed their appreciation of her advice about getting by in the city of Nouvelle Orleans. But these were a special threesome to her. Of course, Mademoiselle Yarico, her ease with the language, was something rare at the heart of this family. Well, that called for some little gift for the day of Epiphany coming up—something for them to remember their time in the Vieux Carré. And maybe one day they would come back for a visit.

That morning, Madame asked the three women to come out on the walkway in front of the inn, if it was not too chilly. Fortunately, the sun was shining as it had done for the last several days. When Adeline saw Gaston, guiding his carriage horses their way, she grew tense. She would have to beg Madame's pardon and let Aunt Maggie go for a tour of the neighborhood, if that were the gift she had in mind. But there was someone hanging onto the back of the coach, a black man with a funny brimless cap pulled down over his ears. His shirt was woolen, but of a deep red which was unusual for anyone's garment. His pants, though, were the same nondescript brown that would have been worn by any field hand back near Macon. He had on woven sandals with what looked at first to be brown socks, but were just his dark feet.

"This is Eli," Madame Genet said, "He belongs to Mr. Winstead—the man that has the sugarcane plantation on the southern edge of town. But it's the free days—you know, Saturday and Sunday—even a slave can trade peppers or polish a boot for coins." She was trying to read the expressions of the Harper women.

"You have no such free days in Georgia—free to do, after their days of sweat?"

She could see the answer was *no*.

"Monsieur Eli is going to draw your picture this sunny January morning at the Avignon—I pay!"

"Oh, no—"

"Now, Madame Linder—it is for Epiphany, just a little *cadeau*, even my friend Yarico will sit by the trellis—yes?—and embroider for the portrait."

"Well, we can pay Mr. Eli—"

"As a gift, *non*, from me. And Eli here will have himself a happy Saturday. He is some artist, you know."

"Yarico, if you could run up and get the sewing bags—"

"Yes, you must all sit and sew, he will not take long—then you will always remember the Avignon. You will come back to see us after Texas gets too hot, *c'est certain!*"

It was such a nice drawing, that Adeline took it out of a flat leather folder and looked at it again and again as they sailed along on their way from New Orleans to Anahuac, where they were first to land in the country of Mexico. The way the man Eli had sketched them all was just right.

The girl in the picture had her hair up in a twist as Maggie had managed to make it do with two extra combs. The girl, or young woman now, was the only one looking up and smiling. The plump, graying, lady sitting beside her was giving her attention to her needlework, but the artist had been skillful with the reddish brown pencil marks. The older woman was smiling, as well, and looked—just the way Aunt Maggie often did—as if she could set down her work and take the time to look up and comment on the lovely sunshine. And behind them, because she would not come out into the same daylight that the other two enjoyed, was the only person as pretty as the French building facade and the streaming sunlight itself. Yarico had been, Adeline thought, beautiful the whole time the three had been in New Orleans.

In the drawing, the third woman sat in the dark of the courtyard shadows, and her face did not give in to any half smiles, as had been drawn on the other two. She was a quiet, serious presence, who would not have had to smile to be lovely, Adeline was realizing. And though the artist, Monsieur Eli had not needed to portray the needlework the woman in the picture concentrated on, no doubt Yarico's work with thread was the most exquisite piece of art anywhere near the Avignon that day.

When the Harper women's schooner turned inward toward the Texas coast, they were able to make out a shoreline, sometimes rolling, sometimes rocky—but never, though they were reluctant to say, as inviting as the banks of the Ocmulgee. But this area was, like New Orleans, coastal, and they had learned on the caravan of steamships from Mobile that ocean shores are often not as appealing as a riverbank. How could any land retain its original gentle form with incessant onslaughts of surf and sharp wind?

The women knew to expect what they had never seen before, but—after the jewel Avignon in its protected nest—it was impossible to suppress their disappointment at seeing the northern coastal town of Texas for the first time.

"Give it a while under American control—that's what it needs." Aunt Maggie was trying to sound cheerful, but even she worried about the date on the last letter she had received from her nephew. Gonzales, further inland and a settled colony for several years, surely looked more appealing than Anahuac.

On a promontory stood a shapeless fort of drab stucco exterior. As their schooner neared the log piers, the women could see that all the streets—and there appeared to be no more than four or so in the whole town—were rain slicked mud. The pathways were crowded with dully clothed individuals, most carrying wet travel bags. Half the structures, homes for the most part, looked to have been scooped up from the streets on just such a muddy day. Maybe twenty buildings along the main thoroughfare posted signs, some in Spanish, some in English, indicating that the place housed a service or store. Adeline and her companions could see the word *Hotel* on one square façade. To counteract their worry over available lodging, they reassured themselves that the next stop—Harrisburg—would have to be more inviting on first sight.

A single room remained at the hotel. It was on the north side, and since the split logs had been poorly plastered from the start, the irregular space felt only slightly protected from the elements. A chipped basin sat in the middle of a rotting floor to catch the drip of rainwater. Besides the pottery bowl and a roughly nailed stand, the room offered one stool and one unprepared mattress. The exhausted women moved it against the wall, so that Yarico could place bedding on the floor near the inside edge and feel somewhat protected from the chill. Adeline asked if she wanted to slip under the blanket where Aunt Maggie and she were stretched out straight and falling asleep, but Yarico stubbornly shook her head. There was no point in arguing or ordering.

They had swapped some American currency for Mexican scrip and paid a hotel fellow to keep a watchful eye on their wagon and trunks. That exchange had cost them almost as much as the lodging itself, but as the innkeeper said—and not in the friendly way Madame Genet would have advised— "If it is to be yours in the morning, you must pay a guard tonight. Luis will do as you pay him."

Tired as they were, the women slept fitfully. Impossible to dismiss during their first night in Mexico was the dull fear that shooting would erupt. Who knew when another madman like this Travis they had heard of might charge in to antagonize officials? Who knew where Santa Anna himself might charge in to assert control?

During the night, Luis apparently hired out his job to yet another man willing to take on work one task at a time. He didn't look as sturdy as the original luggage guard, and the next morning the Harper women were relieved to see this new person, Aaron, leading a stout burro that eased their wagon and trunks toward the water's edge. At least whatever soil this coastal town had been built upon, it was not as easily worn into ruts as it was made slippery by winter rains.

"You need to catch a steamship, is that it?" the new help asked.

"The hotel owner said there would be one going up farther into the bay."

"Where you headed then?"

"We told my nephew, if he got my letter," Maggie was explaining, "that we'd spend the winter in Harrisburg."

"Harrisburg?"

"He wrote that it was the trading town where everything comes in that goes up to the colonies—"

"You plan to spend the winter in Harrisburg?" Aaron was looking back over his shoulder at the main muddy path of Anahuac, and at the nameless hotel where the women had just checked out.

"I'm sorry your hearing is poor," Maggie said.

"It's all right by me."

"It's all right? Harrisburg is all right then?" Adeline couldn't keep from asking.

"I wouldn't want my burro to spend more than a night there, but— what you ladies plan to do is your own business—it's all right with me, but—"

"Just tell us what direction Harrisburg is," Maggie cut him off. "Get the wagon to the docks and we'll take on our travel from there."

"It's over yonder."

Aaron was just pointing up into the farther inlets of the bay. If Monsieur Eli had been sketching, he might have put a little smile on the man's face.

"You might be back later tonight," he said.

"We're on our way to where we can winter."

"Until sizeable land lots are offered to newcomers again," Adeline added. She wasn't about to mention how much American money the women had in their sewing bags and bonnet linings.

No matter how unappealing Harrisburg turned out to be, all three felt they had seen the last of Anahuac. Only Adeline, perhaps, was on the verge of asking Aaron if he had a surly relative by the name of Gaston residing in Louisiana. Nevertheless, they waited half the morning for an unpainted, sputtering steamboat to take on enough passengers to make a trip up the bay worth the captain's trouble. He was unhappy about the effort it took to roll the Harper wagon onto the deck and set log stumps so that its wheels would not roll. The wagon had seemed an unbearable burden most of the trip, even in New Orleans, when they had only fretted from time to time about its being adequately secured in storage at the wharf. But what they were told at Montgomery, they still felt was good advice. *Take the wagon*—sold to them at a good price from one of Macon's sympathetic farmers.

—Take the wagon, and don't be tempted to sell it. You don't know when you can get another, and neither freedom nor land will be worth squat if you can't hitch a couple mules to your belongings and move out of a flood's path.

Adeline, her aunt, and Yarico were inwardly recalling their blessings, when the little grinding steamship brought them around a dark turn, past a small island. They came up a cove where planks had been built out from the grassy bank into the calm water. Maggie was fiddling inside her handbag to feel for her tonic bottle, but she made herself speak to the captain anyway.

"How much did you say it would be to take us on to the next little colony this place trades with?"

"If you're talking about Brazoria, m'am," he laughed, "that's inland almost forty miles. I was so scared when the Mexicans came a while back—not ours around here but the Centralists—when they came aimin' to throw that wildcard William Travis into jail, that's the last time I thought I'd see if my boat could run on land." He took a grimy pipe from his mouth to point in the direction he would have fled. "If you're talking about Velasco—that's farther yet on down the coast. But all the water travel this ship can handle is back to Anuhuac—if my luck holds!"

When the women were deposited two hours later in the town, such as it was, called Harrrisburg, no one had the stomach for chat. Only a gristmill and a sawmill distinguished the settlement. A handful of log structures bore more resemblance to kindling accidents than to what anyone from Georgia would call home. They had to knock on the front door of one such domicile to ask if there was any building among them that functioned as a boarding place. Lookout arrangements were made with a hulking man, dressed in what Adeline deduced had to have been buck colored skins some years ago. He was not as communicative as either Luis or Aaron. But he knew how to reach out for a few coins and to plant himself near their wagon in an attitude of watchfulness.

"It's more travelers—I told you the season would start early!" The woman who'd eased open the door closest to the dock shouted to someone within the one-room cabin.

"Are you sure this is Harrisburg?" Maggie had to ask.

"If you're looking for the one in Pennsylvania, it's a sight more pretty—but you won't be gettin' there by nightfall." A man inside the cabin laughed and wheezed at the same time. The sky drooped in gray wrinkles, and Adeline's aunt had a bad feeling about how quickly night would fall.

"I must have been picturing the other Harrisburg."

"It was the grandfather of Mr. Harris, they say, started up the first one." The woman had a red striped blanket over her shoulders, and when she saw Adeline and the servant woman shivering, she felt guilty for making light of their predicament.

"We don't usually have settlers moving through until spring, or close to. But Luz Erlich has the stables. There's hardly any stock in there now, I don't think. He has the room, if you don't mind the smell."

"In the stables?"

"Over yonder—" She was pointing to a building twice as long as the others. "Usually, Miss Honeycutt puts up sheets and makes her cabin a lodge of sorts, but like I said, that's not 'til after threat of frost. Besides, she took in an Alabama family last October that hasn't gone nowhere, as far as I know."

"Mr. Erlich?" Margaret Linder was not too tired to berate herself. She felt criminal for allowing Adeline and Yarico to run off from Macon with her. The woman in the striped blanket pointed again.

94

"Yonder. Good luck then."

By nightfall, the Harper women sat in a stupor in Mr. Erlich's stable. He had been the nicest person they had dealt with in the last two days. His English was not good, but his meaning had been easy to understand.

"Ya—is warm. You women stay. Sleep in *zah* wagon. Cook breakfast *wiz* me in morning—keep your moneys."

It was lucky he had the one work horse in a stall. With the two younger women pushing the wagon from behind, the horse had been strong enough to drag their belongings into the enclosure. Fresh straw had been strewn recently and no dung was visible, but dampness enhanced the stench of livestock. Maggie and Yarico sat slumped on a trunk that they had lifted out onto the dirt to make room for sleeping. They looked too worn and discouraged to do anything but sit, transfixed like cemetery statues.

Inside the wagon, Adeline struggled to arrange quilts and blankets. When she heard one jar crack against another, she took a spoon from her handbag. The evening meal would be primitive. At Anahuac, at least Maggie had been present enough of mind to purchase a hard loaf of bread from the hotel bakery and to wrap a link of white sausage in cheese-cloth. Mr. Erlich thought to bring a water pitcher to the stable before staying to hear them latch the door from the inside.

"Drink—then wash. Don't forget, douse the candle," he advised, before shuffling off.

Adeline tore the bread into nine pieces. One small hunk apiece went with a morsel of spiced meat, one with a scoop of corn relish. A jam slice passed for dessert. Texas water tasted good, they decided. As delectable as their suppers had been at the Avignon, they had never devoured a meal more gratefully. Relieved that their first days away from American soil had not reduced them to despair, they cried from laughing. They passed around the water pitcher, splashed their faces, climbed into the wagon, and lay down like links of sausage.

In the morning, they dozed well past their first stirrings. When the sun finally fought its way out from overcast skies, Adeline sat up in alarm. She perceived light, but one eye would not open.

"Addy!" Aunt Maggie cried out, "You've been beat up!"

"You've been eaten alive," Yarico, said moving the girl's hair away from her swollen eye, before she looked to see how the older woman had fared. "All down the side of your neck and face, too, Maggie—"

"Am I snake bit?"

"Skeeters," Yarico said. "I'll go ask Mr. Erlich if anyone in Harrisburg keeps anything akin to baking soda."

"My eye—"

"It's all right, Addy," Yarico said. She pressed the girl's hand and gave the aunt a look to caution her from prattling. She put on her boots in a hurry. "I heard 'em last night but I was too tired to swat. Your eye'll be just fine." Maggie was shaking her head. "This seaside kind pestered us all in Savannah when I was a young'n even in winter. Especially your mama, but don't you worry—" The girl's aunt still stared and could only sit with her hand over her mouth.

Yarico rushed to the stable door and was outside before Maggie had time to invent any comforting words of her own. The girl's eyelid was knotted with red bumps, and the older woman couldn't remember if chicken pox had played any worse tricks with the symmetry of Adeline's dear face.

"I must look pretty bad."

"You don't look yourself—but—"

"Yarico doesn't go off on her own like that, unless—"

"She'd rather cut off her arm than watch you suffer."

"They got the side of your face as much as mine, it looks like."

"You're the one getting doctored first," Maggie said. "My looks went a thousand miles *yonder* quite some time ago—"

Adeline laughed, and both her eyes shut. She was relieved that her eyelids still worked at all. When Yarico came back speedily with a cupful of whiskey from Mr. Erlich, as well as an envelope of baking powder, Maggie reached for the cup.

"If Texas is going to be like this, I'll just take to drinking, thank you."

Adeline's aunt kept the girl humored while Yarico dabbed gingerly at her forehead. Bites on their arms could take the whiskey directly, but swollen spots near the girl's eye wouldn't safely allow for anything but a weak paste of powder and water.

The doctoring was done by late morning, and Mr. Erlich was occupied with breakfast preparations. Miss Honeycutt kept chickens, and the semi-mute man in buckskin collected enough eggs for Mr. Erlich to scramble a pile. He handed a plateful out his cabin window to the lookout man. Hearty nourishment would help the women on their day's journey farther down along the coast to Brazoria. Splatters of rain would not deter them. The Harpers could not bear to stay longer in Harrisburg.

"If you can fly—you go to San Felipe now. But no wagon can take *zah* hills. Not in mud we got now. Beautiful hills, you will see."

"It's flat if you go to Brazoria?" Adeline asked. She thought she could spell Yarico in managing the reins. They were resorting to two mill horses that Mr. Erlich helped them purchase, but he was in doubt of their disposition.

"Ya. It gets you the river you want. In spring, you follow river trail to San Felipe and see what is *zah* climate."

"If it's warm and dry enough to manage the trail from there to Gonzales?"

"Santa Anna, he makes his own climate," he said, not wanting to state his fears more graphically. "You go easy to Brazoria. Lots of your people there. Then you see what happens next month, maybe March."

"There's no danger from here to Brazoria?" Maggie couldn't help asking again. Meeting the oversized mosquitoes of the Texas coast was one thing. If she regretted letting Addy risk coming along with her, and Yarico, she most surely didn't want the future regret of not having stayed in the Texas spot where at least one nice person lived.

"Plenty settlers on same trail. It will turn warm enough, you'll see. And you don't have sleeping with *zah* horses!"

Adeline gave Mr. Erlich a jar of scuppernongs from their trunk. He was so delighted he handed them the jug of corn whiskey he had poured from to treat insect bites. None of the women could refuse.

On the path to Brazoria, the three talked little. Only Adeline, despite her hampered vision, was energized enough to manage the mismatched horse team. At least the light rain subsided, and with the sun directly overhead, the path—flat as Erlich had promised—began to dry. Mud that wrapped itself around the wagon wheels peeled off, allowing the two older women a ride smooth enough for brief napping. Yarico, after settling her mind that the girl's eye looked less swollen, drifted off estimating the number of miles between her and French friendliness in New Orleans. Maggie dozed off imagining what Matthew Linder might look like at age twenty-two, and wondering whether he might not already have chosen a bride.

Eli's drawing, already memorized, was tucked into Adeline's coat lining. She visualised the pencil strokes he had taken to produce it.

She worked to remember words to any of the Methodist hymns she had learned in Macon. Next, she tried putting those words into French that Madame La Salle would approve. The girl who had begun to wear her hair up like a lady, was trying very hard not to look at or think about, the land on either side of the damp, chalky road.

Her vision was powerful, and she had been unable to spot a tree in any direction within ten miles from Harrisburg. Trees like those inland in Georgia and Louisiana, dense forests like those they passed through in Alabama, might have been the figment of an artist's imagination. Here, they were on a prairie, which undoubtedly would appear more charming in any season other than winter. But the predictability of the tan stretches with tufts of lanky brush wanting to be green—the bruising monotony of the coastal plain—could have driven a horse to sip corn whiskey, she thought.

Only one pleasure began to counter the melancholy landscape. Erlich told them there would be travelers on the road. She had wondered how true it could be in the middle of January, though he had not told Adeline how friendly the passersby would be. She might not have believed him.

"You get beat up?" An ungainly, open wagon was coming their way.

"Just bugs."

"You stopping as soon as you get to Brazoria?"

"Yessir."

"Would you tell Harlow Massey when you run into him that Randolph is the one who left two bags of cornmeal in front of his store?"

"Massey?"

"You'll see his store when you get there. He can pay me back in June!"

Adeline was almost out of earshot when he hollered back.

"You seen whether Erlich has anything brewed?"

"Some!" she shouted over her shoulder.

A broad-shouldered man and a freckled boy on horseback pulled up alongside and rode at their pace for a mile.

"Panther swat at your eye?"

"Mosquitoes got to it."

"Staying long in Brazoria?"

"Until we can get up to San Felipe—then to Gonzales if it's safe."

"Huzzah Texas! We showed 'em in Gonzales! They can't come take away the rightful cannon they gave us for protection!"

"That's where it all started?"

"Folks was ordered to hand the cannon over, let the soldiers take it—"

"I heard—"

"Buried the dang thing!"

"We read about Stephen Austin," Adeline remembered. "He was in New Orleans while we were there last month."

"Shoot, he was on his way to Velasco and then on to New Orleans in December. He come right through Brazoria and had a speech ready."

"We're from Georgia! We rode with two hundred volunteers—"

"Land o'Goshen!"

"The whole city of New Orleans came out to see them off," Adeline told him proudly. The little boy had taken off his hat and was waving it.

"I got to get on, then, tell my wife the good news," the man said, kicking his horse. "This whole country's gonna come our way once and for all!"

"Is Massey's hard to find?" she called out after him.

"Can't miss it!"

One rider passing them up would call out "Texas!" or "Come and take it!" Someone in a wagon wobbling in the other direction, would holler "Hey there!" or "Steer clear of anything that bites!" or just "Howdy!" When one woman shouted, "Where you all from?" Adeline got the chance to say "Georgia!" Her husband answered "They're comin'!" Another shout would go up, "Tell Brazoria to dig in!" or "Now, we got the Alamo!" or "On to Matamoros!"

The river crossing was not their first, since they and the Georgia volunteers had taken a ferry to cross the Flint after Knoxville. But that first water barrier had been so near the start of their trip that they'd all believed energy would keep them afloat should any mishap occur. At the Brazos, the ferry-man was amiable enough, but his raft looked as if it had not gone through complete repairs for the coming season, and the Harper women, this time, felt buoyed by no special vigor. To see the Macon cart make it to the other shore of the Brazos gave them little sense of triumph, just relief.

The town, when the women rolled in at late afternoon was hardly Macon, Georgia. But some founder had at least made the attempt to lay out streets, and they'd been told there was a center to it all, though no courthouse like those started up in so many Southern towns. This was Mexico, however, not the United States, Adeline kept reminding herself. She did not really know what the typical Mexican village looked like, Anahuac having been such a mixture of Spanish and American influence. Most of the Brazoria buildings in view were log structures or split wood, and a half dozen had even been whitewashed, so there was a sense that many inhabitants originated in frontier not too different from the latest Georgia territory to be divided into counties and opened for land lots.

But since crossing into the coastal waters of this Mexican territory *Texas*, all three women had experienced the sensation of stepping back into the eighteenth century. Whatever enterprise "Massey's" was, it was not a Macon shop where ready-made dresses could be examined. It was not a tin-ware shop where one could browse for candleholders, or a mercantile store that could display sharp German scissors. It was a general store, of the most general kind. The man "Randolph" had left two bags of cornmeal in front.

Adeline left Maggie and Yarico outside to stretch their legs, to work feeling into their feet. Inside, she noticed more sacks mounded in a corner. Aromatic coffee beans and a dozen packages of sugar rested in piles behind the counter. Dried beef sticks were packed into a glass container on the counter, and tin cups lined the window ledge. Adeline was glad they had meticulously packed their sewing tools and materials. She didn't think blue silk and embroidery thread—even durable stitch, cotton thread—made it to Brazoria on a regular basis.

"Mr. Massey?" The heavy set man she spoke to had white hair, but a young face.

"Harlow—See what you need?" When he looked up from the counter, he asked, "Skeeters?"

"I'm on the mend. I told a *Randolph* that I'd let you know where two extra bags of cornmeal came from."

"Out front? He owed me three—"

"He said you didn't need to pay him until June—"

"Pay? I don't pay him—he owes me! When did you—" Mr. Massey was starting to compose himself, since he realized he was talking to a complete stranger, a very young newcomer who had obviously been on the road from Velasco or Harrisburg. "Aw, he's a practical joker. Told you to say that—come June he'll be asking you if it made me mad what you told me—owed me three, anyway."

"Is there an inn or a lodging house in town?"

"How many you got with you?"

"Not as many as we started out with—all the Georgia volunteers— There's only my aunt and…our woman who helps—"

"Well, I'm goin' to thank Randolph when he shows up again in June, after all!" He was taking off his clerk's apron and folding it on the counter. "You staying a while?"

"Until spring weather anyway, and whenever people say the danger is cleared—"

"I gotta find me good folks to stay in my brother's house while he's gone off to Louisville. Take him a month, I reckon, to get on over to New Orleans and up the Mississippi. You stayin' that long?" The man judged the low angle of sun at his window and lit a lamp.

"I don't think we could travel to another town soon if you were to tell us the mud there was all turning to gold."

"Well—you'd go, I guarantee, but that's the right answer. You ladies follow me," he said.

He was on his horse after shaking Margaret's hand. Down the main thoroughfare and over two roads was a house somewhat smaller than Sweet Pine, but not backing into a hill or tree of any kind. Nevertheless, they could appreciate by candlelight that the inside was the most inviting quarters the three women had seen since leaving the Avignon.

"My brother wanted me to get someone to watch his things—you're it, and it's a godsend."

"It is for us, most surely, Mr. Massey," said the girl's aunt.

"Yes, thank you kindly."

"I'll leave and let you to settle in, see what you need and everything, but I have to ask one more thing—Either of you ladies good with your letters?"

Adeline and Maggie were trying not to look at Yarico, who had taken on her air of invisibility.

"I was starting lessons at an academy—"

"Why I'm asking is our main teacher, Mr. Henry Smith—he's up at the convening, one of our delegates in all these independence talks." The store owner seemed to be carrying on two conversations with himself.

"Mr. Austin stopped on his way through here just weeks ago—said to expect a contingent from Georgia!" He clapped his hands, before getting back to his first point. "If you can just teach the little ones their letters and sounds, I'll be off the hook for both obligations that have been making me lose sleep lately."

"I know English and French and some geography, mathematics—"

"The position is yours! What'd you say your name is?"

"Adeline Harper."

"Well, I won't ask your age—we won't send you any older than eleven— how's that suit you?"

"I'm older than—."

"Will you take pay in sacks of flour and cornmeal? Coffee and such?"

"How can we thank you, Mr. Massey?" Aunt Maggie was beginning to cry, so he rushed on to get out of their way.

"Well just make yourselves at home. Whatever my brother's got here, you all make use of. He just doesn't want it burned down while he's gone. I'll show you the school house in the morning. Rosalia lives next door to it—she's got the key."

"We can't thank you enough."

"It's that jackass Randolph we can thank," he laughed shaking his head. "Telling you to say I can pay him in June. Don't you tell him come summer it made me mad, you hear?"

"Sir? Mr. Massey?" Adeline who had been nodding, but without speech at his departure, had suddenly made a connection. "The steamboat man at Anahuac told us that Velasco was—*yonder* down the coast. Does that mean we're not far from there?"

"They've got the post running pretty regular between us and them just recently. They're not more than forty miles from here, south down the Brazos toward the coast."

"Then our Georgia boys are there! That's where they were headed, and—"

"Sure, we got word of their arrival. I reckon they'll stay a while, but Fannin's bound to go get after any threats from Matamoros before too long."

"Matamoros—how far—"

"I forget the miles—it's where the Rio Grande meets up with the gulf."

"But if they're still in Velasco, I could get a letter to someone?"

"I wouldn't wait too long. Our boys are already holding San Antonio. We're fixin' to get us a governor at the convention just now going on. And with Fannin's army growing at Velasco and ready to counter any threats, this whole conflict will be over in our favor before ink dries on a page of stationery!"

Chapter 8   There Art Thou Happy

The Georgia Battalion had been encamped at the Mission Refugio for over a week. Winter rains were sporadic, but the cold did not let up. Under Lieutenants Lamar and Patton, Bulloch's company—certain now that the measles would keep their captain from joining them—had steered in whatever direction Ward took. The entire battalion had flung themselves down in a row of narrow, dank rooms adjoining the chapel.

When Fannin's soaked volunteers first straggled in, the small, well scrubbed sanctuary was already occupied, except for a clearing at the altar and crucifix, by a Captain Ticknor's group from Alabama. A number of other small companies also waited for the colonel at the mission. Still more found their way to Refugio—men worn but feverish for action, men with British and Irish accents, speaking quiet Spanish, talking a Scottish brogue, switching from French to broken English—a tattooed Tonkawa man, an advisor of Sam Houston's, they said, who would not speak at all.

Their variety of attire reminded Francis Gideon of the strongly individualistic ranks in Louisiana legions. But there was hardly any spit and polish to the final appearance of the mission volunteers. They all wore a dull veneer from sweat, splattered mud and rainfall at every angle.

With the whole of the regiment at the mission, except for some of the Lafayette group left at Velasco, and another fifty holding Goliad, Bulloch's First Sergeant was figuring there to be over five hundred soldiers waiting for further direction from Fannin. One of the colonel's officers was assigned official commissary duties, but he often sought out the Macon man to double check his estimate of provisions.

"Surely we'll get a post from Velasco or Copano, today—tomorrow," he said to Francis. "They know we're getting critical—there's still flour, but there won't be bread of any kind without some lard."

"Did you add the Texian company to the count?"

"If you can call them a company." Fannin's lieutenant looked down the center aisle in the chapel where a cluster of woodsmen in dark, slickened buckskin were gesturing emphatically as they talked. It was hard to tell where their beards ended and their leather shirt fronts began. "I don't know whose order they'll take."

"I can't say I'm sorry to see them—that's another ten anyway. We were wondering where the soldiers of Texas were." Malacai's cousin looked with envy at their moccasins.

"Some had a hand in getting San Antonio into our control, but by now they've left the Alamo, or passed through Gonzales and then San Felipe, to get on home. They've got fields to get ready for spring." Francis couldn't let himself think about what duties his father and brother Thomas might be undertaking in the rich, red dirt of home.

"They can get back in the fight if it heats up?" he asked nervously.

"I'm not saying many will jump on a horse and ride to catch up with us in Matamoros, but—"

"So you think it's certain that's where we're—"

"Hey— the boys are crowding up over at the north windows!" The officer dashed toward the onlookers "Maybe it's someone from Goliad. Could be Colonel Fannin himself!"

It was a messenger, confirming that Fannin and Houston—along with a Dr. Grant and Captain Johnson, who had come on in to the mission from the south near San Patricio— were now wrangling at Goliad over command discretion and strategy. Some stubbornly different views heated the dispute, as far as troops loyal to Ward could discern.

"The only orders yet are from Johnson and Grant," the breathless messenger was able to say. "This one for sure—whoever's fit— to take their mustangs out daily, give 'em some regular practice with the bridle, or else they'll go back to being only half broke."

It was not the information Francis was looking for, but he thought some of the men in Bulloch's Company, including Joseph and Malacai might wish to take a turn with the fine little horses Johnson and Grant had brought in from the southern ranges. They were smaller than the typical Georgia farm horse, but spirited and nimble. The men were growing far from spirited. The loss of Captain Bulloch, the draining march from Copano, and the unsettling paucity of food were demoralizing developments. It was too cold and too dangerous to ride far, but the last couple days had been sunny, and Francis thought that saddling up and getting out of the meager mission quarters might prove invigorating.

Step-brothers Joseph Tidwell and Malacai Mulholland were indeed happy for the chance to ride, though Malacai borrowed another fellow's boots, fearing the heels in his shoes might drop off in the stirrups. Within the mission were kettles and fireplaces, and the soldier who had lent his boots, one of the few pairs in camp, was promised a tub of warm water for soaking his feet.

Outside, the Macon men found the same sunshine they'd forced themselves to march in earlier that morning. A small corral off the back edge of the mission was where Dr. Grant and Johnson had led a string of newly tamed horses just five days before. Joseph and Malacai immediately selected a pair of dark brown mustangs that appeared attached to each other and as friendly toward bridle and saddle as one could expect. They did not care where the ride took them, but the men were slow to bend their stiff bodies into riding position and slow to come around the southern perimeter to a lower rock wall protecting cemetery stones and crosses. The memorials were more comforting, oddly, for their uniformity than the rugged partitions of the church interior.

"When we first wandered in, that dreadful afternoon," Malacai said, "I was so tired, I was ready to find a little spot on the ground—just go lie down next to one of those markers."

"It looked like relief, after some of what we've been through."

"And I haven't even raised my rifle—can't say if it still works."

"You'll be glad you saved the powder," said Joseph.

Maybe the mustangs were a little depressed, too. The men gave them near free rein, but they were content to turn together at the main pathway in town and amble in the direction of least resistance.

"If Colonel Fannin can only get word finally from Governor Smith about—"

"You mean Governor Robinson," Joseph corrected him.

"No, I'm sure t'was Smith they've been sayin' is—"

"That *was* the man chosen, but he wasn't in agreement with his Council or some elected group."

"The Texians already held another election?"

"Seems the convention has—off away from all the Santa Anna threat in these parts."

"Washington on the Brazos, I know I heard that," Malacai said. "I've yet to picture where the river is."

"There's a whole string of them as you go east."

"So what you're tellin' me—you're saying there's a new governor."

"Only Smith won't step aside, so it's a matter of opinion whether Robinson is now—"

"Well, maybe Fannin ought to take us all over there and bring the Texians to peace terms with each other!" Malacai always made Joseph smile. He was chuckling now, and he hadn't felt so cheerful since New Orleans, since Mobile maybe.

"If that strikes you funny, then you might fall off your horse when I tell you how well Fannin and Houston get along."

"You don't say—"

"Heard Francis and that commissary officer just today." He wanted to put it calmly, because Malacai could exaggerate if he were to go on to tell any others. "They have opposite ideas what to do next, but the upshot from the new governor is—Sam Houston now commands all the Texas Regulars—supreme command at least on paper and still loyal to Smith, by the way—Fannin, it looks for sure, has his own say over us volunteers."

"Well." Malacai had stopped in front of one very small wooden house, where smoke was curling from a plastered chimney at the back. "Ward's our man. If he's in with Fannin, then that's what we'll—Bless me, Joseph, do you smell chicken roasting?"

They had been told that the colonial settlers, well over a hundred families from southern Ireland had left the area for Victoria when General Cos, Santa Anna's brother-in-law, came through on his way to San Antonio. Then, when the Texians had turned it around and defeated Cos, many Mexican settlers in town had fled their homes, too, pulling back as far south of the fracas as they could.

Joseph and Malacai had not anticipated crossing paths with any inhabitants of Refugio. If they hadn't remained so long in front of the odd little house, they likely would have missed any interaction. But a towheaded youngster, a boy of eight or nine, came out with his hands in his pockets and a pistol clearly nestled in his waistband.

"We're only stopping to smell the lovely cooking."

"Is that so," the boy retorted.

"If I could feast on lovely smells, I'd be stuffed like a roast piglet right now."

"We're having chicken when it's done."

"Don't tell me any more."

"And potatoes and cabbage."

"You know," said Malacai, who was as hungry for a home meal as he was trying to be jolly. "It's a poor sin for an Irish lad to make an Irish man cry."

When the two soldiers were invited in to join the family of seven for dinner, they weren't sure if they could stay calm during the long prayer over their crocks of chicken and potatoes. Whatever self-discipline a soldier needs to hold fire until he's sure to hit target, it took equal restraint for the two Georgia men to bite into their portions slowly. They struggled to eat as they would have in the Tidwell dining room with their own mother at the table.

Mrs. Finnissee crossed herself more than once as the men told parts of their story. There were portraits with halos and statues, other signs of Catholicism enhancing the soldiers' sense of being in a foreign land.

"We're mostly Methodists and Episcopals in Macon, where we're from, m'am," Malacai commented. He seemed to hesitate. "Don't ask how me dad ended up where he called home—I was never told—but I think he may have been the only worker in Cork who— when he'd take the Lord's name— wasn't obliged to make confession—"

"Don't say Cork—*We're* from Cork!" Mr. Finnissee wanted to talk about the city in southern Ireland, and Joseph just took small second helpings while his step-brother and this agreeable Texian family swapped tales. "Home is home," the Irish settler kept saying. "Jesus loves every blasted one of us!"

They felt guilty bringing the mustangs back into the mission corral around dusk, especially since Francis had begun to worry that they'd lost their way in the repetitive, rolling mesquite plains around Refugio. There were two creeks that could easily be confused. They'd brought their sergeant a cinnamon pastry, but he wanted them to keep it for the next morning.

"It was just your good luck," Francis said. He was relieved to see Malacai regaining some of his natural disposition. The good-natured cousin was enough full of merriment to bring some of his comrades out of their malaise later that evening.

"I've been thinking on a literary matter—and you know any thinking on my part is fairly dangerous," he started off. "Sergeant Gideon will know the priest I'm talkin' about—that one in Shakespeare who can't stand to hear young Romeo whine about his problems—"

"Friar Laurence."

"The very one," Malacai went on. "And he keeps sayin' to the upstart, who just goes to weeping about his sorry lot—'There art thou happy!'"

"I remember the other parts better—"

"Well, here's my little list for remembering blessings—you good men are the chorus—just finish off with the priest's happy line." Most of the Second Company men were only beginning to open their eyes, having nodded off early. Some were already smiling for any attempt at cheer.

"At least we're not tipping and diving the waves on the jolly old schooner *Pennsylvania!*"

"There art thou happy!" one man answered him.

"And at least we're not picking slithery-dees from our rice on the icy banks of the Brazos encampment!"

"There art thou happy!" more chimed in. Malacai was in his sock feet, having returned the borrowed boots.

"At least we're not trudging through the most miserable rain that's fallen on the planet since Noah packed up his beasts!"

"There art thou happy!"

"At least these pitiful rock walls are the walls of a friendly Texas mission and not the walls of a Mexican prison in view of the equator!"

"There art thou happy!"

The men took up the refrain until a number of other contingents and clusters in the mission wondered what it was keeping the Georgia group so merry in light of the tense inaction.

It was an evening of encouragement, Francis thought looking on, that might keep them fit to survive what lay ahead.

Colonel Fannin did arrive at Refugio the next day, confident that attacking Matamoros was the way to deter Mexican aggression. Brimming with confidence, he had held out among closest compatriots for the command he desired. Even though Sam Houston had not thought much of the Matamoros approach, and even though he was still the supreme commander, the new governor had officially given charge of the volunteers to James Fannin.

Dr. Grant and Johnson would stay at the Texians' southernmost foothold, and the division and assignment of volunteer forces would be Fannin's to call. The colonel announced his intention to hold official officer elections again within the week, since the convention's new government required updating all commissions. He was still well aware, as commander of the volunteers, that soldiers not in the regular army had the right to elect their superiors.

The chance to reiterate their trust in company and battalion leaders brought new vigor to the mustered men. And if only news would come from either port, about well equipped ships for supplying or sailing down the Gulf of Mexico—the attack would be on!

The next day, however—February 6—a courier did come riding the trail from Copano with news that was hard at first to fathom. It was about Matamoros, and there had been enough soldiers standing around Fannin when the message was brought into the mission, that the immediate shock and silence spread faster than grassfire within the ranks.

It was all about Matomoros. General Urrea had already taken control of the city. Any citizens there who were sympathetic to the colonists' cause—twenty per cent of the port's population was American!—had conceded control to the general's Centralist troops. What was worse, and impossible to visualize, was that General Santa Anna himself was there and had amassed upwards of five thousand prime troops. Mexico's supreme leader was forming up to head an expedition right into the heart of coastal Texas!

Colonel James Fannin's scheme of attacking across the Rio Grande abruptly came to an end. There was no reasonable response for the regiment he controlled, except to withdraw to the sturdier fortress at Goliad, and to prepare for holding Texas lines as they were. The election of officers the next day was   hardly an event to draw out and relish. Five hundred approved unanimously of Colonel Fannin and of Ward as Lieutenant-Colonel, with a Columbus man Dr. Mitchell, taking control of Georgia's battalion.

The official order of retreat came from Fannin on February 11, and two days later as the exodus to Goliad was about to be undertaken, every man in the mission knew his own assignment, and little more.

"Who'd you say is staying here in Refugio? Father Orlando wants to know, now that most of us are clearing out of his chapel."

"It's Amon King." One of the Bulloch men was somewhat sure. "I don't know that he's too happy about it. He'd rather go on up to San Antonio and see if the Alamo is steady."

"Houston already sent Travis up there to see Bowie in person—looks like Bowie has had pretty good luck so far— runnin' off Cos from the town, and whipping them at Concepcion before that. But if Mexico's first general comes up this far—"

"Santa Anna took it pretty hard about his own kin getting ousted there —"

"How many thousands are coming?"

"Don't forget what *Señor Napoleon* did about Tampico in November—he wasn't even angry so much then, but "pirates" he called the captives. Had 'em shot is what he did."

"What did you say Houston's calling for?"

"He's gone to Gonzales with what's left of the Regular Texas—they'll probably head back further east—"

"You figure the Grant and Johnson men are staying put here?"

"Most of Grant's went on with Houston, but those two, they won't give up the southern parts near San Patricio—that's the latest word. They're taking some of their horses back south with them, and some new patrol that's been assigned there—Shackleford's, I think-"

"No, that's the company going back on the road to Copano—making sure we still hang on to the ports—"

Members of the regiment hoisted their knapsacks and picked up their rifles. A few, including Joseph, were getting comfortable with the new yagers and were lugging two weapons. They had put on second shirts if they had any, buttoned their coats well, turned up their collars, pulled their hats down around their ears. Many used lengths of the baling twine brought along to add some assurance of their shoes holding together.

"Have they got provisions waiting for us at Goliad, do you think? I know there's new artillery in some of the wagons—Fannin was waiting on that, but have they been fortifying—food—and supplies at Goliad?"

"That's what most are thinking—"

"At least the place is bigger, on a hill, they say, and much better set up for defending—"

"There art thou happy!"

But the five hundred men under Fannin's lead could not rejoice much as they left Refugio heading north on the road to Goliad. Under other circumstances, they might have been grateful that the roads were less muddy than they had been on the first march inland into the mission town. No rain had fallen for several days. The path leading to Goliad saw no rain on the 13th of February, 1836.

But in the freezing temperatures, sleet fell without mercy.

What should have been a welcome sight, the presidio at Goliad coming at last into view after the frozen, thirty mile march, was akin to a cruel hurdle on the homestretch. The mission fort at Goliad sat atop the highest point of land overlooking the San Antonio River and its woodland banks. The rocky incline was as iced as the soldiers' shoes and coats. Any sense of triumph was absent as the regiment struggled up the brutal slope to shelter. Beyond exhausted, the proud volunteers staggered through the mission entrance. They were spent and could meet no further challenge. Inside the presidio walls, they looked at one another, for proof that they were not dead. They looked away—at the deteriorating stone walls, at their raw hands—in order not to read from one another's expressions, that death might prove a lesser punishment.

Chapter 9   Give Us This Day

Officially accepting command from Captain Westover, who had been in charge of residual men and several cannons, Colonel Fannin allowed his regiment forty-eight hours to thaw and to rest. Then he put the Georgia Battalion and all the other forces at Goliad to work. The presidio, though occupied continuously by one faction or another in the peaking conflict, had fallen into disrepair. Walls needed to be strengthened, defensive trenches needed to be dug, towers for artillery needed to be constructed at intervals. The commissary officer managed to transport enough corn, flour, beef, and coffee— amassed at the last minute from Refugio—to feed a regiment respectably. The enlisted men were marshaled and set to tasks.

"We need six volunteers—whose shoes are in best shape—" Not many hands went up. "To bring in stones from anywhere beyond the wall, even down by the river and woods, and out behind the barracks on the south end." Lieutenant Patton and Sergeant Gideon were told to assign duties to privates. "Stones this big," Patton said using both hands. "You and you, your shoes look in fairly good shape."

"If your hands have started to heal—you can use some cut up flour bags to wrap them—" Francis was saying. "We need you to help build up the perimeter wall. It should be ten feet and it's crumbled to three in places. It'll be better protection for us all—"

"Mobile and Kentucky are starting in on the parapets, so we don't know whether we're to sign on with them when we finish or take our turn on the trenches—Anyway— who has hands that've quit bleeding?"

"We got the lard in we were looking for," Francis thought to add. "That or corn oil might ease any cracks in your fingers."

The soldiers had been standing as they were addressed. The company understood its orders, but there were a few moments when Francis was afraid he might be witnessing a mutiny, a fierce, unspoken refusal to act on stamina beyond what had already been demonstrated. But the fearful moment passed, and the fellow with boots began to pull his coat around himself for the scavenging effort. Joseph Tidwell was positioning his extra pair of long-johns down along his neck and inside his shirt for additional protection. Those who knew rustic masonry to be their best skill looked at their hands for the most vulnerable wounds in need of wrapping.

Private Mulholland wouldn't let himself think of the kid gloves that went to the family man in Macon, the one on his way to Texas himself in a Gideon cotton wagon. Malacai knew his shoes wouldn't hold up much longer. He began to tear a flour sack into strips, thinking he might wrap his feet, as well, after handling heavy rocks where the wall had gaps.

Stone by gray stone, Fannin's men began to make Goliad's La Bahia respectable again as a fortress. Two weeks of toil made the presidio look a formidable three acre compound once more. Some of the men from Louisiana were especially creative in the commissary, and their efforts fed spirit back into the recovering men. Jorge Cruz and his wife Consuela, who helped Father Guillermo at the chapel, shared basil, cilantro, and ground cumin with the battalion cooks. A ration of brandy was offered to celebrate completing fortifications, and though no one openly presumed milder weather—a blessed new season hinted at moving in.

A white silk flag with an azure star was raised at dawn the next day—*Where Freedom Abides.* The sight brought to mind that blushing Georgia girl who'd sewn the banner together, *There is my home!* When the colonel began to call his outpost *Fort Defiance,* such an attitude reestablished itself among the volunteers as well.

It was the end of their first fortnight at Goliad. The day was as convincing a prelude to spring, as any the cotton planters from the banks of the Ocmulgee River might have enjoyed at home. Mild daylight temperatures consorted with dampness from the last month's rain. Brilliant sunshine raised from the earth a distinctive smell that farmers recognize. Joseph had volunteered to take night lookout on one of the parapets. And since Malacai was interested in what stars such a clear evening might bring out, he wrapped a blanket around his coat and followed him.

Francis came a little ways behind, measuring in his mind how many quick steps his cousin took in comparison to his own. Malacai's shoes dragged from the weight of dried mud. But an alarming color where seams fell apart, and stained twine, fixed the sergeant's attention. He had been given an officer's bottle of port, so he was thinking to ask Cruz or his wife if anyone near the mission might swap an old pair of boots or moccasins for such a treat. His cousin arrived just below where Joseph stood looking out beyond the dark hill.

"What can you make out, brother, besides the moon?"

"It's a fair country, you'd have to say—if you meet her in a fair season."

"But *winter* and *war* starting off with the same letter—no mystery why—"

116

"They haven't got a tree that can stand to one of ours in Georgia," Francis spoke up. "The roll and stretch of the fearsome place, though—it begins to grow on you."

"If you go to waxing poetical, I'll thrash you with my blanket."

"A thrashing, then—"

"The place is growin' on me all right," Malacai went on. "I've got half the dirt from Copano to here stuck between my toes!"

"Hush him up, Francis—some ready-aim on the next artillery mount will get rattled and point our way. He'll get a hole blown in the three of us—and this beautiful new wall."

"It does look sturdy," Francis said. It was a tribute, he felt, to some power higher than military rank.

"You think word'll get out? That we're well fortified here—"

"And too much for the Mexican troops to tinker with?"

Joseph had heard other mutterings traveling through the garrison— that General Houston thought it wisest—was ordering—Goliad, as well as the Alamo, to be abandoned for the time being. Join up strength at Victoria, was what the general had tried to order. Some in the battalion were wondering whether the governor, whichever one it was, had a superior understanding of the threat than these officers, or greater influence over subordinates. The question had gone unanswered, so Joseph asked again.

"Do you think we can dissuade the passing Mexican lines, or not?"

"We'll hold them or drive them off," First Sergeant Gideon replied. Malacai shivered and moved from foot to foot.

"All I can say is, they better give us every one a pretty piece of land for all our trouble."

The two soldiers not on official duty walked back toward the presidio church entrance. When the three cousins were together, one of them always managed to bring the mood around to determined optimism, but it was hard to hold back misgivings from one family member at a time. Malacai put his hand on his cousin's shoulder and made him turn to face him.

"I didn't want to say this with Joseph on duty and needing to concentrate."

"That's good..."

"Lord, how he handles that new breech loader—- already workin' it like a third arm—"

"Most are struggling to make the switch. Not him." But it wasn't weapons that Malacai wanted to talk about.

"I think it's these cats that run the place at night—"

"Cruz gives them kitchen slivers, from cleaning his knife."

"I was thinking about their nine lives—thinking about all the lives I've already had—"

"Malacai—"

"No, listen to me—I'm not gettin' maudlin, I just—"

"Everyone's worried—"

"No, but me in particular, I was thinking how many lives I've already had, like the cats—losing my first father, then me dad and mother. There's lots of orphans never get heard of in Ireland after a thing like that." He was looking somewhere to the east, in the direction of both homes he'd known. "Then I survive crossing the ocean, and come to live with fine new parents and a brother, all with open arms—"

"You can talk to Father Guillermo, you know—not about which church—"

"My nerves are fine, that's not it," Malacai said shaking his head. Francis thought the both of them might break down, and he didn't know if he could listen to any more.

"He's teaching me Spanish—one word a day," the company sergeant said, " *frio*," he recited, shaking his arms—*gato*," he went on, pointing to a feral cat that darted near the entrance.

"Francis—I'm just sayin' it so there's a witness—if my luck runs out on this adventure—I want someone to witness that I wasn't bitter. I've had myself quite a life—"

"Cousin—"

"It's the bloody waitin' I can't take any more of!"

In the morning, First Sergeant Gideon came out with an honor guard from his company. It was their turn to raise the flag, "Liberty or Death." And he was happy when the coastal breeze took Miss Troutman's banner the other direction, and he could think of Georgia, the dear people who woke up worrying about him and his cousins every day. "There is my home," he told himself.

You need such moments as these to draw inside from the deepest well, he had gone on thinking. A man needs a few moments when something beautiful reminds him of what's eternal, when the peach colored sky and the sunshine itself could feel like the richest gift in the world. A soldier needed to remember tenderness maybe—a morning when he picked up a baby—in order to brace for cruelty that would not be in him otherwise. He, too, had already been a man with quite a life. Francis Marion Gideon was steeling himself for that instant, should it come for him —eternity, *where freedom abides.*

About mid-morning one of the soldiers on the parapet off the barracks side saw a man on horseback. He was not wearing the white pants of the enemy. He was not on a Spanish pony, but the watch knew it was no time to relax. The rider had put his horse to a test coming down the San Antonio road at that speed. If it had been good news, the man in buckskin would probably have been waving his hat and whooping.

The last time a galloping post had come, it was news from Copano that Matamoros was a lost cause. Soon, the rider did begin to shout. He had been saving his breath until he thought his voice might be heard. Somewhere down by the river bed, as his horse waded through the frigid current, the brutal words fell on the ears at several Goliad lookouts.

"Santa Anna's already at San Antonio! He's here! Santa Anna's already coming up near the Alamo!"

Chapter 10   Home, Over One's Shoulder

One piece of news in Brazoria conflicted with the next. Some said General Sam Houston camped in Gonzales with mounting Texian forces. Others swore that General Sam Houston was rallying forces at San Felipe or farther up the Brazos. The post coming in regularly from Velasco, however, was certain. Santa Anna forces now controlled Matamoros. Even hotheads in Brazoria quit talking about storming the big city just south of Texas territory. Let the despot have it.

No further news was good enough.

Common wisdom held that established settlers could remain north and east of any confrontations. If no farther south than Victoria was safe, one had only to mind that boundary. If families beyond Gonzales felt little security, it was foolish to strike out past that stronghold. Townspeople admonished newcomers on the move to shelter with Stephen F. Austin's colony, as a precaution. No matter where Houston might position himself, the Brazos colony San Felipe would provide certain protection.

Settlers itching to head north before spring storms included the Harper women. Having arrived in Brazoria on January 20, they'd grown wary of getting too comfortable a month later. Adeline, Yarico, and Maggie had begun to tap that settled feeling, the comfort that routine engenders quickly enough in any place where necessities are within reach after hard work. They were sensing the promise they had begun to enjoy in Macon's streets. Sunrise to dusk offered some balance—time after hired sewing for cross-stitch, time after chopping kindling or onions for sketching a fashion bonnet, time after printing on slate tablets for one's own reading.

If they intended to settle in Gonzales—home of Matthew Linder—there was no point in dawdling past the first redbud blossoms. With the Brazos River bottom and the San Bernard likely to bog down even an oxcart this time of year, their wagon master Mr. Hanson planned to take his small caravan up the middle path. A stretch of land between the two rivers would eventually connect to the main San Felipe trail. At that point, Margaret Linder and the younger women could decide whether to cut out west for Gonzales or shelter with the bigger colony.

Harlow Massey's brother Oscar was already back from Louisville but was kind enough to put himself up in his brother's store until the Harper women's departure day. He didn't mind parking himself where there was a steady stream of news.

"Henry Smith is the Texas governor, fair and legal!"

"Last word is he's been impeached—"

"By what authority? That dang Council?"

"If Robinson thinks he can supplant our Henry—"

"I think Henry should've stuck with bein' a school teacher—"

"He's born for bigger than that!"

"Well, we're stuck wrestling with the same big question—Who's fit to teach?—with young Miss Harper goin' off soon—"

"If no one aims to stay, I don't know what we're collecting for—"

"I'm bettin' it goes Robinson's way by planting time. Won't be any youngsters in the school house by then anyhow."

"Hope Robinson likes getting an earful—if he lets any of Santy Anna's tax collectors march in to shake our pockets!"

There seemed to be more consternation among town folks about whether this fellow Robinson would succeed in supplanting their Mr. Smith than there was about whether Santa Anna was going to make the whole lot of Texians walk a plank.

No one the Harpers spoke to was really very worried about that.

Worry served no purpose, everyone felt. Shaping up the independence government would take time, but Brazoria was proud of what Texas already held! The Alamo had been handily grabbed from the Mexican army by Ben Milam—*God rest his soul and may the sniper who felled him burn eternally!* And two fighting legends no one seemed brash enough to challenge, Jim Bowie and William Travis, were still there, still firmly holding the fortress. Besides that, volunteers from the states flowed in steadily, as anyone from Georgia could swear. The settler stronghold from Copano all along the San Antonio River to the Alamo seemed no more likely to waiver than the north star.

The night before their departure, the Harpers weren't going to let any female inclination to fret alter their plans. Had they not first driven their wagon two hundred miles out from Macon? Then floated with it down the Alabama River? Chugged and sailed alongside it across a gulf of saltwater? Had they not already camped in the confines of their makeshift wagon tent? Adapted to big city life when it came to that in New Orleans? Weathered the shock of Anahuac and even been grateful for a stable in the odd, but friendly trading town called Harrisburg?

They worked at reassuring one another.

Yes, they admitted to themselves, it was hard to leave a place as hospitable as Brazoria, and a place sentimental to Yarico as well as to Maggie, because it was the town where they had celebrated Adeline's thirteenth birthday.

"From now on, Addy," Maggie smiled as she had in the artist Eli's drawing, "you'll have to keep your eye on such fellows as young master Zeke in your primer class."

"I told him he's too old for primer—most are seven years younger—but he says he needs to start at the beginning, says his folks were always moving too often for him to get one letter straight from another."

"I shouldn't say," Yarico started. After a month of sharing Oscar Massey's one-room cabin, she was speaking her views again. "What I'm going to offer as opinion is the opposite—do *not* keep your eye on that boy. If a boy has his eye on you, then you work to do the opposite or he'll get his lock on you all the harder."

"You don't know the first thing about boys," the girl answered. All three were laughing. "But you ought to know me better than that. I'd rather get entangled with that silent— buckskinned giant—who watched our wagon outside Mr. Erlich's stable in Harrisburg! There is no possibility my student Zeke can get locks on me!"

"That was before your birthday came 'round—"

"Sounds to me like Yarico knows *something*." Maggie looked up from her stitching again. "Don't forget, Addy dear, right here in Brazoria there's two girls your age already wearing a ring—"

"Wearing pitiful expressions, I'd say." The thirteen-year-old wasn't done. "But no worse than some married as many years and worried sick they might both live to be a hundred—"

"Now, Adeline, I am sorry," said Maggie, "if bringing my own true story to light has turned your stomach on the idea of finding a husband."

"Your mama had a good one, I'll vouch for that." Yarico put down a velveteen bonnet she was tacking lace to. She had transformed a clump of material one Swedish lady left her to work with, but words were seldom as easy to piece together. "Whatever your mama loved, whatever made your mama happy, that's what your papa wanted her to enjoy." Then she laughed out loud, and Adeline looked up from her book even though she felt she cried sometimes too easily when both her parents were remembered at once. "Mr. Harper was in favor of whatever Delphine Harper enjoyed—even if it was *my* company!"

"I'm not saying you should put an offer in the newspaper for a young man—" All three went into giggling at Maggie's notion. "Just between now and when you turn—eighteen—you ought to have your list made up of what's required and who's in good standing."

"Could be there aren't but two available men standing around in Gonzales when it comes time—"

"Well— I won't wish for any duels to come into the picture. You might be all caught up again in going to an academy, anyway—I did hate for you to pull out of all your lessons in Macon—"

"That's what I mean, Aunt Maggie. I have different plans from holding hands with any moon-eyed fella."

"Oh—"

"I've been studying anatomy for one thing." She didn't move her attention from the page to see what look Maggie might be giving her. Yarico was shaking her head.

"I'm going to put my hands over my ears if your Aunt Maggie starts in on what parts the boys might wish you to study."

"I may very well be the first female graduate of medical college." Neither of the older women said anything. It was best not to counter a thirteen-year-old of either gender who took on that tone. "Maybe you didn't notice Dr. Judkins showing me how to sew stitches, while we were going down the Alabama. He told me how they soak boar hair in alcohol and make little crosswise tucks, just like a ladder—and after ten days you can pull them out and the skin will hold nice as you please."

"I'll testify the man was a good doctor," Maggie said, getting control of her voice. "I did feel proud he showed you such kind notice."

"He said I had a knack for stitching—"

"We can all agree on that."

One evening remained for such aimless conversation. They bedded down quietly. Travel by sea, if they were honest, made them less nervous than their looming venture onto swells of Texas land. Mentally they checked and rechecked their preparation list.

The Harper's money—Adeline's money—had been holding up. Because Madame Genet in New Orleans had noticed their sewing skills and approached individual vendors and established merchants on their behalf, they had sewn their way into a small profit during their month-long stay at the Avignon. And at Brazoria, they quickly made up for the horses they'd needed to purchase in Harrisburg. They again earned cash for supplies listed as essential for Texas travelers.

Brazoria was not the tiny settlement they had assumed it to be upon first meeting Mr. Massey in his bare-bones store. Two hundred buildings popped into view closer to the river. At a large operation, Mills Mercantile, every basic necessity was offered— though any of their clerks might guffaw at an inquiry about light blue silk or an autoharp pluck. But there were oxen yokes, camp-stoves, earthenware vessels, fire pokers, bolts of canvas, oilcloth, tallow, lye, whips, lead, axes, cast-iron skillets, knives, whetstones, and heavy yarn. Currency with their stamp was trusted among the colonies and as far away as the states.

Mr. Massey's one-room house felt more like a one-room chiffarobe on the eve of the Harpers'departure. Boxes and packed satchels left little space for a walk-through. Since they were partnering with an older couple whose wagon was superior in every aspect, Margaret signed to swap their hometown cotton transport at Mills Mercantile for a set of six oxen yokes. That contribution, as well as their willingness to take charge of the team would be enough for the Czech couple to call the joint venture even.

The Kolars were from Cincinnati and their Texian son had sent for them. They possessed a fine double braced wagon with a custom made canvas top and wheels that were close to three inches wide. Even its reinforced spokes would be tested, but its chances on the rugged trails were fair. The women also purchased a small open passenger cart, since that could be pulled by one of their three pack horses, in case the coast looked clear for going on to Gonzales.

Though two Harpers would always be at the reins, space in even a big wagon was minimal. One of their trunks had to be left behind. Yarico breathed easier seeing that the family mistress would not part with any books, no matter what they added to the load. They chose to take along only one quilt that Delphine and her own mother had worked on together—a rosebud appliqué they could not part with. Oscar Massey kept the trunk with the others, as well as hand-painted plates, porcelain cups and saucers, small framed paintings, and delicate shawls that they'd originally pictured surviving the trek to Texas.

The storekeeper's brother was a confirmed bachelor, he swore, and had not one chance of turning over his cabin belongings to the discretion of a wife. He told them over and over that it was his pleasure to keep watch on the Harper's pine trunk. If they didn't mind, he intended to use the top as a footrest or basin stand

When Pavel Kolar and his wife Rodina pulled up to the little cabin on the outskirts of Brazoria, the three women loaded up their remaining trunk and three knapsacks they had constructed from canvas. Their bedrolls—flour bags sewn together—went on top. Cotton batting would have made inexpensive stuffing, but the feathers they had spent some money on were less likely to mold if exposed to moisture. They planned to sit sometimes on the folded bedrolls while taking the reins, since their previous wagon excursions had taught them the worst meaning of *seat-sore*. The Harpers figured some tales of deeply rutted, upland Texas trails to be exaggeration. They hoped any such treacherous sinking of road surface would not come into play until they were safely *at home* in later spring.

No throbbing drums or crowds of townspeople cheered the Kolar wagon as it steered through town. Only the pack horses on a tether and the empty cart followed. Still, Pavel and Rodina wanted to drive as far as the other side of Brazoria, as a matter of pride, and the Harper women were happy enough to squeeze inside. The flood of feelings at departures made them more emotional now than they cared for these tough Texians to observe.

But many people in town knew what the arrangements were and who else was going along north to San Felipe with the Kolars. School children and their parents had found it hard to bid adieu to the resourceful teacher. Some came out to call their good luck wishes. Adeline dreaded last good-byes, but was especially uncomfortable predicting what Zeke might do on departure day.

"I know you're in there!" His hoarse voice was unmistakable. He had come riding up to the back of the wagon. "Open up, Miss Harper, so I can give you a letter."

"She's dizzy for air right now, young man, but I'll take the envelope." Aunt Margaret had leaned out and accepted the paper from the red-faced boy. He looked as if he might have shed some tears over whatever was written inside, and Adeline's aunt was grateful the girl was spared that final image.

"The possibility of dying somewhere out on the far trail," was what the thirteen-year-old in the wagon started saying a few blocks later. "I've thought about that. Never considered passing away of embarrassment right here in the middle of Brazoria."

"You aren't going to read what's inside?"

"No. I don't know what to do with it."

"Well, put it down in your boot, so you won't lose it," Maggie suggested.

"That's what I'd figure Yarico to tell—" She stopped, because she shouldn't have known about anything hidden away by Yarico, who was obsessed suddenly with smoothing her apron.

"What—"

"That's a good idea, Aunt Maggie. It'll be easier to look at by campfire some night when we're too tired to sleep."

The caravan of seven wagons rolled and lurched on, but the Harpers could gain no sense of distance covered. The flat, nondescript terrain was much as it had appeared between Harrisburg and Brazoria. Winter had robbed the landscape entirely of color, but apparently Texas could produce only the most pale shade of green even on the edge of its prime season. The loss Adeline felt in the absence of forests was a pain she dared not mention to anyone. In no way could she fix the blame for this bereavement on anyone but herself.

Aunt Maggie had certainly tried to make her escape from legal entanglement a private ordeal. Adeline's yearning for trees was no one's fault but her own. Whatever maturity was infused on her thirteenth birthday gave her another reason to keep a trifling sorrow to herself. Together, the three of them had lost their dear Delphine. All future loss would have to be weighed against that catastrophe.

Adeline was pondering the kind of rigorous daily adjustment God intends creation to withstand, when the caravan came to a halt. A family was sitting on their trunks and boxes, next to a wagon whose broken axle had left the front end bent against a flat rock. Their unhitched horses chewed tufts of grass nearby.

"How long you been here?" their leader Mr. Hanson asked the father.

"Since yesterday 'bout this time."

"We're nearly a day out from Brazoria. Can't say as anyone is willing to turn back."

"You got three more days on this soft trail before you make The Place at the Bend," the father said, gesturing north, but he didn't appear to consider returning there.

"You all have water and enough edibles?"

"My wife seen a hog out in the tall grasses." He lifted up his rifle. "We'll start walking in a few days if no one comes along goin' our way."

"Don't let the children follow you into the brush—"

"Andrew and I have took down hogs before." Both men looked over at the oldest boy, maybe ten, who had stood up next to where his mother sat.

"They can charge meaner than you'd think." The wagon master had something more to say. "Like as not a mountain lion to be stalking the same meal." Both parents stared out briefly where the thick grass quivered.

"We can just leave everything here but food and water. We'll start walking in a few days if it comes to that." When the caravan began to move again, Yarico reached over and patted Adeline's hand.

The Harper women knew they were luckier than some women they'd gotten to know in Brazoria. Few heartbreaks, they felt—notwithstanding loss of life—could hurt more deeply than the disappearance of every personal possession. Some in the town they were leaving had watched a wagon roll back and off a cliff, all fragile mementos inside breaking or tearing into unreachable parts, past mending. Watching a shed with one's precious belongings go up in flames, with only ashes and acrid smell remaining—not much could be worse than that.

Adeline went back to giving thanks for trees. She taught herself by the end of the first day to scan the horizon for a single tree trunk, to scavenge in her imagination an image of that lone, wiry live oak as a seedling, to admit—given this crushed shale and tough coastal clay sediment—what a miracle it was for any sprout to climb so tall and survive for decades. By the time she offered appreciation for one solitary tree, another survivor could be spotted off in a different direction.

Rodina Kolar had picked up very little English during their year in Cincinnati, but her cooking was a kind of language in its own right. She was an expert at the camp-stove, a wrought-iron square heavier than many settlers wanted to travel with. But on the first night she coaxed a delicious roast from the box, and the next evening a crumble cake that rivaled any the Harper women might have driven in to Macon only a year earlier to purchase for a special occasion.

Attending to other members of the caravan made for slow-going. On the third morning, a husband and wife with three skinny offspring feared their daughter to be coming down with measles or influenza. When a sheep farmer and Adeline consulted, they concluded that contact with a nettle had caused the irritation. The little girl's fussiness was due to itch, they thought, rather than fever. The rash subsided almost as suddenly as it had appeared. Then a portly man pleaded to stop and help him replace a wobbling wheel. He had to get belongings up to the colony before trying to bring along his wife and baby next time. A premonition, he said, had made him think to purchase a make-do spare wheel in Brazoria.

By late that afternoon they reached a little encampment on the northern trail, where the main path neared the Brazos but was equally near the San Bernard River, making the distance to a westward crossing very short. There was, unbelievably, a forest stretch of sorts with deciduous oaks, elms, and hackberries, as well as redbuds and what people called the beginning of cedars. The Place at the Bend provided time for those in the caravan to stop and settle on their next move.

Most had no doubt about going on up the Brazos to San Felipe, but the Harper women—and a wagon driven by a man named O'Brien, father of a young son—were considering taking the turn to Gonzales. After a vicious spurt of wintery rain in the first half of February, the weather remained chilly but promising of spring. Newcomers with kin in Texas were warned not to get too lackadaisical about coats and blankets, though. It was certainly not time to cast off any layers by the roadside. But they took relative mildness as a good omen.

And news about the freedom fight, as far as they had heard on February 25, was encouraging. People coming down the road from San Felipe said Sam Houston was no longer at Washington on the Brazos or their settlement. He had gone to treat with some Cherokees in northeast Texas. However, some of his regulars still camped in Gonzales—*where the whole struggle for independence had started, don't forget! Come and take that cannon, if you can find it!*

The trip so far, just two-thirds of the way to San Felipe had proved strenuous enough. When Maggie, Adeline, and Yarico pictured lurching on northward, they couldn't tolerate the thought of doubling back in rainier months to try again for Gonzales. Besides, even if there were altercations between Mexico and Texians out that way, it appeared that the entire muster list of regulars was stationed exactly where the Harper women were headed. They would certainly be well protected by militia in Gonzales—just as they had been on the way from Macon to Montgomery.

That night Aunt Margaret and Adeline stayed up by the campfire after the Kolars bedded down. To make sleeping space each night, trunks and boxes had to be moved under the wagon where they also served to brake the wheels. A width of canvas helped create a second privacy area where two of the Georgia travelers stationed themselves under several blankets. Yarico was adamant about placing her bedding in the passenger cart, pulled up close enough to the end of the Kolar's back wheels that portal flaps could extend on sturdy walking sticks. An oilcloth formed a night canopy over the make-shift addition.

Yarico had taken the last turn with the oxen, and fatigue consumed her. She laughed at herself for once believing horses difficult to win over. Exhausted, she turned in when the Kolars did. Whatever Adeline and Margaret Linder decided was what she would go along with. The last time she enjoyed any sense of ownership over her hours or direction was way back at Sweet Pine, when the fire box had been hers to start up. There, it was her own decision to leave or move her collection of blankets from the scuppernong porch, her decision to pick or let grow the basil leaves in Delphine's garden. Sweet Pine was another life that she would keep in her memory, much like a folded paper, secreted away. Three American dollars the Swedish lady had slipped to Yarico for the velvet bonnet, she kept at the bottom of her other boot. If she should lose just one shoe—or one leg—she'd have either document or cash to speed her recovery. It would not do to contemplate either very often. Whatever Miss Adeline decided, that was where she would go.

"There's the two river crossings for sure," Maggie was saying to Adeline. "It's only the Colorado that makes my stomach churn."

"Mr. Hanson knows for certain of ferry landings, and the post rider coming down from San Felipe said the same thing. He used to live out westerly—says he might move back now that settlers never have Karankawa attacks like there used to be."

"Tellin' us don't be affrighted if the Indians with tattoo ink come along—"

"The Tonkawas—one of the ferries is run sometimes by them." Adeline had been holding back on a question of considerable importance. "You think your nephew is in the least expecting you? Or, even if he's overjoyed to see you, what about all of us—what if his place is half the size of Mr. Massey's one room?"

"The thought never crossed my mind, particularly in Macon, about how people get word. Never considered a country without regular newspapers or post to count on." Such privation had taken several weeks to sink in. "We've been right fortunate so far—"

"I'm not trying to fret over what's unknown. It's been good luck up to now, all things considered."

"I'm just going to tell Matthew you're my niece from my husband's side—hanged husband or some such—if that's all right with you." Addy was nodding. "I'll be the one to say it, don't worry. So it won't be marked down as your lie. Just make life easier when people there hear you call me *Aunt Maggie.*"

"It's a habit I won't be breaking."

"Dear sweet girl—"

"Then let's go on to Gonzales. Huzzah for spring 1836!" They both laughed at Adeline's handiness with Texas talk.

"Let's go on and get some good sleep. You and Yarico will have me thrown over a horse and lashed to a saddle, if I'm too sleepy to hold the cart reins!"

In the morning, Mrs. Kolar made a crumble cake to go with their coffee. She fussed with mixing it more than she had the first one out of Brazoria. Adeline pictured the Kolars' son and how his ranch east of the Brazos might appear to his parents at their reunion. Then, she wrestled her mind back to the pack horses, detaching them and repositioning belongings. Her copy of *Robinson Crusoe* and a leather-bound volume of Swift essays, she tucked down in a corner of the Kolar wagon. What the women took with them had to squeeze inside the one trunk and into their own cart. Adeline and Yarico slung their knapsacks across the pack horses. Maggie wanted to help them, but she was best suited to assist Rodina in making coffee and to ease the parting for the older couple.

Good-byes were getting too common and all the harder. The Harper women took some solace in knowing the Kolars would be at home soon, too. For the Macon family, one last piece of wilderness stretched between them and Gonzales, where Matthew and any other Linders would receive a happy surprise.

And they were not entirely alone on this final leg of their trip. Sean O'Brien had his little son Padraig with him, and his presence helped all the grown-ups maintain a show of confidence. The four-year-old was quick and excitable, and quite enamored of the females traveling behind his father's wagon. He often jumped from the driver seat to the back of the home-styled four-wheeler to wave and then shy away behind the flaps. Adeline and Yarico should have been the ones easily embarrassed, since they had resorted to wearing their fullest skirts and straddling their horses. Only Maggie, managing the cart reins, looked ladylike.

Between the encampment and the San Bernard was farmland that reminded Adeline of the plantations along the Ocmulgee. The earth had been newly plowed up, and she thought the next step in the coming weeks would be to trace distinct furrows, and then to anticipate the first good rain and sow seeds at just the right depth. Yarico, who had managed to get a better night's sleep than Adeline Harper, was leading her family as they passed alongside the last quarter mile of the plantation. The two women riding made out figures toiling near the edge of the field, and when the workers came more clearly into view, Adeline could see Yarico stiffen and straighten up in the saddle just ahead.

Three white men on horseback rode up and down the newly upturned ground, getting down periodically to examine dirt clods. Field hands were looking at dirt clods, too, and breaking them up with their hands or taking a hoe to any that had utterly resisted the plow. The laborers also glanced over at Yarico, riding a horse as a man would and in front of the others. They looked, but they didn't dare for long. Their gaze moved only briefly from the crumbling soil, but as O'Brien and the women travelers passed by, there was a perceptible movement among the workers, turning so as to see the striking figure with reins in her hands.

"I feel bad sometimes," Adeline said catching up to Yarico, "never asking if you wanted to come up to the top of Sweet Pine with me."

"I expect I wouldn't have."

"If I'd been taken to Savannah," she went on, "I don't know what my uncle would have thought you were good for." She suddenly preferred to look down at her fading calico dress skirt and smooth the fabric over her knees.

"Good folks take care of their people." Yarico could see Adeline was still troubled by the field help bent over their task. "You brought me a birthday present, I haven't forgotten—an Indian needle you found there. Only you and your mama did such things as that."

The San Bernard River was down, fortunately, and there was an easy place where the glistening pebbles made the crossing shallow. After Yarico and Addy helped Maggie and their trunk into the back of Mr. O'Brien's wagon, their cart bounced along behind the tall gelding like a skipping stone. The settlers had been told that the last two rivers, the Navidad and the Lavaca were nothing to dread. If they met them, all they needed to do was turn north briefly to circumvent their source. There was no worry about crossing either of the last two barriers between them and the town of Gonzales.

The Colorado River was another matter. They had been told it was long, and wide at every bend. There was no crossing without a ferry, and though the Harpers had been all the way down the Alabama River by boat—not to mention travel by ocean—they and Mr. O'Brien would have to find a reliable ferry operation. Since the river went even farther north than the distance south to where it emptied in the gulf, they would need to risk a decision about which direction led to the nearest ferry. The path they were on was far less traveled than any they had seen off the main Texas trail system. But so far, that had only meant more grass growing across the way. When O'Brien's wagon stopped abruptly, the man directed his son to a parting in the side growth, where he could find a spot for relieving himself.

"Don't you wander out of sight," Maggie warned.

"Then don't look." The youngster was as single-minded as he was shy, and he slipped away into the tall grass anyway. His screech a minute later brought O'Brien and the women running. Flailing arms wouldn't do much to get a wild cat to let go of a child. But it wasn't a panther or a boar. Tan burrs speckled the boy's shirt and trousers.

"Get your clothes off, son. Hand 'em to one of the ladies." The thorny brown seeds clung to every inch of wool and chambray. "Stick-tights," the father said. "Can't be rid of except to pick 'em off one at a time."

Minutes later, Maggie put her hand under the wagon flap and reached for Padraig's coat and trousers. She could see he was cold and humiliated. When he tried to free his shirt cuffs of the clinging needles, a finger bled and he started to cry. She climbed in to hold a blanket around him while the younger women dislodged the menacing thorns.

"You just hold the edges," Adeline said to Yarico. They braced themselves near the wavy grasses and were trying to keep wind gusts from blowing any fierce burrs back onto their own skirts and sleeves. The child's clothes could not be cradled in one's lap like folds of embroidery.

"This'll eat up precious time."

"Just try to hold out the edges." Adeline said again gently. "It's *your* fingers and hands we can't allow to go bleeding." Her own hands had suffered painful jabs. "What else is sure to put us in favor with the ladies of Gonzales, if not your artful sewing?"

During the hour it took to purge the boy's clothing, all three women felt their optimism in need of mending. The lanky grass was a pretty feature of the changing countryside, but they had to grasp now that appearances could be deceiving. When they lurched forward again, they reminded themselves that shorter green tufts still meant a sturdier surface for the wheels to roll on, less likelihood of mud ruts and washed out patches from wear. More aware of troubles that the land could hide, they hoped their faint prairie trail would connect rather directly with a ferryman at home and in possession of a trustworthy raft.

Maggie took to keeping the boy company in Mr. O'Brien's wagon. With Yarico managing their cart, Adeline found herself riding at times alongside Padraig's father. The man in the group chewed on a twig. Worry, no doubt, made him unwilling to chat, but he seemed to be the kind immersed in his own thoughts in any circumstances. His son had an opposite disposition and was drawn to Maggie. In the O'Brien wagon, the two swapped Davey Crockett tales, and they were both napping when the five bound for Gonzales eased up to the banks of the Colorado.

As the woman in charge, Adeline swung herself down from her mare to have a look with Sean O'Brien at the riverbank. She knew the Ocmulgee and the Alabama. She recognized deep river water when it flowed before her. Trees and brush sprang up thickly all along the shore, and at first she did not notice the dark skinned man approaching them from a footpath to one side. She heard Mr. O'Brien's firearm click before she saw the stranger at all, but she was more startled at first by her traveling companion's firing posture than she was by the presence of the Indian.

The people at the San Felipe trail had said not to worry about traders with tattoos. Adeline was taking them at their word. But tattoo meant to her what she had seen on a barge captain's arm at the Macon wharf. She was transfixed by this man's appearance—tall with a long black stream of hair in back, a feather hanging from one side off his ear, and tiny black lines traced across one side of his face.

"River cross this way," he said pointing, back from where he'd come.

Mr. O'Brien brought his weapon to rest across his arms.

"Adeline Harper," she said, holding out her hand.

"Your woman?" the Tonkawa man asked O'Brien.

"No. I'm with them," Adeline said pointing to where Yarico had climbed down to the ground. The cart was more interesting to the ferry man than the settlers, and he walked off to examine it. After satisfying himself that he understood how the odd cart was attached at the gelding's yoke, he next looked at the black woman.

"You stand like *free*," he announced to her.

"That's Yarico," Adeline explained. She and the tattooed man seemed the only humans capable of speech. "I'm Adeline, and Margaret is in the big wagon. We all need to cross the river. Have you got a ferry that can take us all?"

"River cross this way."

"Your raft will hold us then?"

"Across river, I make your little wagon more good."

The crossing took three trips, because the ferry man's raft was not much longer than the length of Mr. O'Brien's wagon and horses. It and the tan pack horse required a single trip, the five people went across next, and the ferry runner brought his own pony on the last crossing with the Harper cart and animals. It was not clear what the Tonkawa man had meant by "fixing" their cart until he hitched it in the reverse direction, with the package rack on the back edge equally fit to drive from, but with a wheel angle that took the road much more smoothly. Maybe, Adeline was thinking, the contraption had been designed backwards from the start.

The ferry runner did not want paper money for his assistance, and Mr. O'Brien let him lift two sacks of sugar out of his wagon. When he looked at the rosebud quilt, the women held their breath, but he was pleased with a blanket and an earthenware bowl in their trunk. He did not seem to be expecting more river travel, and without further swapping he agreed to escort them along the path to Gonzales. Adeline wanted to know his name, but he declined to talk along the trail. *Gonzales* was the only word he would repeat and nod to.

Their Indian chaperone must have heard the sound of hooves long before Adeline could hear anything but geese overhead, squawking on their way back north. Their volunteer guide came suddenly to a complete stop. His standstill came as such a jolt that Mr. O'Brien had a hard time reining in his team, almost colliding into the Tonkawa's gray pony. When Yarico said she could hear galloping, they were all straining their eyes as well for the first details of who might be coming at them from the direction they were headed.

"English horses," their road companion said.

Two men, finally, could be seen riding toward them. Their red pants were the first distinctive feature anyone in the group could make out.

"Turn around!" was the first shout that the women distinguished. "The Alamo!" was the next thing.

"What's happened?" Adeline was riding up to meet them.

"You can't come this way!"

"We're trying to get to Gonzales—"

"We just came from there, and any of the regulars there are out and on the northern path to San Felipe—"

"Santa Anna's all up around the Alamo already!"

"But, it's Gonzales we're getting to," Adeline countered, "there's family—"

"You can't go there now, we're on our way to tell General Houston—"

"What?" Maggie was calling from the back of O'Brien's wagon—I got a nephew there—"

"M'am—" One of the red-legged soldiers had taken off his hat and was trying to catch his breath. "I'm sorry m'am, we're going to have to help you turn around."

"There's no trouble at Gonzales is there?" Adeline's aunt had a pinched sounding voice.

"No trouble there right now, but it's all the men, m'am—"

"Did the men go get General Houston at San Felipe? Are the women leaving for San Felipe?"

"The women are staying to see how their men fare..." The first rider looked at the other soldier to see if he could break the news any better.

"The men from Gonzales all went up to the Alamo. It was just four days ago, on the 25th, that Travis sent out a letter, saying it was do or die for holding San Antone."

"And General Houston will gather his soldiers from along the Brazos, past San Felipe—up in Washington?"

"Yes m'am, that's what we're guessing, once he hears. We're headed there on express, so we can get Houston the news—" Aunt Maggie was letting the wagon flap fall back down, but she was still wanting to ask what the soldiers knew about her Matthew.

"Just answer me—about Matthew Linder— about the men in Gonzales—"

"Almost all the grown males saddled up and rode on in to the Alamo anyhow—"

"They couldn't be stopped, ladies, like we said—read the letter from Travis and spent a day or so talking with their women folk, maybe youngest sons here and there staying with their mothers to help."

"Not most, no matter how many mothers and children were left alone in town. Said they were going on to throw in with Colonel Travis and fight the whole lot under Santa Anna—him with his blood red pirate flag flying! Those Gonzales boys said they was busting in to the Alamo to help Travis, even if he's down to five men—"

"I think she's dead," came a small voice from Mr. O'Brien's wagon.

There was a dark bottle of smelling salts down in Maggie's bag next to her tonic. But it seemed a cruel thing to bring her around only to tell her again the probable truth about her nephew young Mr.Linder. And while the Alabama express soldiers were getting their second wind, the Tonkawan ferry runner was already taking the gelding's reins and turning the cart around for the fast ride back to the Colorado.

Chapter 11   For Love of Finnissee

The report that came to Goliad on the 23rd of February was about thousands of well fitted Mexican troops under General Santa Anna approaching and pressing in closer to the Alamo. That so many could have marched from faraway Matamoros so quickly challenged credulity. But the gasping messenger, who risked his life galloping around enemy encampments to find the trail to Goliad, had to be believed. That the number—six thousand?—could be so nearby, with the intent to exterminate anyone taking up arms against Mexico, challenged fortitude in a way that made sleet or slow starvation relatively appealing.

If Mexican numbers had been four hundred and twenty-three, the same count as volunteer soldiers under Colonel James Fannin and Lieutenant Colonel William Ward, the response would have been ready aim. But such nightmarish odds! Stoicism slowed reaction. There was stifled panic—and denial.

Whether Fannin might have made his mark at Matamoros was moot. Whether there would ever be supply ships arriving at Copano or Velasco, as Fannin had requested—was moot. Whether a better relationship with Houston could have produced a wiser strategy, whether agreement to the governing powers of Henry Smith would have better unified the Texans, whether a less grueling use of his soldiers in the rebuilding of *Fort Defiance* might have left the men more resilient and the food supply less starkly depleted—all hypotheticals were moot.

Even before the messenger's report, Fannin was sleepless over immediate worries. Only a small amount of dried beef remained in the compound, no fresh cattle— unless one were to consider the oxen used to pull artillery carts. Out of what seemed abundant provisions just three weeks earlier, he knew supplies had dwindled to a measure of rice. For the next forty-eight hours Fannin and his officers debated and swore, argued and threw up their hands, pleaded for action of some kind. Should they attempt the aid of Travis, whose courier James Bonham had already been refused once? Or retreat—if to retreat, to where?

"What the hell are they workin' out with all their talk?" a Macon boy asked.

"How to tie wings onto our feet," another private answered.

Something had to be done, all four hundred knew. They oiled rifles, wiped down canons, stacked grape, accounted for powder and pellets, tested carts, and secretly prayed. Captains threw themselves into preparation drill. Major Mitchell, in charge of the Georgia Battalion after Ward's promotion, paced from one company to the next. No grousing came from the worn volunteers under his command or in the La Fayette Battalion. Something had to be done.

Since Captain Uriah Bulloch had never recovered enough from the measles to leave Velasco, First Lieutenant Basil Lamar and Second Lieutenant Alexander Patton carried that weight of responsibility for Georgia's Second Company. First Sergeant Francis Gideon relayed orders to his men— to retie with twine any shoes that could still be held together that way, and to each take as many as two pieces of beef jerky to stuff into back pockets. Front pockets were for worthy pieces of flint if they could find any—the thin baling rope could be used for a tourniquet if dire need arose.

"How far did you figure the march to San Antonio?" Joseph Tidwell was asking. His mustache kept his face from looking as thin as the others, Francis thought.

"Adds up to— near ninety miles."

There was a muted groan from the weary soldiers gathered before him. Close to four dozen American Southerners were still present and accounted for in the company. No one spoke of the few thought to have deserted in January. The inspired movement to help in the Texas Revolution had not developed as anyone predicted. Who could fault an intelligent man for departing without leave as early as Velasco, before the first muddy march? Retired military men back in Macon were known to toast their comrades regularly, and to conclude any report of defeat with the absolution—*No Blame! No Blame!* Whether those now deleted from roll call had been ethical in dissolving sworn duty—as the Texian government and military seemed prone to dismiss orders—who could say? All such inquiries—moot.

"Can we scavenge for shoes? Or socks?"

"We're still under orders not to stray from the mission proper. When we move out, it's as a regiment."

"The carousing that night—that wasn't any of us—" a soldier no older than sixteen protested.

"Lamar and Patton and I know that—Mitchell and Ward, they know it wasn't any of you—"

"One of us could stand guard—we'd just go in for shoes, if they have extra—"

"Don't disturb Mexican townspeople for any reason. Their homes are not to be approached." Francis repeated. He didn't think it would do morale any good to talk about which privates in which companies were thought to have been those drunk one night, and terrorizing the village women. Thankfully, Cruz was still on speaking terms with the Americans when Francis offered to swap the bottle of port for a pair of moccasins. The Texas native's wife had a friend, an older señora, who owned well made moccasins hanging on a peg, unused.

Malacai look away uncomfortably from the talk of shoes. He wore fine Indian sewn leather, and his feet felt on the mend for the first time in a month. He implored Father Guillermo to get word to the Mexican couple, to thank them. Then, even the priest left to join Father Jose Valdez at one of the safe ranches outside Goliad's walls.

Joseph sat woodenly on a bunk not far from his step-brother. He hesitated to ask a question of odds again.

"How many trained soldiers did you reckon are following Santa Anna?"

"There'll be more on our side when we get there, and when the regulars get there," Francis said evasively.

The men nodded quietly and looked at their shoes. They oiled their rifles and checked their powder flasks again. They all began to take on the same features, Francis noticed. Even Malacai's curly brown hair fell in dusty straggles. There was nothing to do but look down and work at something. Nothing could be done but wait for word from Fannin.

Word came not *from* but *to* James Fannin on February 24. A second short note written by Colonel William B. Travis at the Alamo, was handed directly to the commander at *Fort Defiance*. This time, the messenger was accompanied by Captain Juan Seguin, an independence advocate that Santa Anna would surely shred as a scourge if ever he were caught. No doubt he kept his own pledge to go *where danger was greatest!* And several soldiers on horseback had gone carrying a longer document, an impassioned plea to Sam Houston and the Regular Army—a desperate message to the people of Texas. The couriers were sworn to get the letter through *or perish in the effort!*

Travis had only one hundred and fifty men inside the mission at San Antonio. He importuned Texans for help, and at the same time pledged his life for their cause. Those cognizant of the odds already called him a hero. But Colonel Fannin could not bring himself to move immediately toward the Alamo. Though James Bowie, his fellow officer at the Battle of Concepcion, braced for death behind the menaced Alamo walls, another evening went by. What grim difference a few months had made! In the first real battle of the settler revolt, it had taken just thirty minutes for Bowie and Fannin to jointly claim victory against madly dispersing Mexican troops only two miles from San Antonio!

The next day, Fannin gave the order to move to the Alamo. But the regiment delayed until King and his men from Refugio joined them. They delayed as the artillery was tested for movement in the worn wagons—then retied and tested for movement again. There was further delay when the commissary raced to amass provisions. They waited for half the rice to cook. Unopened sacks were then loaded, on the unlikely chance water could be boiled along the way or within the Alamo. The messenger swore that some beef remained within the barricaded San Antonio mission. And if the regiment could make it across the turgid river, and if the men could trudge ninety miles west with or without shoes—if only—something might be done.

On February 28, when the regiment finally struggled out from Goliad's mission, it was the struggle of Sisyphus. Nothing was fated to end in triumph. Cattle pulling the artillery carts strained to budge wagonloads of leaden cannon pieces. Rocks and mud on the slope down to the San Antonio River would have strained a well-shod army to its limits. Jagged edges ripped any leather seams still holding. The cruel precipice broke the spirits of those making do with baling twine.

"Halt the wheel!"

"His arm's in the spoke!"

"Set a damn block to it!"

"Easy now—where's Dr. Judkins?"

"Keep the wheels locked!"

"The blasted thing's sliding!"

By afternoon of the first day, Colonel James Fannin's regiment had made it only several hundred yards from the Goliad mission. Wagons and men crumpled to the ground just the other side of the river. Officers converged near Fannin, and even Lieutenant Colonel Ward, spoke of the obvious. Their leader maintained no differing view from the candid assessment of the captains, so a unanimous vote called to rectify the disaster as best they could. The order was given to move in reverse. Soldiers who had thrown themselves into pushing and pulling wagons and beasts were allowed to straggle back up the hill and collapse into exhaustion. Men on horseback helped those incapable of further movement. Artillery was left under guard until the next day.

In the middle of the night, the oxen strayed away. With no food of any account, chances of recovery shrank over the following day and evening. Someone thought to turn the calendar page. It was now the month of March, 1836.

"Francis? Have you been sleeping?" The sun was at Malacai's back, and his eyes disappeared in the shadows.

"Just barely—how are your feet?"

"Still there, thanks to you and Cruz."

"Any word yet, from the Alamo?"

"No."

Other bleak facts punished the sergeant's senses. He knew not to speak of other developments, but his cousin's proximity made him set aside the reserve of rank.

"There was another post about some men at Gonzales—"

"Is it the regulars then? Francis?"

"No...Some soldiers there, but mostly settlers."

"What is it?"

"About thirty or more from that one town." Francis rubbed his eyes. He looked as if he were still asleep. "They went ahead and rode on in to the Alamo."

"Just people?"

"Older men...and some boys from Gonzales..." The company's First Sergeant could not say more, and Malacai let him turn away and move aimlessly in another direction.

Birds other than sparrows began the next day to return to the coastal plains. Wandering sandpipers hopped in the dirt. Mockers and doves landed on the mission's new masonry work to peck and inspect. Bees hummed in the grassy patches around the chapel where Father Guillermo declared that mounds of pink and blue would burst forth in another six weeks.

As he sat outside, leaning against the southern barracks wall, Malacai watched a hawk soar and dive. The air warmed by mid-morning, and he felt that with another month of sunshine and a meal one day soon, he could revive. His feet were feeling so much better, though he needed to keep rubbing them through the soft leather—almost as soft as those gloves from Ell's back home. If only he could eat, he was thinking, catch something substantial the way a hawk could. But that was when he perceived the thundering hooves, a horse from the south this time, from the village Refugio, where the Irish family lived. Even with a feast laid before him, his appetite would have disappeared. Malacai knew, along with all the Goliad men, that the sound of galloping meant bad news. A crowd drew near the rider before he could dismount his foaming horse.

"It's Johnson and Dr. Grant!" was the man's first cry.

"Have they come on in from the south? Are they at Refugio? Are they going to join us here?"

"Both of them run down!"

"What are you saying?"

"Down far southerly near San Patricio—they got to Johnson and his men first—caught and killed as far as we know—"

"Get the colonel! Somebody go get Fannin!"

"Then it was Grant—they think he was on his way up to warn us—"

Lieutenant Colonel Ward stood by the entrance of the mission. He strode out among the familiar men.

"Let's give him a hand, brothers" he said nodding toward the express rider. Two men in Bulloch's Company helped the stiff messenger to the ground. "What did you say about Grant? On his way here?"

"The doctor set out to warn us, they think. Him—they got, sir—it's sure! Dragged him to pieces." The rider hid his face. For a long moment, the officer from Georgia could do nothing but give the soldier a consoling pat on the back.

"Did anyone say how many of Santa Anna's men had peeled off to head down that far?"

"Not Santa Anna, sir." The rider was getting his breath. "It was a second army entirely. They're under that General Urrea, they called him. They're headed straight for us!"

Second Company men in the Georgia Battalion had been given outside duty that day, and as stricken as they were about the San Patricio forces—who must have been lost along with Johnson and Grant—they were grateful that William Ward had been the ranking officer to come out and meet the messenger.

Could it have been less than four months ago that a portion of this group stood together at the courthouse in Macon, Georgia? How many among them had been there that November evening? They had listened by candlelight to Milledgeville officers—McLeod and Ward—extol the virtues of American revolutionaries, call on patriots to aid Texian colonists similarly oppressed? The Georgia boys were both heartened and heartbroken to see Ward up close again. He was so distracted from the battalion after taking on higher duties. Of necessity, he kept closest counsel with Colonel Fannin.

The battalion's original leader looked, just then, as if words were of less use to him than they had been at gatherings and dinners on the trek to Texas. The soldiers in his presence knew that panic only depleted energy. They allowed each other a space of silence in which to endure shock, in which to acknowledge dire apprehension.

First Sergeant Francis Gideon worked at a button after the news sank in. When the men began to attend to the messenger and his horse, he approached his commander and dared to speak.

"Lieutenant Colonel Ward, sir?" he started.

"Yes...Sergeant?"

"I know you need to...inform Colonel Fannin, but I was wondering if Lieutenants Lamar and Patton are expected back today—"

"Not today."

"Your orderly reported to me—three days ago when we gave up on our march to the Alamo. He said Lamar and Patton had gone on horseback to take a message."

"Fannin wanted to make sure the council—and the governor—Smith—that they know we tried and failed to get to San Antonio. We wanted some officers to ride to the convention—to ask what Texas wants us to do at this point."

"They won't be back today then?"

"What's today—the 2nd? No, they've only just made it to Washington on the Brazos today, if they're lucky." Ward saw that water and breathing room were helping the rider recover. Fannin had to get an official report before rumor flooded the barracks. "These are my *little brothers* you've got here, Gideon—they're all good men—you're in command of the company until Lamar and Patton return."

In the days of slow, aching recovery since the failed approach to San Antonio, Francis had known himself to be senior in rank. But men in his company were doing what they could manage automatically. They were not capable of much. He had responded "Inside" or "Outside," as they looked to him for directions in the absence of their lieutenants. Since their arrival at Goliad, the senior officers had frequently been consulted when superiors met, so much needing to be reckoned with and decided. Francis had often taken on the duty of daily commands, easy enough to give when tasks were routine—

Those last two stones you set in the top wall—they look shaky—they'd better be reset…Let a drink of water and a bite of jerky do for midday, boys. We'll be glad we waited for rice and pintos later tonight…Help me hold that brace while the parapet gets stable.

It was different to be told by Ward. To be "in command of the company" was to be solitary in a way even Francis Gideon's innate self-possession could not make feel natural. The news about the slaughter at San Patricio was sinking in slowly to a lonely expanse, like the dark ocean floor.

Whoever was standing in front of him, Francis didn't recognize at first—he was so lost in thought. The light inside the brick and stucco barracks was so dim that the men looked different when they stood upright out in open daylight. The drooping mustache Francis knew well, but the eyes of the man had changed, and Francis began to smile from embarrassment at seeming not to recognize his own kin at first, his cousin's step-brother. Of course, it was Joseph. Of course—although those eyes had taken on a sharp and grim look that Francis did not know.

"Sergeant Gideon?" Joseph Tidwell was among the Second Company privates standing off to the side while Ward had spoken with their lead man.

"Tidwell…Yes?"

"Whatever you need us to do, Sergeant," he said. He waited for Francis to settle on words.

"Joseph—*you* know—*you* were in some fighting down in the Floridas—"

"Yes."

"…I was trying to remember. Just hearing Ward's voice again—"

"We remember why we came."

"You know we need to stay together. It could all get…" Francis was thinking orders needed to be shorter, and unequivocal. He took off his hat to get his hair from his eyes. Joseph reached out and put his hand on the sergeant's arm.

"Don't worry, Francis, your head'll get clear." He took his hand away and stood more erect. "I just wanted you to know—whatever you need."

The next day, a final appeal slipped through from William Travis at the Alamo. The courier who made it to Goliad said another rider had gone in the direction of Gonzales in case there was word at last of General Houston's advance. The message of Colonel Travis—echoing his first two—spread among the confused and exhausted men at Goliad's fortress. *Duty and Honor! To sacrifice all for freedom—! The Lord on our side!*

Outside *Fort Defiance*, the flag cut from petticoat silk, the white Troutman banner with the azure star—*Liberty or Death*—was still flying.

In the second week of March, a barefoot volunteer straddled a horse and galloped from Goliad toward San Antonio to scout for any news about the outcome at the Alamo. Another frantic scouting party, from Houston's forces building around Gonzales, also ventured forth. A few women and children were found wandering away from the San Antonio calamity. One man, a personal servant of Travis, was among them. They alone survived the onslaught. Travis, Bowie, Crockett, Bonham—one hundred and fifty—and the family men whose home had been Gonzales—all bloodied, all dead.

That Santa Anna's thousands—seasoned veterans, for the most part—had suffered casualties in disproportionate numbers brought no solace to any Texian or American. The Goliad rider waited one day in a clump of hackberry trees and cottonwoods for the death notice to get to Houston. Whatever the general's written order now, he would carry it back to Colonel James Fannin.

The next morning, the Goliad command anguished over the terrible outcome at the Alamo and over Sam Houston's order as well. The general's reasoning came with the command. So many losses had been dealt to those in Santa Anna's service—many badly wounded left near the battle site—that the remaining thousands had encamped at some distance to take stock and slowly recover their own strength and senses. They would not be fit to march again for several days. *Now* was the opportunity *for Fannin to abandon Goliad!* The colonel was commanded to leave behind a demolished fortress, to remove the volunteer regiment to Victoria and await further word of the Mexican dictator's next target.

The Georgia Battalion and the LaFayette Battalion had a day to tear down proof of all their efforts in the last month, if they were to obey General Houston. The council and Lieutenant Governor Robinson, whose directives Fannin preferred, no longer figured in. Goliad had barely twenty-four hours to render the fort unusable by Urrea's or Santa Anna's troops. News from the previous week, that Texas had formally declared itself a free and independent republic, did little to enable the colonel's response. The Alamo defenders—all perished!—died without knowing of the Declaration of Independence, a vote taken far north on the Brazos River. The Texian cause was officially the same as any American's in 1776, but William Travis and Colonel Fannin's field partner Jim Bowie—all those men— had fought and perished without knowing.

"What in heaven's name have they decided?" a New Orleans soldier asked Malacai.

"That your battalion and ours are already met in hell—if all this bloody confusion—"

"They're sayin' we still hold Victoria—"

"Driven to wits end there, too, no doubt—"

Still no order came from the colonel to destroy the walls and fortified parapets of the mission. In the atmosphere of grief mixed with rage—controlled frenzy—he had not decided on a justifiable command to his troops. Then, yet again, came a fast riding messenger horse. The galloping came again from the south, and the alert from Refugio was urgent, so desperate as to break through and crumble the walls of denial.

Families—those few who had not departed when King left them unprotected to join forces at Goliad—were threatened. Settlers of the Irish colony were stranded. Hostile ranchers and the encroaching troops of General Urrea tormented them. This plea was not from a military man whose chain of command Fannin might have questioned. This message came direct from parents begging Fannin to save their children. He was their only hope for evacuation.

Captain Amon King, Refugio's former protector, immediately saddled up with his company and rode south toward the stricken citizens. They took with them what wagons and oxen the fort still possessed in order to transport the families, who surely would not be able to march to safety.

148

Forty-eight hours later a courier from King was spotted by Goliad guards. Ward's original troops, especially Bulloch's men watched tensely. King could not do it alone—he needed immediate help!

This time Colonel Fannin reacted swiftly. Or Lieutenant-Colonel Ward might have already called out for his horse. The summons galvanized the Georgia Battalion into motion. They had sworn their oaths of service to such a cause.

"Ward," Colonel Fannin told him, "We won't withdraw to Victoria until we've heard from you! Get the settlers out of there! We're not abandoning Goliad until you return!"

First Sergeant Francis Gideon and the officers of the Georgia Battalion—Captain Winn, Captain Wadsworth, Captain Ticknor, others on horseback—as well as Major Wallace and Lieutenant Colonel William Ward mounted up and made their way south alongside their men. Some of Captain Horton's company, those who did not go with him to secure more wagons and oxen from Victoria, also marched on the southern trail. If ever adrenalin and anguish combined to crystallize purpose, such was the case as one hundred and fifty men forced themselves south, back to Refugio. Since arriving on the coast of Texas—since all the weeks of confusion, deprivation, gloom, and menace—they had not once, as a unified band, regained their original zeal for action. Finally, on March 12, they undertook the rescue of desperate families!

"This is why we came, Sergeant!" a man yelled to Francis.

"Don't worry, Sergeant Gideon—We'll get there in time!"

Francis was riding next to his company, sorry the regiment's wagons were already ahead at the little church in Refugio, where terrified settlers were surely gathering for safe escort. Most in his company would themselves have qualified for transport. Some of his men had sprung into movement as one would envision a wooden doll's jerking response to being wound. But they were marching, and they wore uniform looks of purpose, in spite of their ragged clothes.

"Good Lord, Francis—*you* should trade shoes with *me!*" It was Malacai calling up to him, over the clamber of hooves and marching. "I didn't know it was baling twine holding your own together now—"

"It's working—my horse's shoes are in good shape—"

"Never you mind—a sergeant needs his shoes—"

"I'm okay—we'll look out for the others—" The soldier in command was acutely aware of the need to encourage his men equally. He was about to move on.

"Do you think the Finnissees made it out to Victoria already?" Malacai shouted. "They're the ones Joseph and I had a meal with—"

"All we heard was *several families*—"

"This is why we came!" It was Private Tidwell making his voice heard from another direction.

"Damn if it doesn't feel good!" was what the sergeant's cousin called out as Francis turned to check another row.

Despite their own state of heightened purpose, they identified panic as they approached one of the creeks near the Refugio mission. Several American volunteers, maybe King's men, were letting their horses trot in zig-zags, it seemed, near the mission wall. Pockets of women and children gestured wildly, some running to grasp bundles, some just trying to hang onto toddlers. Father Orlando appeared at the church door, and then he was just as suddenly lost from sight. Townspeople, upwards of fifty amassed near the sanctuary walls. And off—near the horizon—a scouting party of soldiers soon clustered—white pants, dark blue coats, and the distinct flat hats of the Mexican army!

The settlers wailed in relief as they grew aware of the approaching battalion. Some raced immediately away from the church, back to their homes to retrieve further provisions. Frenzied movement proved their final decisions to be the agonizing kind. Escape now hinged critically on time. A delay for one more bundle could mean disaster for them all.

"We thought they would just leave us alone—we've been good citizens of Mexico!" one older woman lamented to Malacai.

"Are the Finnissees with you? Did they make it to Victoria before?"

"You know the Finnissees?" the woman said, setting down her blanket loaded with clothing and loaves of bread.

"Are they here now, or—"

"Poor Missus Finnissee!" the woman cried. Joseph Tidwell had walked up to join Malacai. During the march, he mastered his fatigue. For him too, it was not a nameless citizenry he'd come to rescue. He had sat at a home meal just once in three months. Like his step-brother, the plight of a particular Irish family compelled him.

"They think it was an accident about their littlest boy—"

"—the lad—"

150

"The boy just walked out the front path…when a Mexican soldier came scouting the town—"

"They didn't hurt—they didn't kill that boy!" Joseph shouted.

"It was probably what some of the rancheros said," the woman went on tearfully, "that the poor boy's gun just went off—he was always tucking it in back under his belt, his older brother told a neighbor."

A toddler drew close to the woman and reached to be picked up.

"But that doesn't help his poor mum and dad—"

"Not the little lad!"

Malacai and Joseph were in a rage, and Father Orlando came up mildly to tell them that the Finnissees were all back in a private room off the chapel. Everyone in the family was terrified, but the mother especially, and the father who felt it was his fault—the older sisters and brother—they were all paralyzed with grief.

When Privates Mulholland and Tidwell stormed into the mission, where they'd recently spent three weeks thinking cold mud to be their worst enemy, they found stony silence and furious whispers among the battalion.

Captain King and Colonel Ward were arguing, behind doors that were hardly impervious. The companies knew something of the Finnissees' tragedy, but countless other tales of strife swept through the shelter, threats brought on by Refugio ranch dwellers in sympathy with Santa Anna's Centralist cause. One resident of the mission area, a De la Garza, without doubt had sent spies to alert Urrea's scouting parties.

Behind the chapel doors, King and Ward battled about seniority.

Captain King wanted to take his men out on a mission immediately to find the spies and anyone terrorizing the Irish townspeople! He wanted to show the enemy the consequences of dastardly action against civilians!

Lieutenant Colonel Ward argued that the Georgia Battalion was to rescue those very civilians—there was no time for punitive action—barely time to round up innocent families and rush them from worst peril!

Captain King stormed out and gave orders to his men to saddle up for retaliation!

Ward denounced the move, adding that his Captain Mitchell could later slip out to locate spies. But Fannin's order was to rescue settlers and return to Goliad!

Captain King countered that he'd been at Refugio longer than Ward—longer than any of the blasted other volunteers in the entire regiment. It was his command that should be obeyed!

Ward, as King's superior officer, ordered him to desist—to conform to steps in the evacuation plan!

A dangerous gloom hung in the crowded sanctuary. Divisive posturing could itself prove lethal during a crisis. In the heated throng, men inched toward the captain or the senior officer.

First Sergeant Francis Marion Gideon felt a queasiness from having witnessed such a crisis before in Texas. A sickening realization came to him— that he would do as Lieutenant Colonel Ward commanded— direct men under him to get families into functional wagons, to get on with Fannin's order. But he had the gut-wrenching premonition that he was likely to have to press rank against members of his own family.

William Ward stood grimly, as if expecting one more round of rhetorical fire. King shouted that dusk was settling in around the chapel, and the retaliatory excursion—what the bastards deserved!—would be conducted on horseback by torchlight. Discussion was finished, King swore, and he summoned his own men, as well as any of Ward's who weren't afraid to show judgment's fury to the enemy! Anyone, even among his own avowed company, who tried to interfere—let them try to stop him!

In the convulsive rush toward the chapel door, First Sergeant Gideon tried to account for men under his authority. He couldn't be sure who had just left with King—surely not the sixteen-year-old, who should never have left his own mother in Macon. No, he saw now, the boy was still among most of the privates in his charge. But, just as his gut had warned him, Malacai Mulholland and Joseph Tidwell were moving to a spot directly before him, and they faced him, with such eyes—even his cousin—eyes that he had never seen before.

"I'm going, Francis. They'll lend us the horses," Malacai said.

"You are not."

"This is what we came for—"

"I'm ordering the both of you—and the whole company!—to stay—"

"Dammit all to pieces!

"Sergeant—" Joseph's voice was always deep, though he was reaching inside for something, and the gravelly timbre came from forced control—but Francis Gideon cut him off.

"We came here to help people—" their sergeant said. "We all came here from Georgia to help people just like our folks at home! Lieutenant Colonel Ward has commanded us to action that saves families—and we're going to abide by his orders!"

"Damn *you* then!" his cousin Malacai shouted back, shrugging off the hand that Joseph had placed on his arm. But the two did not follow King and those who rode off in the growing dark. The sergeant spun around to see who next in the company would dispute his say, but the rest of his men had turned as if absorbed in calmer tasks. The ranking man was left to pick up a settler's provision box and see what room could be made in a wagon.

Ward's battalion could not return with the colonists to Goliad's mission until morning. The crowd at the church finally slumped into a kind of repose, while sporadic gunfire sputtered in the darkness. Pounding soon reverberated on the mission door, shattering a subdued rest most had fallen into.

A boy no older than the Finnissees' first son had raced his pony from the outskirts of town to report a horror! "King's men!" he shrieked, waking the sanctuary's fitful sleepers.

Lieutenant Colonel Ward couldn't make sense of what the boy was saying. The officer told him to slow down and start with what happened to—how many Mexican soldiers?

"I was following on my pony, along the creek bed—Timothy, the Finnissee boy was my friend, so—"

"King went out to find De la Garza."

"It wasn't him they found, but ten or so soldiers sitting around a campfire," the boy cried. "They were just sitting at the campfire, and one was even laughing about—" His voice stopped, as if it could not articulate the images coming to mind. "Someone with King said it was *them* anyhow—someone started—the Mexican soldiers ended up shot—in the head and—everywhere!"

"They killed some soldiers—"

"And the rifles were loud— so you could hear shouts in Spanish coming—from down farther along the creek."

"Where did King and his men go?" Ward was asking through his teeth.

"They weren't sure which direction to go—I think they went the wrong way—"

"What happened to King's company, son?"

"They got run down —I think they got caught or killed by all the others coming from the creek!"

Two hours later Bulloch's Second Company braced for another wave of attack from the infuriated soldiers of General Urrea. Gideon and the Georgia men crowded against the low perimeter wall in the churchyard where they'd been stationed. They'd chipped through the rock structure to make firing holes for their rifles, and now they were sitting flat against the cold solid segments for protection. Joseph Tidwell had mastered the breech loading yager he was issued. He could pick off two soldiers charging the churchyard for every one the others in his company took down. During a lull, he loaded his rifle as well. He couldn't relinquish the firearm he had come back home with from the Floridas. That they should all be looking at headstones in the mission cemetery took nothing from the respite—a logical backdrop! Cautiously, they tapped out powder and reloaded, barrel or breech.

One of Francis Gideon's men had been grazed in the first rush. The others had answered his hushed call and were still there and ready. They had not all fired at the same time, but in succession— as Ward had instructed—and not until the white pants and flat hats could be clearly seen. Inside the church, Ward's   Battalion blocked the church's entrance and readied their rifles at back portals.

The sergeant outside in the graveyard was thinking that Ward sounded and comported himself this evening the way he had by candlelight back in Macon—just last fall. It seemed far away, like a previous life, but he still recognized a steadfastness in Ward's manner. He and Captain McLeod both, the West Point men— they had summoned in themselves something Francis admired. It had made him step up to the front of those gathered in his hometown and sign his name to a list of volunteers. It was clarity of purpose—a marriage of past sacrifice to present necessity. It was a kind of fierce love that an honest warrior exudes. McLeod's and Ward's speeches had drawn from and inspired intense dedication, like what had driven agrarian colonists to thwart the King of England! Now Ward was methodically directing his battalion in deadly action. Gideon was praying he too could calmly tap that depth of courage.

154

"Francis?"

"Shh…"

"Did I ever tell you about the work bell in Cork?"

"Are you hurt?"

Francis didn't hear anything else from Malacai, and he slid down on his belly to move in the direction of his cousin's voice.

"I'm all right," he said.

"Everybody, stop your talking—that's an order," Francis whispered hoarsely. There was no noise at all for a while, but an odd sound came from the same direction, and Francis realized it was muffled laughing.

"As I was saying about the granite quarries—I wish to hell the bell would clang and we could all call it a day!"

It was all right for the men to laugh softly. They had their rifles reloaded, and it was all right for Malacai to give them something to smile about. The bodies of a dozen soldiers lay in the road beyond the mission wall, their white pants contorted by final twitching. One of the slain was close enough for any to see that he had impulsively reached for his hat as it rolled away. It was best for those within the churchyard to wrest their attention, however briefly, from the spectacle. More attackers wounded by the Americans had stolen away to find cover or able comrades.

"Francis?"

"Dammit, Malacai!"

"Sorry for swearing at you earlier, dear cousin," he said.

His men were still chuckling when rapid footsteps and hoof-beats came from the far end of the street again. The next hours and the next half day went by as in an eerie dream. A minor interlude of reloading and crawling for water was cut short by another furious assault from Urrea's army. More corpses sprawled in the street. Some bleeding soldiers made feeble efforts to drag themselves out of the range of fire. Among the volunteers in the mission cemetery, the pitiful scene was much the same. Three men in the Second Company sank to the dirt in uncanny sequence. All were lost in an instant, so that the nearest soldiers firing through holes in the wall, knew to keep loading and firing. With his shoe, Joseph slid one slain man's rifle close enough to grasp. If he could handle two firearms, he could make use of three. There was nothing to be done for the dead.

The ghastly thrust and parry went on into the second full day, and when Francis sent Joseph to ask for more powder from inside the church, the answer came back that there was almost none, except what was being reserved for a last effort. Sergeant Gideon's men were to fend off one more attack from Urrea and then retreat to inside the sanctuary with those in the First Company. There, Ward desperately considered a night escape, since the settlers fared better in the care of the impartial priest than with the soldiers.

Another onslaught came and went. Dusk descended, and Francis knew his men would need to move quickly into the cover of the church before Urrea's forces surged toward the wall again. Some of his men ran, hunched over. Some crawled, pulling themselves along with their elbows. Joseph had his arm at the side of a soldier who needed steadying, and Malacai was in the shadows of the wall, still leaning near his firing position.

"Malacai!" Francis called. "We've got to move now!"

"Is there water?"

"Inside!"

"What about the dead ones?"

Francis intended to stay calm, but he crawled over to Malacai and was about to grab him by the collar and shake him.

"Dammit—"

"I'm shot, Francis." He'd been sitting a little crooked, was all that Francis had thought. They had all cramped up from the tense positions. And Francis only thought that Malacai had sat at a funny angle to get the circulation going.

"Where—" But even in the dimming light, Francis saw how pale his cousin was. The blood oozing from a place above his belt was dark red and was spreading across his shirt.

"Maybe, I could just stay here—"

Joseph came out the church door where others called for great haste. There was movement at the end of the street again, and the next attack would be closer to the chapel entrance. Francis and Malacai's step-brother dragged the wounded man inside. There was no time to see about him until after Urrea's men had charged and forced a sustained response to exploding rifles. Mexican artillery pounded the mission. The windows and walls of the church began to quiver and shed dust, and the Georgia Battalion stayed at every portal, trying to conserve their powder for shots they knew would hit mark.

Families crammed themselves into the side and back rooms that once had been barracks, and Malacai was carefully pulled away from the entrance and back to where Father Orlando and some of the settlers looked after those injured.

"Your friend is not long in this world," the priest said to Francis.

"He's my cousin."

"I thought he was gone—but he's started to speak—shh—"

"Francis—take the soft shoes— where's Joseph?"

"He's up near the door—he's our best shot—"

Father Orlando crossed himself, and he was taking a rosary from inside his pocket. Francis brushed a strand of hair from Malacai's cheek and unbuttoned his collar. A little chain he had never noticed was loose around his cousin's neck, and he lifted it to see the gleam of a tiny gold cross.

"Your cousin is Catholic?" the priest asked.

"No—I don't think—"

"My first mother was—" Malacai's eyes had opened partly. The priest moved the candle closer to Francis. "Tell Joseph—what a lovely family I have in America—"

"Malacai..." Francis rested his hand lightly on his cousin's head. "Malacai..."

"There goes one now—"

"What, Malacai?"

"One of those stars I was telling you—"

When Lieutenant-Colonel William Ward gave the command to move out in the cover of darkest night, there was feverish movement and a silence as if throats had been gripped and even lungs immobilized. But the shuffle of worn shoes was steady, down to the back of the chapel, around behind the little altar, up to the threshold of the rear door, and out across the dark field into the night and the creek beds leading away from Refugio— where there was occasional cover from stands of cottonwoods, where Ward ordered them to disperse but keep watch of each other in the water, in the woods, in the bogs, in the lower creek that would finally wind up toward Fannin's men, surely on their way now to Victoria.

Chapter 12   Within the Whirlwind

Margaret Linder fell too ill to travel as rapidly as the Gonzales couriers had been riding. The two cavalrymen took time only to tell of the town's sacrifice—men and boys who had defied mortality together, and ridden on the first of March straight into the Alamo. Following the less worn path to Washington on the Brazos, the soldiers were racing toward the main colony trail. Two rivers after their encounter with the Harper women and O'Brien, they planned to cut due north to alert those at the convention. Sam Houston and the entire Texian government would be there. They told the man and Adeline Harper to stay with the Indian as far as the Colorado and then to retrace their route and find their previous encampment just south of San Felipe.

"Get close to the Brazos," they said before spurring their horses on. "You'll be able to shelter with settlers anywhere on the main path." They had taken another look at the Tonkawa man assisting with the Harper horses and cart. "It looks like you'll be all right with him along. You see mostly the friendly kind in the center part of all this storm."

The Tonkawa man was helpful, though he didn't show much willingness to converse, except that he'd already addressed Yarico as *Stand Like Free*. There were no further utterances from him until the party reached the Colorado again, only a guttural sound indicating the women should be escorted across first. But Adeline's aunt was drifting between unconsciousness and hysteria, and the two able women moved their odd cart into the shade of a live oak and urged their traveling companion, Mr. O'Brien, to take his larger wagon on across.

When the ferry runner helped the man get his wagon wheels free of a mud rut on the far bank of the river, the traveler set about foraging in his provisions again to find sufficient payment for the reverse river crossing. The Indian shrugged him off. From his own horseback storage, the Tonkawa man retrieved the young father's two bags of sugar, and handed them back. The raft went immediately back in the current.

"Are you coming, or not?" the father shouted to the Harper women. "Do you think you can come across?"

"You go on ahead!" Adeline called, after reading Yarico's expression. Aunt Maggie was not in any shape to be bounced at top speed along the grass and pebble trail. As the heavier wagon began rolling away on the other side of the Colorado, the rear flap moved and a boy's face and hand could be made out. The two women just waved, thinking it best not to call out *Goodbye, Padraig* at a time when their Maggie was so stricken from the near certain loss in Gonzales of her nephew Matthew.

Immediately the ferry runner undertook to gather long sapling sticks from the river banks, and when he showed Adeline the size of thick brush he also sought, she began to collect what sticks and shrub pieces she could. She and Yarico had released the harness from the tall horse and managed to hoist their single luggage piece up from the floor of the cart, so that Maggie could lie down more comfortably on the feather ticking.

The Tonkawa man came back with a stone the shape of a small squashed pumpkin, and he motioned for the girl to go back with him for another. They and Yarico worked to set the stones against the rear wheels of the cart, and at the same time to rest the harness bar against the live oak trunk. When the cart was steadied at a safe incline, the man in leather leggings secured some of the longer poles with rope that looked to be made from horsetail strands. He was making, it was clear to the women, a reasonable shelter for the night they were to pass on the banks of the Colorado.

They hated to pull out the rosebud quilt for any reason and risk its getting soiled from riverbed splatters or foliage stains. But they were sure to need their woolen blankets to keep warm in the March evening, and they needed some partition which could provide a woman's privacy. Yarico used their axe to dig a narrow trench for a latrine, and she and Adeline took turns guarding modesty. With Margaret more alert late in the afternoon, they thought she might undertake a short walk in the direction of the privy. She appeared steady on her feet, and she refused any assistance beyond the quilt.

The afternoon shadows were shifting and Adeline, as she looked to the west, thought the evening—contrary to the distressing day—might prove to be quite lovely. She thought she might enjoy this muted Texas landscape, where now more frequently majestic oaks commanded respect, and riverbed woodlands had to be acknowledged. She thought she would be able to say grace for the relative peace of the spot, except for the hunger beginning to gnaw away any other sensations. The dark-haired man had gone off up the riverbank out of sight. Adeline thought he might be searching for some fish she had noticed in the deep current earlier that day or for some pecan shells she had spotted under trees along the banks. A sudden scream and an abrupt scrambling sound came from behind the hanging quilt.

"Snakes! Sna-a-a-kes!" Maggie's shriek pinched off to a yelp. Holding her skirt and underskirts up above her knees, she bolted from the brush. All three women shouted at one another. And then a violent thrashing came from the north, grew in proximity and urgency, and finally descended onto the area where the older woman had just emerged, red faced and in tears.

There was a singular sharp whack behind the partition, and then another thrashing jostled the quilt.

"Two!" the man called. He came out from behind the rosebuds with a beheaded rattlesnake in each hand. "Teeth still kill very bad. You move flower blanket." He put both snakes in one hand and sheathed his knife. "Sick woman make good shout. Now we eat!"

This was not how Adeline and Yarico would have pictured the end to a day that had begun with a cast-iron camp oven and Rodina Kolar's painstaking crumb cake. For the time it took their Tonkawa escort to make the women a fire and set some limber green sticks so that they were close, but not too close to the flame, for that hour Adeline was thinking one jar of scuppernong preserves could be shared three ways and made to stave off stomach pains until they reached the Brazos encampment the next day.

But the roasting snake meat began to smell good to the women, in spite of their sensibilities, and when Adeline's appetite sharpened her thinking as well, she went to wrestle a skillet from their trunk. This added equipment delighted their escort, and he stole off in a direction that Adeline thought would surely be pitch dark without any candle. He must have spied something earlier in the afternoon, since he came back soon as if he had followed and retraced mental steps that needed no further illumination. The man had three pieces of cactus over which she and Yarico exchanged thoroughly skeptical looks, but he began to pluck the spines with a tool from his pouch—pincers made from bone or antler. When he had finished with one, he handed the instrument and the next prickly section to Yarico. Then he peeled the first cactus slice, and after swabbing the pan with an unroasted rattler scrap, he put all the pieces—white meat and green cactus—into the pan to stir.

There was still a half loaf of coarse brown bread they had brought from Brazoria. Adeline had forgotten it, and Yarico smiled after she sniffed to make sure it had not gone moldy. Using sapling slivers that the Tonkawa man had made for spearing the food, they began to eat. The meat was tender. The concoction would have benefitted from ingredients

161

in the herb garden back at Sweet Pine, but it tasted good, and the tangy vegetable was as welcome as any of the sweet peppers Madame Genet had introduced them to at the Avignon. The Indian had tasted preserves before, but he wanted to know what startling berry was inside the jar from Macon.

Maggie was present, but she was not all there. She ate absentmindedly and would not respond in speech, except to ask without any prompting or connection to the dialogue around the campfire, "Could I have misjudged his age?" Minutes later she would add, "My Matthew could be just twelve or thirteen...too young to go." And just before she lay down in the cart, under the makeshift shelter that had been constructed, she said, "Those riders were from Alabama. It didn't look like they knew..."

Adeline was too tired to sit by the fire for long after dinner. She half sat, half leaned in the cart next to her aunt. She drew around herself the blankets that were her share, and drifted in and out. What the Tonkawa man and Yarico were saying, the Harper girl could only partly make out. The man had addressed her—the odd child in charge—to straighten out some basic questions of identification.

"Your mother?" he had asked, pointing to where Maggie was.

"—Yes," she'd lied.

"Your slave?" He indicated Yarico. Adeline did not want him to consider anything but what was in their trunk as possible payment for his added help.

"No—my *other* mother," she had said, shuddering. This information caused the man to study them all more closely. "I'm Adeline, that's Yarico, and over there is Maggie." She turned the subject to his name. "You?"

"English call me *Walker*," he said. "I am *Walk Far*."

Then he'd pointed, repeating *Adeline*, *Yarico*, and *Maggie*.

"Tonkawa call you," he had said with a faint smile, "*Two Mothers... Stand Like Free...* and...*Snake Scream.*"

Each time Adeline shifted in the small cart, Maggie edged in the opposite direction. Light from the ebbing fire made the overhead branches ripple like ocean waves. Sporadic croaking off by the riverbank blended with two human voices and the last crackling of flames.

It was Yarico, by nightfall, with whom Walk Far grew willing to talk. She was clearly not a child, nor was she an older, sickly woman. The two spoke about this place—Texas—and what could be found off in every direction.

The man made a sweeping gesture south and east and said "Two, three days—big water, no end." Walk Far pointed north and he said, "Two, three days—lonely buffalo, too many Comanche." When his arm stretched out more directly east, he said. "Many rivers—many more trees...thick like wolf fur." Yarico was making a noise as if she couldn't believe that. He gestured south and west, and he said. "Mexico horses and rifles. Big danger for English, like hundred rattlers." Anyone listening might have wondered what direction the Tonkawa himself would take to escape such commotion.

"Which way is your home, your family?" Adeline heard Yarico ask.

"Half day north. Many women...Some rattlers," he laughed. "Your home is how far?" Adeline was turning so that she could hear, because she had lost track herself, and she wasn't sure how many miles the three women had gone. It was a minute before Yarico made an answer. She had needed to figure it up, but also to speak in a language understood.

"East... three or four days land...four or five days big water...three days river like Colorado...three or four days land...home." When she finished, she had to stay silent, because Maggie had already taken the day for her turn to cry, and it was not like Yarico to let her tears be witnessed anyway.

"Your home very far," the Tonkawa ferry man said gravely. "Stand Like Free very far from home."

If Aunt Margaret had not recovered by morning, she had at least located some fortress in denial that withstands intrusion by facts. She talked blithely about Matthew from time to time, about how he was only twelve by now—she must have miscalculated. She shook her head about just missing her nephew's family when she and Addy had *called on them in Gonzales.* She spoke merrily about coming back in a few weeks and writing a letter of intent in the meantime.

There was nothing for the others to do but get the little cart and the three horses back across the Colorado. Once more on the bank where they had first encountered Walk Far, the two younger women tried to put their gratitude into words. This ferry runner had turned out to be so resourceful and kind.

"We thank you for your help," Adeline started. "Please keep the bowl," she said to him as he tried to return the original crossing fee.

"I keep blanket for home woman." Their blue wool blanket was around his shoulders. It hung down comfortably like his long hair. "You take bowl—too much."

"I have something," Yarico said. Maggie and Adeline opened their mouths, but could not imagine what to say. They watched her reach into her plain brown pocket and hand something small to the man.

"This—very old." He was examining the stone needle from Sweet Pine.

"It was a gift to me...now it is...for you...from my home."

He lifted a slim leather lace from his vest and tied it on.

"Thank you for letting us use your ferry raft!" Adeline called back, as she pulled herself up onto her chestnut mare.

Yarico rode the tall gelding pulling the cart, and their third horse was strung along as pack animal and spare. Aunt Maggie settled in, smiling at the tan pack horse and talking to herself.

"Not my raft!" Walk Far called after them. "Just borrow!"

The closer the Harper women came to the San Bernard River, the easier it was to see that twenty-four hours had changed the plans of many people. Settlers and sometimes soldiers were going in both directions on the trail they had thought of as secluded the day before. Small clusters were crossing the San Bernard toward Adeline and Yarico, with the intention apparently of taking the less muddy path to the coast down between that riverbed and the wide Colorado.

"They're going to have ships in three days at Matagorda!" one military courier on horseback claimed.

"You say you started out from Brazoria? What's it like there—they still getting the post in regular from Velasco?"

"I don't think anyone can whip ole Crockett and Bowie at the Alamo," one older woman hollered from the back of a wagon, "but I got my grandkids with me so we're angling for Columbia, and on to Harrisburg if there's any bad news."

"You hear anything about San Antonio? Are the Alamo men holding out?" a wagon passing them wanted to know.

Originally, the Harper women had planned on two hard days at most and one night as the time it would take them and Mr. O'Brien to get from the bend in the Brazos trail to Gonzales. Now, they might have considered turning southeast themselves in the direction of Brazoria.

164

The Masseys would have the latest word, from their hometown delegate Governor Henry Smith himself, if no one else. But the Macon women were down to some aging bread, several pieces of jerky, one jar of corn relish, and the whiskey bottle that Mr. Erlich had given them in Harrisburg. They needed provisions, and the closest source was the settlement in the narrow strip between the San Bernard and Brazos rivers. Supplies were said to come up the bigger river.

The San Bernard seemed harder to roll across returning to the east. Of course, they had been with the O'Brien wagon the first time. Even though they were every bit as steeled for travel hardship as that man, they still had enjoyed the additional layer of confidence that any company lends in risky endeavors. Or maybe the pleasantly distracting interlude with Walk Far made their sense of loneliness in this solo river crossing more intense.

"It's just plain higher than it was when we came over it yesterday," Adeline said to Yarico, still riding the cart horse. Maggie had been helped up side saddle on the pack horse, who could just manage her weight, as well as the clothing knapsacks and sewing bags. But they didn't want to risk anything more precious than their trunk to the cart in the deeper water.

"I expect it's been raining upstream, somewhere over close to San Felipe or Washington—" Yarico said.

"They're going to get it all straightened out," Maggie broke in. "When I get my letter written and in the post, it's going to say, 'Now, Matthew—you're too young to go off fighting, so just stay put until we get there, and anyway General Houston is taking the whole army down to your parts, so just—'"

"Yarico—after we make it across—can you take the reins again from the cart seat?" Adeline was thinking about the plantation that was not far along the trail on the other side of the river. "It might be best if you're driving Maggie when we get on into the encampment."

"It'll be best," was all Yarico said. The cold rushing water came up almost up to the axle, and though they hadn't wanted to risk letting Maggie cross in the questionable rig, they were glad their trunk weighed enough to steady the wheels. The riverbed was still more pebbly than muddy, and despite the higher water level they crossed to the other bank without screams or losses. If rattlesnakes were fond of river banks, they had not wanted to remember what Oscar Massey and his brother told them about the poisonous varieties that swam in the rivers of Texas.

Adeline, Yarico, and Aunt Maggie had been so absorbed in their work while members of the wagon caravan, that when they'd first reached the bend in the Brazos trail two days before, they really hadn't paid much attention to their surroundings. They could have described only the Kolar's splendid wagon, and O'Brien's pared down model, as well as their fellow travelers, the pack horses, and oxen. Rolling back into *The Place at the Bend*, alone, they felt caught in an eddy to nowhere.

Their sputtering boat ride along the bay from Anahuac came to mind, when Harrisburg had peeked out glumly from behind a little island. Their first impression of Brazoria came to mind, when they'd met up with Massey in his stripped-down store at the town's edge. The scattered dwellings here gave loneliness a sharper edge. Seemingly lost forever was any sense of belonging, that feeling one takes for granted—when running down a hill to the welcoming sight of one's own back door, when driving a cart up to the hitching post right off a familiar front porch—home seemed but a dream.

Still, Adeline was reminding herself—not just on this day, but several times recently—that she would have been lost in a permanent way that she'd once heard a preacher describe hell, if she'd ended up in Savannah, wondering in what direction her uncle had sold Yarico. Blood relative—or not—had Maggie been thrown out of her life—or behind bars—for the sin of leaving a harsh husband, or the mercy to stay with a dying mother and her child, Adeline would have suffered infinitely. Even *The Place at the Bend*, as melancholy as it looked, could not make her wish she had stayed in Macon to take such chances.

She doubted, however, that anyone noticed where the Harper wagon finally came to a stop. New Orleans, they had heard, sometimes included transients in their population count. In this place, coming and going looked to be the only two threads holding the scene together. There was no sign of the O'Brien wagon. Travelers pausing at the periphery waited for word to head out, for word to stay put, waited on supplies, or for raids to lighten up, waited for land lot contracts. In these last few days, they waited to see what in heaven's name would finally come out of the convention to the north. Not even the word trickling down the main trail from Washington—*Independence*—had power to invigorate the camp.

Among the scattered structures was one shelter part underground with a log roof laid out only waist high. At an edge of the rough clearing, a leaning shack appeared haphazardly started, the effort abandoned before any door was made. Adeline tried not to imagine what kinds of snakes eat snakes, because she thought the shack's dislodged walls with its gaping threshold, could surely house little else than life forms doomed to slither. If the women had not just spent a comfortable night under a makeshift brush roof, they might have been alarmed to see humans entering and exiting from matted doors as if lean-to's had been their only shelter for a while. No structure looked akin to a stable, or they would have been glad to approach an owner like Mr. Erlich and pay to share an enclosure with beasts.

When they had gone past the plantation earlier, there had not been any field hands laboring, and Yarico's nerves had held up best of the three Harper women's. She directed the cart toward the unfinished shack.

"There's still nearly three hours before nightfall. If you wanted to take Miss Maggie to stretch her legs, you might knock on one or two doors and let people know we aim to stay a few days."

It was the kind of direction Yarico used to put to her, back at their own little house outside Macon. She was telling the younger woman what to do, but delicately the way a tender mother does to give her child a sense of independence.

"I'm ready to remove myself from this thing," Maggie said. "Someone here might know about Gonzales—you never know—it could be Matthew came on up here ahead of us, in order to..."

Yarico found only three snakes inside the squat room, plain brown and with no rattlers. They enthusiastically traded the meat strips for a half pan of cornbread and some jerky. The large family living in the mostly buried cabin had been overjoyed to swap for fresh catch to mix with their rice. The Wainwrights were from Natchitoches and could testify to the Harpers about wooded land all the way from their part of Louisiana to northeast Texas. The rather treeless central part of this old Spanish territory had not really suited them, but one month had led to another, and here they were in their second year where the Brazos turned. The newest child in the household was just nine weeks old.

In the first week they spent at The Place in the Bend, Adeline and Yarico—as well as regulars, who were as friendly as they were dingy—steadied the north and west side of the structure they'd claimed. The eastern side was mostly open but facing a swath of scrub trees, which provided some privacy and allowed the sun to warm the interior. Out the south side, the ground was clear, and a fire pit from earlier inhabitants was rebuilt and made usable. They kept their cart pulled up close to the door opening and tethered the horses to thicker trunks in the woodsy area.

What the Harpers learned about the convention was what everyone else as close to Washington was finding out. An amazing document had been written and signed. As of the 2nd or 3rd of March, Texas was declared to be an independent republic! Of course, Sam Houston had been called back to his commission as the Supreme Commander of all Texian forces, regulars and volunteers alike! It looked like all those gathered were going to sign off on a real constitution and everything else a proper country would need to proceed as a land of laws. But the main thing, of course, was getting the official army organized again, so that Houston could face off somewhere and make Santa Anna give up on his northern lands.

"Get ready for a swarm of fightin' men coming through this way," Annabel Wainwright had told Margaret Linder. "They're fixin' to set their plows aside and just sling their best rifles over their shoulders. Just like they went out last fall when the Alamo was stole away from Santa Anna's brother!"

"How do you think Travis is holding up there now?" Maggie had to ask.

"My Abel heard from a lieutenant just this morning, comin' in off the river. He was in a hurry to get to Brazoria, then to get the post in to Velasco…"

"What had he heard about San Antonio?" Adeline's aunt asked again, "My nephew will want the latest word—"

"Travis was a-sayin' his prayers, is what." Two of Mrs. Wainwright's children put their arms around her shoulders. "Bless their hearts, they know I'm fixin' to cry if I talk about it much. There just wasn't much hope for Travis and Bowie. I reckon General Houston's order to get on out of the mission was just too late." She lifted the edge of her apron to her eyes. "I think all the general can do is take the regulars down a ways toward the San Antonio River, close enough to see what Fannin does with his volunteers at Goliad."

"Fannin was at Velasco! We know him, or heard about him," Adeline rushed to explain. "He's from Columbus, near our home—we went through there on our way—his wife Minerva and their girls—they moved to Velasco about when you all came from Louisiana. They got a big army together when our Georgia boys arrived. They went on down to Copano is the last we'd heard, on their way to a little town inland— "

"Well, bless your hearts, you said you was from Georgia, but I didn't figure you'd know them boys—"

"You say they're at Goliad?"

"The most we know is Houston wants Fannin to get on out and over to Victoria. Seems like they could all make a show of force there…And if Travis can slip away from San Antone…"

"How far is Victoria from here?"

"Oh, I don't know where all these missions and forts are, but it's a ways over from Gonzales—right near the coast. All I know for sure from the convention is about Houston and every Texian he can muster—they're all rounding up to add equal force with Fannin's army."

"Lots of the younger boys stayed in Gonzales to help the women folk," Maggie said.

"That's right," Adeline said in a hurry. "We just don't know how things turned out there, so we're glad General Houston has new permission to go on down and help."

"Well, I keep telling big Abel, my husband—out checkin' the river right now— that he does not have permission to leave me here with five children and go off to line up against Santa Anna!" the woman went on. "We're stayin' right here so he can shoe horses and help the children pick berries—I can't tolerate being left right now with the newest one." She held her arms out for the infant who'd been brought to her by the taller girl. "Besides, we're safe where we are, and that's all I can let sit in my mind, to tell the Lord's truth. Just stay put, and you're safe."

That was the message Adeline and Margaret took back to Yarico. She was tidying up inside the log shack, finally unearthing their sewing boxes from saddle bags and trunk compartments. Adeline was torn on most days as to whether staying confined in their temporary shelter was more likely to shift Aunt Maggie's mood to an unhealthy dreariness, or whether hearing news of San Antonio or Gonzales from their few neighbors would be more certain to send the oldest of the three into a need for smelling salts.

Maggie grew hopeful about General Houston's march toward Gonzales with regular troops. And, for a while, they did not hear decisive news about the Alamo.

Yarico, one morning, set out a cross-stitch that Maggie had started in daylight back on the Alabama River. She had forgotten it during paid fancy-work in New Orleans, and the seam sewing that had occupied their time in Brazoria kept the linen tablecloth out of mind. It was good to see Maggie pick up her needle and bundles of embroidery thread. Adeline found time to start herself a new calico bodice to go with her skirt, which was holding up to the workout of straddling horses. Self-consciously, Yarico sketched out the shapes and pieces needed for a bonnet like the one she'd made the Swedish lady. Adeline said she didn't think she would need a Sunday dress any time soon. She insisted that Yarico lay out any length of silk she needed.

News about the Alamo did not reach Adeline and Yarico until a fortnight into March. They could not keep the worst of the message from Maggie, who grew adamant that her nephew had been far too young to ride into such peril. Houston's army, they learned, was compelled to burn Gonzales themselves before pulling back east. No one in the encampment could speak of the implications. Instead, their neighbors emphasized the damage that had been done to the soldiers under Santa Anna. Most Brazos people thought he would have paid too great a price to want to take on Houston's army and the Goliad army, which were now bound to join together.

Even the youngest children could sense agitation rising around them. Rugged farmers and hunters streamed through the encampment. Grim men, crazed men were riding off to join General Houston. Countless wives, it was said, struggled to manage their babies, cramped cabins, and spring fields on their own. Lately, Annabel's husband was making his case to join the general. One night Adeline lifted out their last jar of corn relish to take over, if Mr. Wainwright should be gone the next day.

"What's that?" Maggie asked. Candlelight had made something on the jar flicker.

"They'll need some cheering up if—"

"Looks like a crack."

Now Yarico looked up from where she'd been rinsing blackberries. She was alarmed by Adeline's frozen expression, so she went to lift the jar from the girl's hands.

"I'll go take a candle and bury it, where no children or horses—"

"Don't worry, Addy. One was bound to crack sooner or later," said Aunt Maggie. She had not seen the gash of black mold deep inside the glass container.

Adeline watched Yarico's candle flame shrink out in the woods. If saving settlers depended on someone in dear Maggie's state of mind, she did not want to calculate their peril. Panic, she thought, might set in slowly like mold, and creep into the heart of things, out of sight but deadly.

In the next days, it grew hard to tell how many people swarmed down the Brazos trail from parts up north near Washington and Nacogdoches. It looked to be about the same number of people swarming up from Brazoria, or over from Anahuac in the opposite direction seeking the army's protection. Annabel's view, "Just stay put and you're safe," had not persuaded her husband to stay home.

In the shack, by candlelight, Adeline wrenched her thoughts away from absent men folk. She tried to keep her mind on the tucks and darts she was making in the new bodice. When she reached for her thimble box, she tried not to look very long at the light blue silk that Yarico was turning out into a bonnet brim.

Yarico's hands and fingers were made to sew. They were so graceful and sure in their handling of the fine material, that it was almost too pretty to watch. Other reasons made it difficult to dwell on the rare cloth. That extra length of blue silk had been first sketched out as a proud flag, though not nearly as elegant as the banner that had in fact been delivered to Captain William Ward in Macon's neighboring town of Knoxville. Adeline couldn't let herself look too long at the shimmering blue material that Mrs. Bedeford had bought for her. It felt so long ago that she had resorted to cutting down an appliqué star and moving it to a blue piece the size of a man's handkerchief. And there was no telling what her friend Mr. Gideon might be facing that very moment at Goliad. She could only hope he would find some comfort in reaching to wipe his brow.

Chapter 13   A Banner for Believing

At the creek's edge, where Francis Marion Gideon and the remaining men in Bullock's Second Company had run at midnight, one of Ward's officers handed him the reins of a horse. The battalion decided to stay in the cover of the woods growing thinly along the wetland crevice, and when they reached a northern turn in the creek, they could strike out again for the San Antonio River. Crossing it and another twenty miles of dry plain, they would find their way up to Victoria, not far from the coast. The captains were to stay on horseback where they could be seen and followed by their men, and they were to ride periodically at the rear to ensure no stragglers became lost or attacked from behind.

These were clear words in English, and if Francis had been reading a military manual in comfortable barracks, he might have written out the same order himself. He knew instinctively to follow the creek away from the mission at Refugio—sure to be overrun by Urrea's lancers at dawn. He also knew for certain that Malacai was just then left behind on the floor of the chapel, with eyes that would see no more trees and rivers of this earth, or star-filled nights.

Francis strained to put his shoe in the stirrup, so that the sole would not come apart, at least until he got his leg over the saddle. The effort made his entire body feel more cumbersome than a cotton bale. He was not sure he could order the company to march, to run if possible in the middle of the night toward new battles that would likely be twice the onslaught they'd already endured. But the men were already staggering ahead through the sparsely wooded creek bed. His horse began to follow without prompting. The moonlight that enabled the battalion to make some headway in their determined direction also made it possible for any Mexican patrols to spot their movement, so some privates scattered in spasms toward any live oak clumps farther away from the banks of the creek.

Ten or more had in this way distanced themselves from the boggy trail, and another dozen were in sight just behind the horse Francis rode. A lone man was ahead at a slight turn in the shallow water. He had reached out for the trunk of a scrub oak to steady himself. His head was down so that Francis could not at first see his face, but besides the rifle slung over the man's shoulder was a pair of high-top, leather boots tied together by their laces. This soldier's head was still down, though it was too dark for him to be studying the ground. The man's shoulders were shaking. Despite the scuffling noises all up and down the creek, Francis approached as calmly as he could on his horse and let the reins loose so the animal could take a sip from the current. He could not bring himself to tell the soldier to get going, to move on as fast as possible.

Only a few young privates in the company had a drooping mustache, none as distinct as Joseph's. His shoulders also drooped as if there were only one pose to strike after departing from the Lady of the Rosary church in Refugio. The soldiers behind Francis struggled past him, and the two Macon men were left at the rear of the retreating line.

"I can't think right now," Joseph said, looking up at last, "—what I'm going to tell our mother."

"—He said to me—" The sergeant's voice choked off, and through his shoe flaps he dug his toes into the stirrup. Joseph, now gazing away from Francis, struggled for the power to speak.

"He was partial to you in a lot of ways."

"Malacai said—tell you what a lovely family—"

Francis couldn't stand to see Joseph Tidwell so defeated in spirit. He'd been the only one of the three to know firsthand that not every man who joins a militia returns home. The cousin first to walk up to William Ward's signing table had been Francis, but Joseph was the tested survivor, proof that a man can sometimes parry with death and not be taken down.

"We need you now," he said to Malacai's step-brother. "You're in better shape than most, and you're best with any firearm. You need to stay with the faster moving men in front. Keep up with Ward, with the other two companies, and make sure ours takes the turn…We need you when the battalion gets to the cutoff, and for the dry trek to Victoria."

"These are for you," he responded. "They're off a man who can't use them anymore." Francis reached out for the leather boots.

"That's good. If I can't wear them, one of the other men will."

"The creek edging north—how far do you figure the first cutoff to be?"

Francis reached back into a saddlebag. Whoever rode the horse before had kept two slender account ledgers and a stick of graphite. He tore out a blank page and sketched the triangle that Goliad made, with Refugio straight down and Victoria up highest at the right. He leaned over to hand Joseph the map.

174

"Maybe fifteen miles from here is where we cut north toward the coast, to Victoria. But we'll have to take cover at daybreak. Patrols are crisscrossing everywhere." Joseph stood upright again. He looked down the creek in the direction of those following the soggy bed.

"Two days back up to the San Antonio River—as many as two more across the plain, that makes three, maybe four days up to the gulf at this rate—"

"That's what I count. You go now, Joseph," Francis said. In the pause, they were both beginning to shiver. "Stay at the front. I'll keep up with the company from behind."

"See you at Victoria, wherever the hell it is."

"Fannin might be there already. We'll stay with Ward."

"We'll all tell it together—back in Macon."

"Go on, Joseph."

"Yessir."

During the bitter night Francis angled his horse over toward a clump of oaks south of the creek, and then edged back toward the creek bed. His stragglers were steadily in contact and making progress as well as they could. He put on the boots and hoisted onto his horse two fellows who had been covering the distance in their sock feet. He couldn't look to see which one accepted his worn shoes. They skirted the creek's edge until close to daylight, when the two—both from Milledgeville, they said, swore they had been revived. They could march on, if the sergeant wanted to spell another two men. Francis should keep the boots, they told him.

In the growing daylight, there was no wise action but for the men with him to squat or lie down in a depression near some mesquite trees and try to keep their one horse quiet with clumps of grass they could hand to it or let it stretch its neck out to chew.

Clearly, the main segment of Ward's battalion had gone at a faster pace, and those with the company sergeant had to fend for themselves and find the northerly fork on their own. No one had come up from behind, and Francis tried to cheer himself that it might be true, as common assumption had been about Mexican troop movement. Officers had been tutored by Fannin and others that enemy soldiers, like those under General Urrea, were very unlikely to pursue American fighters. They might be swarming into what was left of the Goliad fortress, but they probably hadn't the stomach for tracking down Fannin's or Ward's flanks converging at the coast.

Signs that Francis read upon daylight the next day, at the creek fork, reversed his optimism. He and another soldier studied the footprints and boot prints in the soft mud where the creek angled in two directions, one a jagged but necessary turn north toward the San Antonio River—the Coleto rivulet. No steps seemed to have gone up this sure course to Victoria. Either the forging currents had already washed away signs of Ward's retreating battalion, or that entire group of volunteers had blundered off course, in the southerly direction, toward territory already in Mexico's grip. The waters trickling away from Refugio had seemed confusing to Francis even weeks before, when they had been able to fill drinking jugs at leisure and in broad daylight. There was no telling what erroneous course Ward's men might have followed as a unit or as splintered segments.

Francis refused to think about what had become of Johnson and Grant's men between that point and San Patricio. Was there some wishful rumor that a handful of prisoners were being held from the Agua Dulce battle, where the doctor had been killed? If Santa Anna's generals were sending prisoners back to Matamoros, maybe the counter rumor— the one about supreme orders to treat all armed settlers and volunteers as pirates, to be shot!—maybe that horrifying rumor was not true.

The dozen men with First Sergeant Gideon trudged and staggered by chilly night and stretched out by day to rest or forage for what nuts they could. Water, that had been a certainty as long as they followed a creek bed, disappeared altogether after they forded the San Antonio River. Once the company stragglers angled off in the direction of Victoria, Francis began to count days. He thought he could remember how many since the battalion had fled Refugio in the middle of the night. He knew they were in the middle of March, but he had lost track of how many nights he and the Second Company had leaned against the mission's perimeter wall and fired rounds at the waves of storming Mexican troops. *Could it be as late as the 18ᵗʰ or 19ᵗʰ?* He was losing his certainty about such accounting, but he was positive about one fact. The men under his command would need food and water soon, or they would be lying face down in the open wilderness, from deadly fatigue that makes further action impossible. He even pictured the horse as the last resort for nourishment, but he wanted to give Victoria another afternoon, or day, to emerge on the eastern horizon.

What, he wondered at daylight as he drifted off from exhaustion, what could Ward's men have found farther south, and what could Fannin's battalion be doing at that moment? Some worrisome, low, rumble was beginning to announce itself in the west. Between the recessed stand of trees where he and his men had stretched out to rest, and miles back toward the western hill where the regiment had fortified Goliad, some commotion was slowly building.

James Fannin had learned of Ward's defeat at Refugio four days earlier, and as soon as Captain Horton made it to Goliad with new carts and oxen, the colonel had ordered his men to demolish as much of the fortress as possible. At last, on March 18th, his battalion had taken advantage of an early morning fog and set out east toward Victoria. Their oxen, unfed in the chaotic departure, were finally allowed to graze at midday. Then the army's cloud cover dissipated entirely. Now in retreat, Fannin and his officers were no more in agreement than they had been at the fort. Dispirited privates tried to maintain fortitude in the confusion. Superiors debated whether to rest or force march to the coast as quickly as possible.

Again, rickety carts plagued Fannin's regiment. The small wagons were never intended to hold the stupendous weight of armaments that the colonel insisted be brought on the withdrawal. On a path made of Georgia sand and quickly draining Ocmulgee gravel, the carts and hospital wagons might have rolled steadily along. But in the sodden spring pathways one found between rivers near the Texas coast, wheels sank. In the clay mud, the oxen had half the strength and none of the will needed to grind out progress.

The troubles of forward movement mattered very little, though, when volunteers at the rear of Fannin's regiment noticed an encroaching swarm of General Urrea's troops. Forward movement ceased to matter, except that a grove of trees just two miles ahead would have provided better cover than the grassy indentation where they found themselves. There, the retreating soldiers were forced to make barriers around themselves in the shape of a square. Carts were stationed, and oxen were slaughtered to form an impromptu wall, backed three men deep along each side.

Gone was delusion. Mexican troops had indeed the determination to follow at the heels of Texas armed forces! Their general had the shrewdness, too, to see that Fannin's men would be pinned down if kept in the tall grass beyond Coleto Creek.

Only a few of Ward's volunteers had been able, quite by accident, to join Fannin's troops in their defense formation. An insignificant shred of the Georgia Battalion had wandered in the right direction to intercept the La Fayette companies. Among the lost segment from Ward's command, were a few starving wanderers that included Joseph Tidwell. They had moved well ahead of their sergeant's group, and had read the river connection correctly to move up alongside Fannin's soldiers on their retreat.

Tidwell, next to a youngster from the Mobile Greys, stayed on his belly during the initial exchange of gunfire. Some survivors from his own company had their firearms ready at nearby carts. Fresh muskets were handed out —five hundred had been transported with the battalion! And powder for another day or two! Joseph had managed to hang on to the yager. He knew he could put it to deadly use again, as he had at Refugio. But the battalion's last meal had already been consumed, and the Macon man understood that hunger was going to be as much a factor in the outcome of the battle as the half-regiment's poor location. Through the fat March grasses, they were unable to see where fire was coming from.

"Don't use your powder unless you see a blast," Joseph said. He could tell the Alabama soldier was young. He'd been firing as fast as he could reload.

"I ain't sure if I got one!" the youth said. He had a peculiar southern accent, but his brown hair was curly, and Joseph couldn't halt the fleeting image of Malacai.

"That's what I mean, brother. Wait until you're pretty sure you see the fire—"

"I might get my head blowed off if I'm watchin' for fire!"

"That's for certain. Just take it nice and easy." Joseph said calmly. "I don't think we'll get them to rush their aim any by peppering this field with wild shot."

"Who's company you with?"

"Bulloch's—we're with Ward."

The younger man raised up enough to squeeze off a bullet, and then he slumped down to reach again for his powder.

"We thought you was all sliced to bits over at Refugio—they said you got beat and run through—"

"Some of King's men—but don't you worry—most of us slipped out the back at night before Urrea knew we had even quit firing from the church yard."

"You had a chance to shoot from the church wall? I remember that little yard in front of the church…"

"Yeah," Joseph said. He lifted his body in order to send a shot in the direction a loud blast had come from. "I think I remember you—when we all came in from Copano."

"We got there just before Ward and you all. Or was it Kentucky men I remember? Seems like a long time ago—nobody woulda thought they'd come and pick up a fight around that little wall. My boys and I had a picnic there one day when the sun come out good."

"The Matamoros plan—we had it mapped out we were going to Matamoros—to set ole Santa Anna straight over mistreating settlers—"

"Where'd this Urrea get his gumption?" the boy wanted to know. He took another shot, and Joseph reached out to hold his arm a moment.

"We've got some good powder yet. Let's not blow it to kingdom come."

"You get a chance to kill some of 'em already?"

A sharp explosion was followed by a thud at an adjacent cart. One man from Tidwell's part of the company fell over and matted the grass. His eyes next to the glassy stare of the ox didn't make a comforting sight.

"Just keep your own thoughts and your sights out on the periphery," Joseph said.

A volley of rifle fire seemed to come from several directions, and the youth crawled closer to one of the wagon wheels. A second round came, and from Joseph's experience, he thought there to be enough Mexican soldiers surrounding their formation that Urrea's men must be outnumbering Texan forces by three to one.

There would be no making it to the wooded area where at least sharpest rifle aims would be able to pick off many of the attacking troops.

"Doctors!" A shout had come from a side of the defense square opposite of where Joseph was stationed. "Doctors—over here! It's the colonel! Over here—it's Fannin!"

The night of the nineteenth proved more murderous emotionally than the day had been. Among Fannin's battalion, several crack shots had belly-crawled out to the edges of the grassy low spot in an attempt to pick off snipers in the farther field. Once wounded themselves, Fannin sharpshooters were stranded. They cried out for water, but no one in the reinforced square could get to them. And water—never mind the creeks and mud that had been traversed—was in short supply. There was not even enough to cool off the artillery in between loadings. The rifle fire, except for retaliation where an explosion could be made out in the dark, slowly ebbed away. Texas cannons, worthless once metal overheated, ceased entirely. Maddeningly, Urrea's bugles sounded for a charge sporadically throughout the night, just often enough to keep Fannin's men from dozing into reasonable rest. Only the piteous cries of the wounded for water went on and on, through dawn the next day.

On the twentieth, James Fannin, already wounded in the shoulder, and his captains discussed what move to make. They figured Urrea to be capable of waiting them out, even if it took a few more days among independence fighters for abject injury and starvation pangs to peak.

Joseph watched across the way as the white flag of parley was positioned on a stick. What the Alabama boy had told him, about the white Knoxville banner getting destroyed before the La Fayette retreat, made truce maneuvers now hard to bear. The thought of their tattered banner was only somewhat less hard to stomach than the thought of Macon's dead. He was not of a mind or a constitution to raise white flags at such times. But he was weary and past hunger, like all the other Georgia volunteers. Joseph thought he could stand giving up the win, if it meant this Alabama youth would get a meal soon and a chance to rest.

He glanced, however, at the carts where another private in his own company had fallen the day before. Joseph scanned the scene from one small wagon to another and tried to count the Second Company men that he could make out. His reflexes still rallied against surrender. There were plenty of muskets! These volunteers could at least make Urrea's soldiers pay in bodies for the victory they were sure to claim!

But, a Mexican officer was walking unscathed through the truce lines. He spoke with an accent, German probably, so that his short greetings were at first as hard to believe as his smile. The enemy officer walked calmly, in a friendly way among the defeated volunteers. The truce flag was waving. And the English that Joseph heard Urrea's official speak was almost too good to be true.

"Just a few days more, men—and you'll be home!"

Chapter 14   Fair Are the Meadows

Francis and his remnant company had spent the night listening to rifle fire and the sounds of artillery just ten miles to the west of the trees sheltering them. They could not imagine the commotion of blasts and staccato firing to be anything but an encounter between Fannin's men and General Urrea's. The blessing inherent in the distance was that during the hours of pitch dark, they had all been able to visualize the bloody defeat of Mexico's troops, the trouncing of those who dared pursue the La Fayette battalion. They had blissfully fallen asleep, hungry as they were, on a final, pleasant dream of Fannin's victory. They had dozed off picturing their imminent discovery and rescue by one of the Red Rovers or one of the Mobile Greys—any of the fighters under Colonel James Fannin!

"Alto!" a shout suddenly went out. One of the men with Francis had awakened before him and was reaching for his rifle. In a panic, he did not stop as instructed and was shot by a Mexican soldier on horseback. The cavalry man already held the reins of the horse Francis had been riding and sharing.

Francis ran impulsively toward the fallen private and must have looked to the mounted soldier as if he too were reaching for the rifle. The bullet that hit Francis went through the upper part of his right arm. A sharp fiery pain jabbed deeply and then disappeared for a time, so that Francis sat up. He gripped his wounded arm and saw the blood coming from a spot high on his sleeve. The first man hit had a dark hole in his forehead, and the others in Gideon's command were shouting and most were holding up their hands.

"Alto!" the soldier in the white pants shouted again. There were three other soldiers in the Mexican patrol, wearing the gray rough pants of lower rank.

"Si!" Francis said. "Si! Alto."

"Ah, Espanol!" The officer scrutinized Francis and motioned the group of stragglers from Bulloch's Company to come out from behind the trees and kneel so they could be counted and tied. "Espanol. Bueno!" the lead man said.

The patrol soldiers allowed their captives to perform a cursory burial of the dead man before moving on. It didn't look to Francis as if they had decided whether to march their prisoners west toward the silenced battlefield or east to Victoria. He and the remaining company men used sticks and slender rocks to dig a shallow hole, to cover the mounded dirt and stones with thin branches of mesquite. Two of his privates in torn socks began to examine the dead man's shoes and the boots that Joseph had brought along from Refugio. In their own indecision, the Mexican soldiers permitted their prisoners the time to determine the best arrangement. Francis ended up with his wrecked shoes again, but two of his men worked to retie his baling string. They also used his blue handkerchief to secure a shirt rag over his wound. Francis thought the bleeding arm would not stop throbbing any time soon.

All these movements among the American volunteers, Urrea's patrol observed with a patience and respect that took Francis by surprise. Maybe they were all ready for a bell to clang, he was thinking. Everything in the last four days had made the First Sergeant think of his cousin, and it was Malacai's voice he heard in his mind—*Let's get the bloody thing over and get on home, for pity's sake!*

When they were tethered together and at last on the march, Francis was sure they were headed north as much as east, either because they knew the surest path to Victoria or because—like officers on the Texian side—they could not reach agreement. The trudging was excruciatingly slow, and two hours after setting out, the throbbing in his wounded arm consumed his consciousness, but thirst among the men was equally intense. It had already surpassed hunger during the night they'd heard the battle. Whichever destination the Urrea patrol had decided on, they would arrive without any prisoners if no water were provided.

"Agua," Francis said to the man in charge. "Señor, agua, por favor."

They stopped their horses and peered into the gourds in which they carried their own water rations. Those in gray pants were shrugging and shaking their heads. The lead soldier cursed, indicating he had none to spare. Francis believed that the miles to coast would be dry for them all.

The officer looked at the First Sergeant's shoes, and he looked at the bandage over the man's arm. He had a little smile that was not entirely unfriendly, either because of the Spanish Francis had picked up, or from the miniscule likelihood that this particular soldier would run off if allowed to go on a brief search for spring water. He handed over a rope strung with three empty gourds and motioned for one of his subordinates to walk the prisoner off in a likely direction, somewhat west, not too far south, maybe toward the smaller creeks running off the Coleto. It occurred to Francis that yesterday's battle must have ended decisively in favor of Urrea's army, or else he and his men would all have been shot in a reflex of retaliation. The battalion with Colonel James Fannin must all be in Urrea's hand, he admitted to himself—why else the generous gesture of letting captives provide themselves with water?

Most assuredly, battle clashes in the west had ended. There were sounds this morning, chirping and the rustling of wings that Francis detected through the louder screen of his own groans and trudging feet. Mockers now sang in the leafing scrub trees and brush. Green sprouts were tempting finches farther north from the protection of the shoreline, and some hopped in the willows to announce their nesting intentions. It was spring, Francis marveled. One full season – almost two—had been lost in a painful blur. But nature had a way of countering human intrusion! No battle was going to halt the steadfast advance of spring!

Francis breathed more deeply, in spite of the throbbing and the hunger. The smell of moist dirt—even the Texas kind that was powdery not far down from the grass streaked surface—a beautiful smell of living earth invigorated the Macon farming man.

He and the patrol soldier had gone some distance, over several subtle rises and slopes in the terrain. There was no sign yet of a water source, but over one more gradual incline and falling of land, there appeared to be a clump of oaks and slim offshoots that Francis felt could signal the location of a creek.

His escort nodded when Francis gestured toward the trees, and the two, now well beyond sight of where the patrol had stopped, went on to the likely spring. Water trickled several feet from the largest tree, whose most mature limbs stretched enough to bend and sprawl. Francis knelt down by the gurgling source and submerged an empty gourd with his good hand. The guard dismounted and permitted his horse to nibble at a patch of rich green. His rifle folded across his arms, the soldier leaned against the big trunk, to rest in the shade while the water was collected.

Francis had not been able to place a pungent smell near the shade of the tree, but he steadied himself as he bent over the spring, and he fought off dizziness from the walk and the hunger. He was most aware of the pounding in his head, so that when a scratching sound registered and a low growl finally identified itself in his brain, he could only look up at the last instant to glimpse the mountain lion as it descended the trunk and threw itself, claws then teeth, into the neck and shoulders of the Mexican soldier. The dominant noise came from the animal, because it had clenched the soldier's throat, and because Francis was too shocked and too thirsty to emit any sound except a rasping wheeze as he vaulted clumsily up from the ground. He waved his left arm and tried to shorten the distance between himself and the Mexican rifle, which had been knocked from the guard's grasp. When he wrapped his fingers around the weapon, he found he had no strength for steady aim and could only resort to flailing at the wildcat with the butt of the firearm.

The mountain lion snarled and backed away a few feet, before loping off toward a nearby rise, and then disappearing. Francis took off one shoe and removed his sock to hold against puncture wounds in the guard's neck. But the man was losing too much blood. Francis searched frantically for a better piece of cloth, a sweaty rag, maybe, for a compress. He was reaching into the man's jacket, when everything went black inside his head. The blow Francis caught while he hunched over the mauled soldier, toppled him onto the dying man. The kick that he suffered in the ribs sent him tumbling in the other direction and left him face down near the roots of the oak. Instinct made him turn half way to see what final assault might be coming, but he a saw a man with a wide hat and a woman and a riding cart.

"Gaa-to," Francis stammered, in case the wildcat had only retreated a short distance. "Gato."

Hours later, when the sergeant came to, it was going on dark. He found himself lying on a colorful blanket near a wooden stool, down on the swept dirt floor of an adobe house. At a table nearby, a man sat with a rifle. A gray-haired woman near a candle was holding a baby, and another woman stirred something over a flame.

"The spring is our water," the man told him. "These days one man can kill a family this way. We have heard such tales. We thought you went to poison our water."

"He is alive, no?" the woman at the stove said.

"We are sorry," the man said, shaking his head.

"You hit him, Felipe—you are sorry."

For a minute, Francis saw two blurry women at the stove and two blurry men sitting at the table. He closed his eyes so that he wouldn't see two tables and two babies.

"We saw the cat marks. We will tell the army you did not kill the soldier," the man said.

Francis wanted to reach a hand up to see if there were cracks in his skull where it hurt so badly, but he was lying on his good arm. The one that had taken a bullet earlier in the day would not move either. He was so light-headed that he could not possibly tell whether hunger or injury was robbing him of complete thought.

"Here, Felipe. See if he will eat some...a little posole."

Francis could only part his lips when the man lifted his head and held a spoonful of soup to his mouth.

"Agua, por favor," he said.

"Si, si—" The man said. "You see, Mama, they are not all so bad—"

The woman holding the child had answered in Spanish that Francis could not make out at all. When he'd taken a sip of water, he nodded his thanks and put his head back down on the blanket. The baby's eyes followed his movements, and Francis could only smile back.

"The rancheros say most are going back to Goliad, the ones that did not get sent to Matamoros."

"Bueno," his wife said.

"In a day or two, I will take him to Goliad."

"Tell someone there he did not kill the soldier."

"This one has the Anglo hair, but not the killer eyes."

Francis drifted off into blackness. He had understood the word *Goliad*, and he had drifted off.

Goliad's fortress was filling up again. The first group of American prisoners to be sent back to the mission and fortress were those not wounded, who could march. Joseph Tidwell and other survivors, arriving finally at the gray stone walls, were crammed into the tiny sanctuary. For a day Joseph's shoulder angled just below one man's chin, and another fellow's cough rattled his own chest. The likelihood of fainting cast a double horror over the defeated men. Pools of filth expanded on the dirt floor, but space between the prisoners was so diminished that any could have perished standing up. At last, they were released at gunpoint to the parade ground within the fortress walls. The regiment had surrendered honorably, but they now had no strength and sank where they were halted. In the colder months, they had squeezed themselves into the barracks at the outer edges, but Urrea's men now occupied that enclosure. Under the watch of armed guards, the Americans collapsed in a stupor, moving only when they had permission to stumble or crawl to see to one another's injuries.

The seriously wounded had been left on the Coleto battleground, Colonel Fannin among them. It was a day after the first march back to the mission, before guards escorted the fittest among the disarmed La Fayette battalion to collect survivors lying in the thick grass. Any American doctors were under orders to first attend to injured Mexicans. Joseph waited among regiment survivors to hear whether the colonel made it safely back to the fort.

He and those few from the Georgia battalion also waited for any word about the fate of William Ward's main contingent. On the third day, some special fuss at the mission's front gates woke the Americans. Any who could stand rose while Colonel James Fannin was carried through the ranks and allowed quarters in the same perimeter building where Urrea's officers were housed. Some wives appeared to be traveling with the Mexican army, and the La Fayette men were left pondering how long it had been since they last saw any of their own sweethearts or mothers.

The surrender, they kept reminding themselves, was on honorable terms. They could regain strength by concentrating on what was assured—that after a deportation to New Orleans, they would all be on their way to family and rejoicing. Such were the honors of war, as long as they agreed to never take up arms again against Mexico.

Never take up arms again in Texas! Joseph wanted to see Francis Marion Gideon come in through the gates among Ward's men, so they could have a subdued laugh together. What grand promise of glory it would take for them to ever come to Texas again and take up arms against Mexico!

But he was not sorry they had come for their original purpose, and maybe they had done some good. Among their guards were several who told them that the Refugio settlers had not after all been harmed, that Urrea was a good general who saw to it that no one unarmed, no settlers were to be harassed by his troops.

The night guard that watched Joseph's area had grown used to the man with the mustache. He allowed the prisoner to come over to the wall near a parapet that his Southern friends had worked on. Though several sections of wall and the other artillery towers were destroyed on Fannin's orders before the retreat, Joseph's parapet still stood. He asked permission to come over to the rock perimeter near dusk to ask if there were any soldiers or wagons heading toward the gray fortress.

"Looking for your amigo?" the watchman asked.

"Yes. Family."

"You will all see family very soon."

"If they get here in time."

The La Fayette contingent filled half the inner grounds of the mission, and Joseph couldn't help envying their camaraderie as they waited for the news of ships and dates for their departure from Victoria—or would it be Copano and Velasco, from where it had all begun? Somewhere on the coast. The Coleto battle had not taken as much out of Fannin's battalion as the siege of Refugio's church had used up from Bulloch's men.

With nothing else to do, and their spirits reviving, they were all figuring the calendar days and predicting what the waves would be like on the travel by ship. There was fond conjecture about parades and receptions at their homecoming. Well, there might not be parades, since the outcome of the effort had not won any rights for the Texians. But the boys from home had tried, and they had the blisters and the stories to prove it! The old men, retired soldiers, would make their regular Macon meetings soon and toast these survivors for a most valiant effort—*No Blame! No blame!*

The Alabama youth from Coleto, Joseph noticed, rested among his own company. Men from Mobile appeared to be taking care of him. He had seen two of the older soldiers hand him their rice cups, saying they had eaten all they could. These Mexican guards—or their superiors— could not be accused of too much generosity with food supplies, he thought with some contempt, but the Southern men had taken care of their own. Every man in both battalions could go home proud of that.

"Hombre!" called the guard from the parapet. "Your amigos are coming, I think. The light is not good, but I am looking just east. Do you hear now?" Joseph winced to think what shape Ward's battalion might be in after a forced march from Victoria. If they were on their feet at this point, though, they could revive. It was the night of the 25th. They could rest for the day or so it would take to have ships waiting at a port. And with their level of eagerness, they just might fly toward home if they found it too hard to walk!

Joseph stood with the others in the courtyard as wave after wave of William Ward's company proceded stiffly through the mission gates and crumpled wherever resting space appeared. Ten men that Joseph recognized easily came through the portal. And many in the next dozen and the next, he was sure were from the first company, Georgians of Columbus, or the third company from Montgomery, all ragged and worn, some skeletal. But he recognized so many, and he was trying to hold back tears at the thought of embracing Francis—rank be damned.

Sixty came through behind their leader Lieutenant-Colonel William Ward. Someone said he had not wished to surrender, but it had come to that desperation near the coast just below Victoria. The city was found already occupied by Urrea when the wandering battalion slashed its way through cactus and mesquite to the former Texian stronghold. They rose against artillery and lances, but it had at last been too much to fend off. Eighty-five men accompanied Ward when the surrender was accepted.

Seventy men, Joseph estimated, and then he'd thought it was eighty or more who'd made it past Goliad's gates into the courtyard. And still there was no sign of Francis Marion Gideon.

Joseph could not bear the thought that Francis and his men might still be out there somewhere, dying of thirst or starving, wounded perhaps. If they were lost with no reasonable hope of help, Joseph did not think he could bear to know. He stayed out near the parapet late into the night. The guard knew him and allowed him to wander down the wall to a low place where he could look out into the dark fields surrounding the fort. American doctors were permitted in late hours to walk among their injured and give what treatment or comfort they could. Joseph noticed Judkins bent over two bandaged and moaning men. Three of the Mexican wives and a woman named Alavez followed with soup and tortillas. One of the La Fayette physicians came over to the wall where Joseph studied the darkest shadows.

"You with Ward?"

"We got split up. I was looking for someone I haven't seen yet."

"A few were put to work—they had some sent to the ship builders in Victoria—"

"Is that right?"

"Others were taken prisoner...loaded into wagons going on to Matamoros." The doctor took out a small cigar and offered another to Joseph.

"I guess he could still be out there." He hesitated. "You didn't hear anyone speak of First Sergeant Francis Gideon, did—"

"Gideon?" The doctor quit puffing. "I know where there's a letter addressed to that name. When King's courier rode in from Refugio, I had to treat him for cactus nettles and he couldn't go back. It wasn't until the day you men got into it with Urrea that he remembered he'd been carrying a letter—somehow made it from Velasco or Copano to the mission.

Joseph was dumbfounded, and the doctor hurried off toward a group nearest the church where many of the Fannin battalion had made camp. When he came back, he had a torn yellow envelope in one hand. He was smiling so broadly, he seemed to have a hard time keeping his cigar in his teeth.

"Poor fellow says he's sorry the envelope came open—says he's sorry he went on and read the letter, but it kept his own hopes up. He wants to come over and apologize to you, but he still can't walk very well." Joseph could merely reach out for the letter. "You need a candle?"

It was only a few sentences long, and at first Joseph didn't recognize the name at the bottom or on the outside of the envelope. And then he remembered the Macon girl traveling with her aunt and servant. They had seen the battalion off at New Orleans. That was her name—
Adeline.

22 January, 1836

Dear Mr. Gideon,

I hope this letter finds you and your cousins well. We have reached Brazoria and hear that Ward's volunteers are already at Velasco. What pleasure to think that we are still neighbors after having traveled so far! I am writing to let you know that your letters home were mailed in New Orleans, as you asked they be. As I expect never to return to the banks of the Ocmulgee, I hope you will let Mrs. Bedford, and any other Macon friends who ask, know that we think of them often.

May the courage of Georgia men deter the brute will of Santa Anna. May God keep you all from harm.

Yours truly,
Miss Adeline Harper

Joseph didn't think Francis would mind his having read the letter. Maybe it was something a more public man could read aloud to the entire regiment. He folded it into his pocket and kept awake a little while longer straining to hear any sounds of stragglers or lone wagon wheels.

The next day muted rejoicing set in among the Americans. It was Saturday, and there was growing belief that the day of departure approached. Even though Ward's companies were exhausted, there was fresh adrenalin. To be at last on their way home! The Alavez woman made sure there were extra pots of soup, and her furtive contributions to the evening meal made up for the meager rice rations still coming from the guards and commissary. Another few hungry days could be survived. The men began to recall the delicacies they had enjoyed back in New Orleans. A few more days of hunger, a few more days of marching—would they go straight across the plains to Velasco?—a few more days of Texas could be survived.

Some who had made the Alabama River come alive with song on their way down to Mobile, began again to try out their voices. Sympathetic guards gave free rein to the prisoners' inclination, though the songs were none they had heard—*Home Sweet Home* and *My Country 'Tis of Thee*. The cheerful verses went on until the men ran out of breath, until there was hushed news that tomorrow would be the day, and brotherly cautioning spread out among the men to get some rest, to conserve their energy for heading out.

Joseph was spending one more night at the crumbled wall where he thought he might spy a familiar figure with two or three surviving Bulloch privates. As the singing died off, one of the soldiers reminded everyone that the next day would be Palm Sunday. Tomorrow! Of, course! It was spring—the fields were beginning to bloom as Father Guillermo had said they would. Of course Easter would be coming up. And tomorrow was Palm Sunday! The choir that started up was almost four hundred strong. Even the wounded who could make no sound were moving their lips. Knowing little English, the guards stood in appreciative silence, and the few ladies—who had already been to bed—came to the windows of the officer barracks to listen.

> *Fair are the meadows, fairer still the woodlands,*
> *Robed in the blooming garb of spring*
> *Jesus is fairer, Jesus is purer*
> *Who makes the woeful heart to sing.*

On a low rise to the northeast, a small cart had rolled to a stop a few hours before, at dusk. There was no point in trying to take the injured man down the rocky banks of the San Antonio River in pitch dark. The jostling trip from his small house closer to Victoria had been hard enough for the pleasant American. The soldier suffered raw inflammation from his gunshot wound, and the swollen bulge where Felipe had struck with a rifle butt was giving the man considerable pain. The cattle worker, who had only protected his water source, felt bad—all this pitiful trouble between rancheros and settlers, the Mexican army and Texan soldiers.

Surely it would end soon and go back to the way it was. He was hopeful from what he heard about Urrea that this leader was more likely to bring a return to peaceful life than the heavy-handed General Santa Anna.

But Felipe did not wish to talk with anyone about the politics of his country. He only wanted to get the wounded man to his comrades, so they could both recover—from injury and from guilt. The man was called Francis, as far as he could understand. After days of delirious weakness, he had been awake when a neighbor rode by to say the rest of the soldiers from Victoria were going to Goliad. They were all being taken to Goliad, from where they would march out of Texas and get on their homebound ships.

Francis was still in and out of consciousness, and Felipe had driven the cart just to the banks of the winding San Antonio when darkness descended. Besides the danger of night crossing, there was the risk of approaching the fort as an unidentified party. He had a wife and baby waiting at home. There was no need to risk getting shot accidentally by his own countrymen in the dead of the night. He had made himself a bedroll and settled next to the wagon where Francis lay.

"Good singing to hear before sleep," he was telling Francis.

"Goliad—is very close."

"When the sun comes up, we will make our way down to the river and up the hill."

"My cousin...would be singing—"

"Don't talk, now Señor Francis. Just listen—"

Fair is the sunshine, fairer still the moonlight
And all the starry host above—

In the eerie dark of predawn, Joseph Tidwell was back at his post near the crumbled gray stones. He had caught a bit of sleep, but he kept dreaming that Malacai's cousin was close by and was going to make it to the mission in time to head home. The guard at the parapet, he noticed, was slumped in the pose of sleep, and there seemed to be no one else stirring. Except for the occasional low groan of an injured man or the fitful cough of a sleeping soldier, the courtyard was at peace. Then, one door from the barracks opened quietly, and Joseph spotted a Mexican officer that the men had called *Garray*. Another ranking man, too, emerged with a candle and a list, and then a couple of Fannin's doctors stepped forward and were whispering. The physician who had given Joseph the letter came briskly, but silently down to the wall where he stood, and Joseph couldn't imagine what he wanted.

"You should come," he whispered. "Captain Garrier says we should follow him, but you must be very quick."

"Follow where?"

"The doctors and a few others—but, please, we are asked only to follow—"

"I'm watchin' for family—."

"He can only take a few—"

"I better wait here—in case my cousin—"

"Yes, of course." He almost turned to go. "Are there any German men in your company? Their foreign man, Holzinger, is looking for any German names—he wants to know before he leaves—"

The man looked pale, ashen, but Joseph thought it was just the strange half-light.

"No?" The doctor hesitated about a handshake, and before turning back woodenly toward the barracks door, he just said, "Well, then—"

Joseph thought it was strange, but it occurred to him that maybe James Fannin had taken a turn for the worse. Personally, he felt more allegiance to William Ward, so if it was about the colonel, he could not make himself feel guilty for not lending a hand.

In another two hours a slight tinge of rose began to suggest sunrise, and some of the women were up and about even before the officers. Joseph saw the Alavez woman talking to a youthful volunteer, even younger maybe than the Alabama boy he had tried to help through the Coleto engagement. All the guards were suddenly awake and on their feet, even the parapet guard, who usually turned in to the enlisted men's barracks at the first sign of daylight.

It looked to be as they had suggested the night before, that today was the day. But then, Joseph doubted, maybe the early stirring was because of Palm Sunday and what it meant to these people, serious about their religion. Perhaps special services were to be conducted. He noticed that one of the wives had her two little daughters with her. He hadn't observed any children before in the parade area, and he thought it was odd how one girl turned her face to her mother's skirt and seemed to be crying.

194

The prisoners' own officers were rallying them as gently as they could, since so many were stiff from sleeping out in the cold night air. It would be a clear sunny day, if one could judge from the brightening sky, but still March nights could dip down to low temperatures, and with such exhaustion and little food, it was hard for the men to jump into action.

Everything was looking as if today would be the day. The guards and their superiors examined their lists of prisoners again, accounting which was routine, except that divisions were being made. Groups were being formed—some were to march out south of the mission. Others were to head down to the river and east of the church in the direction of Victoria, and a third group—was there also a fourth cordoned off to be with them?— readied for a more westerly march toward San Antonio. These divisions certainly made no sense if today were the day to start for Velasco or another port, Joseph thought. But one of the men in his ragged company said they were all to collect kindling and brush to take along, since the trees were sparse nearer the coast. And the group forming up at the front gates was to draw water for the journey.

Nearly four hundred were on their feet, and Joseph thought it was unusual that two of the women came along to the front of Goliad's entrance and stood as if in defiance of their spouse's wishes, since the higher officers were not in sight. But the main worry Joseph had as his unit lined up and was set to a cadence, was that Francis could be close to reaching the mission, and that he might just miss arriving in time to be with the remaining members of the Bulloch Company, as they made preparations and headed out.

The Alavez woman was talking to the Alabama boy when Joseph Tidwell began his march out past the fortress gates. And Joseph thought he had said "Good morning" to the friendly parapet guard who now strode alongside his unit. But the guard's silence, he felt, could be because the man hadn't heard. And anyway, the pleasant night guard should have been asleep, so he may have been too tired to answer.

The Georgia men marched a few hundred feet out in front of the fortress at Goliad. There was no talk among the guards, who were usually inclined to chat with each other, and Joseph thought it could be due to the late hours that most everyone had kept the night before, or to the incredible beauty of the morning. It was, after all, Palm Sunday! Birds stirred and chuckled in the brush. The sun was a crimson ball, rising like a crown over Victoria in the east, as the men were directed along the gray walls toward the south. And just as the kindly priest had told Francis, the meadows beyond the mission were beginning to shimmer in colors, not just hues of green, but a fine golden yellow was emerging, and then, they said, there would be blue and red in some of the later months this spring.

A dozen rifle blasts smashed through the still beauty of the Sunday morning from the south side of the church, where Joseph's group had been taken down the hill toward a creek. From behind him, a southern voice shouted, "They're going to shoot us, boys!" And before Joseph could spin around, the man in front of him had jerked before falling, and frantic men on either side of him were being cut by rifle fire. The rifle volleys grew to a single deafening explosion from below Goliad's hill, and for seconds Private Tidwell slapped his arm where his own weapon usually lay. A finch screeched as it flew from the mesquite nearby, and the strong scent of budding life rose from the damp ground. The thought Joseph had when he looked into the eyes of the guard aiming at him was simple—that it was not the guard who had let him look for Francis. The man aiming at Joseph did not know him, he thought, and never would.

On a rise beyond the mission, where the ravine below met the San Antonio River, and land on the other side angled up to the entrance of the fortress, a man in a red poncho was watching soldiers march out toward the water. He was about to wake Francis Marion Gideon, but the injured fellow slept so well that Felipe hated to shake him into consciousness. The owner of the wagon guessed that the Americans were not on their way off to the coast for their homeward journey yet, so he let the wounded man in his cart sleep a little longer.

He was thinking about the beautiful morning as the soldiers below him marched to a certain point and then halted. He was looking at the little flowers, some yellow and some white, that peeked out around the rocks of the incline, and he thought he might try to put a few in a gourd, with a bit of river water, to take home to his wife. He did not want to stay long in the fort, because he had been missing his wife and little daughter.

When the shooting started, he thought he was suffering from poisoned water. He thought he was seeing something from another person's nightmare. He could not see how many were shooting, but such explosive and futile efforts to escape made him unwittingly reach up and tear at his hair. Rapid volleys and screams came from the ravine close-by, but he realized the same horror was unfolding south of the mission, and clouds of firearm smoke rose from the west side of the gray walls, too. The firing and pointless running made one guard, an officer maybe, down below, step off to the side to get sick to his stomach. The soldier bent over. He was gripping the reins of his horse, when he stared up from where he'd been ill. He looked up the hill and saw the man Felipe with his cart. He wiped his mouth on his sleeve before mounting his horse. The soldier did not look back at all the shooting and crying out, but instead just let his horse amble in the direction of the river, and the rise beyond, and the cart.

"Francis—Señor," Felipe said. His voice did not sound like his own voice, he thought. He couldn't shake a sizzling rattle from his ears, like cicadas, but that season was far away. When he looked down into the wagon, the man from Georgia was lying awake. The American's eyes were open, but when the injured man brought his hand to his forehead and appeared to consider sitting up, his attempt ended with a shudder. "Bueno. Stay like that, my friend." The sizzling rose around them. "A soldier has seen us. Stay very still."

Chapter 15   Downpour

In the encampment at a bend in the Brazos River, thirty miles south of San Felipe, a rare day surfaced in mid March of 1836. Adeline thought it could have been an extra that God spared from Eden to dispense at that time. Despite the morning's peace, broken only by the cooing of doves, a backdrop of sorrow and apprehension stretched behind settlement activity. Last week's news of the final decimation at the Alamo still gripped the camp's inhabitants. Within twenty-four hours, word of General Houston's retreat had swept through. Having ordered his army of several hundred away from the razed area that had been Gonzales, he now made the Colorado River the Texian's line of defense. Couriers confirmed the general's command to Fannin—withdraw the Goliad army east to Victoria, near the coast!

Independence was anything but won. But on a beautiful day, it seemed possible that Texas regiments could hold Santa Anna to the western stretches where few settlers clung to their towns and farms. With Sam Houston's regulars guarding any approach of Mexican troops from that direction, settlers on the Brazos and farther east believed there was time in the middle of March to stay put.

The chill that had pervaded Texas through the first half of March subsided, and after several days of light rain, leaves on oaks and native elms began to bud. Yarico and Adeline rolled two short tree stumps from the fringe of the encampment to just outside their threshold. One of their woolen blankets served as a door flap, and the rosebud quilt provided adequate warmth to their common pallet. All three women had adjusted to spending nights fully clothed. To shut out the stark worries of daylight, they wrapped themselves in routine —the hauling of water from the communal well, the heating of the kettle at the fire pit by their cabin, soaking peas and watching the cast-iron pot, mending, or scouring the cabin for anything with stingers or without legs.

Mornings could be lovely. Adeline had taken up repair stitching while the light made its arc overhead. Annabel Wainwright's two daughters read from a worn primer, while the young teacher nodded and darned their stockings. In exchange for regular schooling and frequent mending, Mrs. Wainwright shared a pan of steaming cornbread she made each dawn as her infant slept. The younger son and the daughters knew where wild onions could be picked in the afternoon to go with rice and any meat—squirrel, rabbit, wild boar, turkey— that others in the camp

199

might bring into bartering. Shipments went up and down the Brazos haphazardly since the movement of Mexican troops in Texas, but the Harpers' neighbors stayed alert to any signals for incoming cornmeal, beans, sugar, and coffee.

On the memorable morning, Adeline was darning one of Susannah Wainwright's gray stockings. She was also spelling her neighbor from watch over the two girls in the brood. The younger sister Cassandra sounded out words haltingly over a page about an eggplant family having tea. Parents in Brazoria had wanted the parting school mistress to keep the book.

"After we read, Miss Adeline, may we copy the pictures? Mama has four stationery pages that took on some dank. They're soiled, but she said we could draw on them, if you have a pencil we can share."

"First, I want to hear you both read again—without puzzling over words you ought to know—"

"That might take until the end of the week," Cassandra said. "These vegetables in the book—they have more time to visit with each other than our Auntie Camille did back in Louisiana, and she was a spinster."

"You're too young to remember her much." The older sister closed her own eyes for a clearer memory.

"I don't even recall what day of the week it is," admitted Adeline.

"You're the teacher, and you don't know it's Thursday?"

"Well, Susannah, I believe I do know it to be the 17th."

"The riverboat *Yellowstone* promises to pause right near us on its way back down the Brazos tomorrow, that's how I remember." The more mature child smiled back, but then her expression grew somber. "Daddy and Ned only rode up toward the Colorado two days ago—that's another way to count. They promised Mama they'd be back within the fortnight."

"I'm certainly going to tell your mother that your arithmetic is superior," Adeline said. She was worried, too, especially about the boy. "Are you the one who taught Cassandra how to read the days of the week?" Both children nodded.

The older girl was probably only four years younger, Adeline thought, than she had turned on her own birthday. Concentration on the lesson dissipated and conversation lapsed. But the silence was pleasing. The younger girl turned pages, and a mockingbird started its repertoire in a leafing mulberry. Some chilly gray days were sure to intervene between this morning and the long stretch into spring, but the day was a piece of perfection, worth stitching into memory.

Aunt Maggie had looked up from her tablecloth embroidery. In the quiet space, she held a needle where she had started to pull the thread through and paused to appreciate how ladylike Adeline appeared with the Wainwright girls leaning nearby. They were seated on one blanket the Harper women allowed to be set down when the ground was dry. The woolen cover could be beaten with a broom if necessary to make it fit again for bedding. Maggie would have sketched the cheerful scene herself if she'd had any such talent as that of Madame Genet's friend in New Orleans. The change that Texas had brought out in Adeline was a story the aunt wanted to brag on to her nephew, who was sure to be heard from soon. Maggie knew the others took special precaution to protect her. But she was capable of piecing events together, and she secretly rejoiced over news that Gonzales families had moved along in the direction Sam Houston took.

The army gathering around the banks of the Colorado now had just come from the hometown of Matthew Linder, and she was eager about what news Mr. Wainwright and the older son would bring on their return. She wouldn't be able to sleep if she spent too much time imagining a third young man coming back to their Brazos encampment in a week. News and reunions happened that way in Texas, she was learning. A person would just look up and see someone on horseback that they hadn't been expecting. A day or a life could change that fast.

Whatever Yarico had been doing inside the one-room shack, she had finished, and she sat on the end of the Harper trunk in the open doorway. Both Adeline and Maggie noticed her presence at the same time, and they read one another's thoughts. When had dear Yarico silently slid the trunk to the threshold for good light? How did she manage to keep that blue silk bonnet down in the folds of her brown dress, so as not to draw attention to it or herself? A stranger would have guessed her to be worrying over pecan shells or bean pods. The two women smiling about her felt she had no need to be so cautious.

Mrs. Wainwright came up from her cabin to join the gathering. She didn't look sturdy enough to have so many children. Despite Yarico's modesty, Little Abel sidled up to the doorway to ask for a peek at whatever her fingers worked. The mother studied their interaction until her girls stood to roll a log where she could sit next to Maggie and nurse Wendel.

"Here in Texas, we don't question how you do with your field hands, much less house help," Annabel said reassuringly. "Bad as things is sometimes, that's what I like about this place. A fair person has a particular way of doin' chores and seein' to children—never mind all these rules, like the wide world knows how it's laid down to be!"

The mother marveled about the ease with which the three women made their sleeping arrangements in the tiny shack. She observed how Yarico never muttered about rinsing out the family's change of wear and hanging wash to dry on tree limbs near the cabin's open end. In her first days around the Harpers, she had wondered if the servant didn't sleep in the little cart stationed now out back, but she wasn't one to poke around concerning private matters.

"I wouldn't mind some good help like her that you all keep, so never mind what anyone from back home might say. My girls are some good with the baby and little Abel," she laughed, "but I'd come near to swapping with you most days!"

Since leaving Macon, Yarico had grown efficient at stanching her thoughts the way Mrs. Bedeford's water pump turned off with a turn of the wrist. When there were other people nearby, even folks as helpful and willing to share as Mrs. Wainwright and her reasonable children, that was time to shut off any thinking that went with the individual named Yarico. It was only during *invisible time*, mornings like the 17th of March—when Adeline was teaching or handling her own needlework, when Maggie was sorting the subtle colors of thread that she had to finish her embroidery—that Yarico could put some tucks into the fancy bonnet she might sell one day. That morning was the kind of lovely free space the good book talks about when it promises heaven will be filled with golden light and fresh green everywhere. She had come out to the threshold for air that was both cool and heartwarming. Yarico wondered if the dark-haired man Walk Far was searching for a place to take his family, away from the stream of Texas soldiers moving east. She wondered in what direction her own home—her real home—might be. So far, in this life, she had never been there.

The next week it rained steadily. The Brazos grew so swollen that the steamboat *Yellowstone* stopped shy of making it back downstream as far as The Place on the Bend, and the Harpers' friend Annabel rationed their rice in case no fresh deliveries arrived from upriver. The alternate clothes that Yarico hung in the cabin to dry remained damp, and since anything but a small snapping fire on the open side of their hut was impossible, the three women chaffed in their undergarments. With only damp branches raising their bedding from the mud floor, their blankets mildewed.

The year before the land had shrunken from drought, the Wainwrights reminded everyone, so spring rains were welcome. But they could not hide their worry about big Abel and Ned up near the Colorado. They didn't want to picture the two having to cross a swollen river, rushing and wild at the turns.

A week after the lovely Thursday, clamoring travelers surged from the upper Brazos trail. Families in soaked wagons wobbled down the path, their donkeys and horses burdened with packs. They said that soldiers from Houston's army were showing up in San Felipe, with some heading as far north as Washington on the Brazos to tell of advancing Mexican armies. A Mexican force destined for Nacogdoches was close enough to soon overtake Sam Houston's army at the Colorado near Bastrop! One frantic woman, alone with three children no older than little Abel, swore she'd left her breakfast plates on the table and a cobbler cooling in her kitchen. She heard that Santa Anna was ordering his troops to set fire to settlers, as well as settlements! On the rain-softened banks of the Brazos, the path sank into ruts. Countless hooves and wheel rims wore ruinous gashes into the trail.

Adeline and Yarico reassured Aunt Maggie as a habit, especially in the last two weeks, but they sensed each other's lack of conviction about safety at the encampment.

"If it were the Kolars coming back down from San Felipe with such warnings, that would be different," Adeline said to Yarico.

"Or suppose it to be Walk Far coming through with his family, and saying there were towns burning just a day's ride west—"

"Remember when Maggie herself used to go into Macon—on a Thursday for the newspaper—"

"I never considered what a place would be—with no news in print to let you know what was fact," said Yarico, "and what could be just whipped up from scared thinking." She spoke softly, because Margaret had put all her sewing into the trunk and was sitting near the cart, staring absently as if she wanted to be ready for bumpy running again.

When two Texan soldiers, both wearing coonskin caps, galloped into the encampment, Maggie might have been the only one who responded to what they were shouting as if she'd been expecting such news. She shrieked as soon as the rain-soaked strangers started yelling and waving their arms.

"Santy Anna's a comin'! He's kilt everybody in six towns back that way! The children and women are gettin' hacked to pieces and the men is all strung up and burnt!"

"Run out now, if you got legs! There's two more armies behind the general aimin' to set fire to anything left that moves!"

Mrs. Wainwright wrapped up her infant, who had not finished nursing and was wailing from the disruption. The thin woman bolted out of their cabin with the baby. Susannah gripped their milk cow's tether, and Cassandra was dragging little Abel by the hand. Their father and Ned had saddled up their only horses many days before to join Sam Houston, and the stranded family fled to the Harper shack. They crowded in where Maggie and Adeline stood ashen and at a loss where to head in the rain. Just outside the open end, their three horses and the Wainwright cow snorted, and shook the water from their eyes. With Cassandra and little Abel tugging at Annabel's apron, the mother began crying louder than her baby. Shouting and cries carried over the pounding rain, and it was clear that the encampment had exploded into exodus. Through a gap where the walls joined, Yarico watched the frantic scattering. Fear could be met, she thought, but panic was something far uglier, and more deadly.

"We're staying here," she stated, in the absence of any other sane speech. "Nobody can set a thing on fire in the rain. And chances are this little place is off any map where an army aims to conquer."

She thought of the musket they'd accepted long ago from Mrs. Bedeford, how it was traded away with their cotton wagon weeks back. But the older Wainwright girl had brought two family rifles, kept dry in oilcloth, each with one shot ready. When Adeline went limp at being urged to take one, Yarico reached for the extra. Something was not right about the shrieking soldiers. Susannah slung a firearm over her shoulder, but her mouth hung open, and she didn't look fit to aim. To Yarico's mind, those two riders were in no hurry to help frantic settlers in their stampede out and on down to the river. Little Wendel quieted down, and the other humans in the cabin could only stare at the woman holding a ready rifle.

"We're going to stay here for a while, if that's all right with the Harpers. Could be we head out in this rain, and that baby will get wet beyond what any church man, Mexican or Texan, could stand to see."

"We're staying here," Adeline repeated. "You all just sit wherever you like."

"I didn't like those men not telling us where General Houston is right now," Yarico went on. "It's few times I've witnessed men liquored up, to tell the truth," she said "Back in New Orleans, I heard some getting loud and full of bragging one night—"

"But soldiers—"

"I don't trust their voices," Yarico said firmly. She was shaking her head and signaling Adeline. "Shh—" She looked through one of the cracks in the rough hewn shack. "Hush now—it looks like everyone's gone, except for us."

Maggie sank onto the Harper trunk. The wispy mother slid next to her with the baby. Adeline drifted down onto the damp bedding with Abel and Cassandra.

"Y'all just hush for a while. Just rock that baby and each other. You hum to that baby, now, Miss Annabel. Susannah—you stand over by the open end, like you've been doing, child. I'm watching this way for anyone who comes near the door."

What Yarico saw was the two men in coonskin caps stop in the middle of the encampment and quit waving their arms and slapping the reins of their horses. She saw them take their time after eleven families had run madly from their cabins and brush huts and rushed toward the Brazos. The one with bushy sideburns wiped dribbling tobacco juice from his chin. The soldiers waited for the scrambling and the screaming to subside.

They had shouted and whipped up the evacuation until the only sound in the encampment was the rain, which had begun to lighten into a chilly drizzle. She watched the intruders ease down from their horses, their dark leggings soaked, and walk calmly if a little unsteadily toward one open cabin door and then another. They came from behind one hut with a mule, a sheet slung over it making a bundle. More bedclothes soon bulged from whatever the men were taking, and Yarico didn't allow herself to say a word when one man went down into the Wainwright's excavated dwelling and came out with a shiny clock that probably had sat near their hearth.

Yarico was thinking about the darkest places in hell that she'd heard about, and she wondered whether she would wait for either of these burly men to threaten the good people in the Harper shack, or if she would just shoot the first that showed his face close enough for a fair aim. The one bullet fired in her life could not miss. She nodded to the girl Susannah. The child gripped the other rifle, but was looking less and less as if she'd have the presence to dispense with a scoundrel like either of these two—much less Santa Anna.

The two thieves climbed onto their horses without looking at the ramshackle dwelling off the settlement's edge. Somehow the Harper's horses had fallen into a defensive quiet in the rain. The cow, too, was silent after the commotion. Nothing about the place attracted the vandals' attention. They had scavenged quickly, taking the best. Even drunk vermin might fret about the quick return of owners who had fled.

After an hour in the crowded shack, little Wendel began to whimper and to shift in his mother's arms. Annabel Wainwright hummed and opened her blouse to nurse the baby. Cassandra came over and drew her mother's shawl over the infant's face. Little Abel put his head down on the rosebud quilt, closed his eyes and slipped his thumb into his mouth.

"It's good we stayed," Yarico said. "I doubt it was anything like what those two said. They were up to no good, but they're gone now." All eyes turned to Yarico, taking in her calm demeanor. "We're going to wait on Mrs. Wainwright's husband and older boy, isn't that right?"

"They'll be back any day, I expect."

"You hear, Aunt Maggie?" Adeline attended to the older person shivering.

"My blanket's over here in the corner," Yarico said. "Maybe you want to put that around her shoulders and rub until she quits shaking."

Mrs. Wainwright was afraid to go back to her cabin, when Susannah came to tell her that the clock and all the cups and plates were gone, that the candlesticks were taken except for one, and their father's heaviest coat had been ripped from the chiffarobe. There was still a bag of sugar, coffee, some rice. And the morning's cornbread had been left in its pan in the cast-iron oven—miraculously not burned.

When no neighbors came back the next day, the mother told Susannah to go on and feed their neighbor's chickens, to wring one's neck so they could all eat well in case they had to move out in a hurry, to keep a list on one of her stationery pages, so they could trade for what they owed those good people if they came back.

Rain fell hard again. Under a canvas rain cloak, Adeline went out on her mare to see what the Brazos trail looked like. In spite of formidable mud and sinkholes, there were even greater crowds of people—mostly women and children—clambering down the way from San Felipe.

"We've been told to head down south for any crossover! We got to all get over east! There's no one left in the capital—It's moved to Harrisburg from now on! Down on the east coast! Washington's empty, and no one's in San Felipe but the army! They're hopin' to steal away, back upstream where the steamboat can get them over east of the Brazos!"

"Are you sure? The whole army's left the Colorado? Did you see anyone you trusted to be saying such things?"

"General Houston was there himself! He's over six feet in his moccasins—you can't miss him!"

"His army's mostly at this river now? Are there lots of men with him? We're lookin' for a father and son!"

"Some went on to help the settlers get up as far as Nacodoches, but there's another Santa Anna general going after those that far north!"

"Has anyone heard about Fannin's army at Goliad?" Adeline shouted. The older woman straddled a horse, just as she did. A white-haired man struggled to steer a small wagon carrying her children.

"Goliad?" the woman repeated. The rain was falling in torrents, and what Adeline thought she heard at first, she just shook her head about, because it was not possible that such words could be the truth.

"They had to surrender to one of Santa Anna's generals!" The woman turned once more toward Adeline, near the place where the trail began to veer and follow the river. "They was all rounded up on the battlefield—all Fannin's men!"

Once when Adeline was about Susannah's age, she'd put her hand down in the wash basket, and had been stung by a yellow jacket. The pain was sharp and searing like the thrust of a hot poker. And before that, there was another kind of worst pain, like when Aunt Maggie explained that her mother would not be waking up, the dull kind of pain that swept over her body in horrible waves.

What Adeline felt, after hearing of Fannin's men, was both kinds of hurt. A need to scream was building inside. She needed to cry out, so that every breathing creature in the territory could hear, but the rain pressed down over her.

By the time she returned to *The Place at the Bend*, a gray speckled horse waited near the doorway of the Harper shack. Some commotion went on inside between Mrs. Wainwright and her older son Ned, who was telling his mother as gently as he could that big Abel intended to rejoin Houston's force.

"He's in need of as many men as can come—there's crowds a-growin' both sides of the Brazos. The boys east are tryin' to get over our way, but not near as many men as President Burnet has called for can get across the other rivers—"

"He don't need boys. He don't need daddies that got five children—"

"That's not so, Mama—just about all with the general has children and wives left in a hurry. Some ran off from Austin's settlement before any burning—"

"Not with just born or barely out of toddling, Ned—"

"Mama—I'm goin' back up the Brazos to stay with daddy—"

"Oh no you're—"

"I know you need Nickel," he said gesturing in the direction of the horse. "You keep 'im. I can walk back up the trail—"

"No." Mrs. Wainwright was looking at her eleven-year-old son, her oldest child. "You got to have the horse."

"General Houston says we can whip 'em, but we gotta wait until Santa Anna shows a weak side."

"You go on and take care of your daddy." She handed Susannah the baby and put two pieces of cornbread in a kerchief. The chicken legs she wrapped in the other pieces of stationery.

"We won't get caught out in the open like Fannin did—even Houston said he didn't reckon we'd see them Southern fellas again—"

"You go on, Ned, while you still got daylight to make it back up the trail."

"If just any of them fightin' kind from east around Neches come over to help—if they just can make it over our way—" He was out the door and hoisting himself back up in the saddle. "Watch out for some deserters that's put the terror into people—stealin' on this side of the Brazos and scarin' the men from leaving their families over on the other side—"

"We heard about their kind," Susannah said.

"Like as not, I'll meet up with daddy soon as I get to San Felipe. Houston was fixin' to move the whole army a little up river, so we can cross by boat. If we can just cross, we've got enough horses to get on down to the coast, to Harrisburg!"

"We'll be followin' the river south first, I reckon!" Mrs. Wainwright called after him.

If the rain had just quit for a day, it might have made a little clearing in the women's thinking, but it only subsided into a trickle and then came in another torrent. Without much deliberation, they decided. They'd take a half day to gather what would make the most difference. Somehow, they would move away from danger, down along the soggy trail.

The bad news sank in, even if there'd been nothing special to pack up. Not only had the Colorado line been broken as the western edge of defense, now even the Brazos River wouldn't be a sure barrier between Texians and Santa Anna's armies. And the capital was now down at the eastern coast, in Harrisburg? None of the Harper women could speak about what a humble, scattering of structures that was! If the Independent Republic of Texas was scrambling toward Louisiana for self-preservation, there wasn't much future to count on. Whatever Fannin's army faced was impossible to contemplate. It wouldn't do to lose one's mind in a puddle off the open end of a three-sided shack.

Yarico, Adeline, and Maggie spent long hours into the evening stitching together several pieces of canvas that Annabel's husband had swapped on his annual trek. Four large sections, they put together in pairs for stretching over the carts. The Wainwright's old wagon was not much bigger than the Harper rig, but it had sturdy wheels. Then the women crafted additional canvas capes that could be draped at the first sprinkle or shed in an instant.

They gathered every soft tote bag, knapsack, or saddle bag that would dangle from a shoulder or rest on a back. The night before setting out, Susannah and Cassandra returned to their dugout cabin, where they mashed the rest of their cornmeal and flour into a stiff yeast dough. One heavy loaf would be consumed in the morning, the other two stuffed into cloth bags. The deserter thieves had stolen a side of wild hog from the smoke shed but had overlooked pork rind and bacon strips.

Water, seemingly a sure commodity, could not be counted on as fit to drink, Annabel warned. The girls took two clean jars to the well. They secured their last bag of rice, a measure of sugar, and beans under canvas. The milk cow would be led along as far as possible, and even that animal carried its own feed sacks. With just three horses, the families understood they would walk alongside the wagons, except for whoever held the baby or neared collapse. A single horse could only pull so much, and the younger mare and pack horse had to be protected for last resorts.

The Harpers and Wainwrights lightened their trunks by half, though the rosebud quilt stayed folded at one side. The children's mother refused to part with a crocheted bedspread, and only the toughest blankets were scattered in the wagon bed. Of the thirty books that had traveled with Delphine Pagnol from Savannah to Macon, Georgia, Adeline selected six not much harder to carry than a baby. Yarico watched the girl stack the rest on a split log up off the muddy floor. Other belongings—bowls, oil lamps, tablecloths, mattresses, and footstools, she condensed into a tidy raised stack. They might all be back in just a few days—who knew? Decent people were likely to leave unclaimed possessions undisturbed as long as they could.

"I've got one tin of matches in my apron pocket and a handful down inside one boot," Yarico said. They needed to disclose what was carried in places not so obvious.

"I've got the hatchet in my knapsack," Adeline said. "My sewing box is in there—it has a knife, my scissors."

"The tonics and stomach cures are down in my sewing bundle," Maggie said. "We've got a half bag of dried peas we'd best save for a day with nothing—a bottle of whiskey if there's any use—"

"Cassandra has tea leaves in her day sack and Susannah is carryin' necessities for Wendel—a tore up sheet for more changings—without washin' and sun dryin' along the way, I don't know—"

The half day spent on preparations was a rainy lull when Mexican troops had probably stopped as well. But there was no reason to expect the next warning shouts about Santa Anna's advance to be false. General Sam Houston himself was on the move out of the way and aiming for the gulf. The Harper women and the Wainwright family had to head out or learn firsthand whether the dictator's edict about extermination of settlers was rumor or truth.

Adeline Harper had once listened to their unusual friend in Harrisburg, Mr. Erlich, talk during a breakfast of scrambled eggs about how much better the trails were getting in the Texas territory.

"Why, zah big horses here, you watch them go fast to the settlement far north on Colorado. What they call Mina, or some say Bastrop, yah.

These big horses from Harrisburg in zah good sun and dry roads—get north in three days!"

In steady rain and impossible roads, progress southeast toward the gulf, toward Harrisburg, might take over thirteen days. A thousand fleeing families converged on one path. Women and children from the scattered and major settlements of the Brazos slogged their way down the riverbanks to find a crossing. If Houston's armed Texians were retreating to the eastern coast, that was the only direction families could head for a chance of survival. For some shred of safety, find Texas soldiers, even if the army expected an eventual face-off with Santa Anna.

To the Harpers and Wainwrights, days lurched by in a numbing blur. No one on the teeming Brazos trail checked off progress at dusk. To be alive was reason for giving thanks at sundown. The women attempted to steer onto the firmer edges of the trail. At the end of each day, a prayer could be said over what had not been discarded to lighten the wagon loads. Grass along the muddy pathway was littered with trunks and luggage, blankets filled with dishes and clothing. Wrecked side boards and shattered basins encroached on the road. Any object might be forsaken for motion forward toward a crossover east.

It wasn't until the end of the first week that the Wainwright's milk cow snapped an ankle in a slick rut that Susannah was unable to steer it from. The shocked girl stood frozen with Adeline's axe before a grandfather in the wagon behind stepped up to destroy the animal. Only a fool would have used a rifle for anything but to warn of Santa Anna's approach. Beef was crudely whacked and dispersed among those fleeing on the same stretch of road. But the children didn't grow hungry enough until the next day to bite into a chunk of boiled meat.

During the second week of grueling movement, little Wendel began to whimper less and less to be fed, and soon Mrs. Wainwright began to whimper that she didn't have enough milk for her baby. Another family, trudging behind them in the ruined path, toiled to lead two burdened donkeys. They had already buried their infant son before the trail angled down. The young woman with vacant eyes sat in the Wainwright's wagon for most of a day, pressing Wendel's listless lips to her breast. Near the third week of exodus, Annabel herself had to nudge the lifeless form from the stricken mother's grasp.

"Nothing was your fault," she told the child bride. "You done what you could. Wendel knows, and your own little one—you done what you could. You're practically a baby yourself." Annabel wore the expression of someone crying, but she couldn't make tears flow, any more than she'd been able to produce milk. "Susannah and Cassandra will sit with you a spell. It's all right, darlin'—ain't nothing your fault."

Adeline and Yarico helped steady Annabel off the side of the road where pale mud was easy to scoop away for Wendel's burying. Little Abel found two wet sticks and he laid down speckled river stones to make the cross lie flat on the mound.

"God bless this good baby," Yarico managed to say. The current of escapees swept them on.

Near the end of the third week, the two families caught a gnawing panic about ever crossing the swollen river by raft. They doubted any ferry landing would be free enough that one could risk the wait. Hysterical voices spread the worst news— that there were three Santa Anna armies charging to cut off settlers and any armed Texians near the gulf. The trail was said to bend even more sharply toward the coast soon, and families had to get to the east side of the Brazos River if there was to be any security near Houston's soldiers.

What a post rider, rushing by, shouted about Goliad, was delivered like an afterthought. The express rider racing toward the general's army said it too fast, as if a person couldn't let such horrible information dwell long on the tongue or in the ears.

All Fannin's men were shot dead at Goliad! All were lost! Fannin himself—Ward and every last one—all executed at Goliad!

At one ferry crossing they discovered two hundred people jammed up near a single raft. Peering numbly from the trail, Yarico and Adeline witnessed antagonism among evacuees as terrifying as any hostility they could have imagined from Mexican troops. A tough, muscular woman straddling her horse shouted down any other individual claiming to be next for the crossover. She maneuvered seventeen field slaves tied by their ankles and shook her rifle when an elderly couple protested about having already waited a day. She cocked her firearm at the ferry runner who warned that the raft couldn't handle the shackled workers all at once.

The muddy Brazos churned along and rose, with road debris and tree limbs swirling past and the torrent threatening to demolish the banks as well. Adeline needed to take Yarico's elbow when the raft began to tip. She jerked Yarico's arm so hard that she thought it might break, when the weighted raft tipped over halfway across the Brazos. The people tied together had nowhere to go but down into the racing mud, while the cruel currents took human limbs and tree limbs down to the river bottom and up and then down, down again.

When the Harpers and the Wainwrights approached the last manned crossing, a wagon that had traveled for three days behind them suddenly picked up momentum on the outer shoulder and drew alongside to pass. The children pitched everything but siblings out the back flap as they cut ahead to secure an earlier turn for the final ferry.

"If we've come to climbin' over each other's reached out hands," Annabel cried after them, "I don't know who's fit for salvation!"

The Harpers and Wainwrights—four women, three surviving children, and their three horses— reached a rise. The last crossing, near Fort Bend—not so far from Harrisburg!— could be seen. The spectacle rendered them speechless. There weren't two hundred people waiting to be ferried. The number was easily two thousand!

Without discussion, Adeline, Yarico and Maggie turned off toward the river and doubled back for a straighter leg of the Brazos. The Wainwrights followed closely. Debris was snarling into a knot upstream, it appeared, and the river was high in one stretch but clearer of menacing branches. They rummaged through their trunks for belongings most precious. Their horses could pull the wagon and the cart no further. Whatever they took would burden the animals as they waded across the river, so an extra book could prove deadly. A bowl of sentimental value could drag down a child. They pared down to what they wouldn't mind dying with.

Adeline draped the rosebud quilt around her shoulders. She slid a thin book with the pressed Avignon drawing down into her bodice. She, Maggie, and Annabel waited on the flooded grass while Yarico hoisted little Abel up behind her on the tall brown gelding. The Wainwright girls shared the spare tan horse, the only creature in the assembly not past spent. Two horses in the water at one time, they believed, made the odds better.

When they got to the other side, Susannah clung to her brother and sister while Yarico plunged back across. This time, Mrs. Wainwright hugged Yarico and Aunt Maggie straddled the spare. On the eastern bank again, Yarico could see Adeline waving her away from a third round trip. The thirteen-year-old had been talking to the chestnut mare, and she now sat atop the reasonably rested, if not the strongest horse. But Yarico rode out halfway on the tall mount in spite of Adeline's protests. Both horses snorted to get enough air the last hundred feet. Yarico had seen all she could bear of flailing arms in turgid water. She was ready for the River Jordan if any violence should happen to Delphine's lovely girl.

On the safer bank of the Brazos, she helped Adeline slide down from the saddle. The girl's skirt was soaked, and she collapsed where the quilt had fallen. Suddenly she put her hands to her face and stifled a shriek. Yarico sank down next to her.

"I'm hurt—" Adeline gasped. She was pale, and her breathing couldn't hold steady, and there was blood on one leg, where the water from her calico skirt trickled down. "A branch must have—I didn't know—"

"Are you cut—where—" Her ankle and knee appeared uninjured, and no cut could be found on the girl's thigh. Yarico just put an arm around Adeline and then reached into her bonnet where she had kept a dry kerchief. "It'll be all right, Miss Harper. You did a fine job of bringing yourself on across the river. It's all right—"

"But—I didn't think—"

"You did fine," she said again. She gave Adeline a little shelter to wipe away the blood, although no one was there to see.

Yarico found no reason, then, to keep herself from crying quietly. Out on the sodden eastern banks of the Brazos in April 1836, it was as cruel a setting as any for a thirteen-year-old girl to discover her body's sure signs of womanhood.

Away from the river, the women and children took turns walking and riding and resting. Any among the scattered settlers who had made it this far moved eastward as if they had already fended off mortality itself. If Santa Anna were to come up behind and threaten them with lances and bayonets, they would raise their arms in defiance, even if they hadn't the strength to scream, much less finger a trigger.

At first they crossed paths with some of their own Texian soldiers—none that Annabel Wainwright had ever seen before. But as families straggled on toward Louisiana, army men were seen less and less. Straggling troops moved more south to intercept Houston and to put themselves as much as possible between fleeing civilians and battle lines. One last bedraggled Texas soldier sat in his saddle, weeping as he watched the women and children stagger east. When he too turned down toward Houston's main contingent, someone shouted to him "Remember the Alamo!" Another person called out "Remember Goliad!" The Harper women and Annabel saw no more of their country's forces for several days.

On the morning of April 22, the sound of galloping barely roused a group of sleeping families clotted together near a swath of trees in east Texas. The exhausted evacuees had strewn themselves along the Trinity River. Only a few miles remained to cross before reaching the American border at the Sabine. But many had gone as far as they could travel in their attempt to escape. Most felt they had already met a kind of hell. The sound of hooves grew louder and there was very little reaction. It didn't really matter to most of the starving survivors what some messenger might call out. Another rider would come along in the afternoon or the next day and shout something else. If it turned out to be an advance scout of Santa Anna's, then whatever executioners might be on their way could make rather quick work of these forlorn stragglers.

"Santa Anna's beat! Santa Anna's been taken prisoner! The Texans have won! We beat them out along the San Jacinto! Texas has won!"

It was all the families of Independent Texas heard for the next fortnight, so gradually the women and children felt it must be true. They could at least stop to rest. When the first few days of May turned sunny and the fields around them began to burst into pinks and blues, the fleeing people could at last dry off and warm themselves. They could tend the weakest among them and sit at a campfire in the evenings to ready themselves for the journey back home, no matter what they might find in ashes, no matter what rebuilding would be in store.

They were already trading what necessities they could—a pair of scissors for a hammer, a blanket for a rain slicker, jerky for honey. The settlers began swapping stories and striking up songs in tentative celebration, since it would be more weeks before most knew for sure what their men had suffered or survived. A fellow with graying hair—truly a Texan now!— took out his harmonica one night as several fires flickered. The somber melody he played gave some inexplicable solace to women and children stretched out on that coastal plain east of the Brazos.

He played his harmonica for a stanza and then sang lines before picking up his instrument again. The lines went on about a sea captain, and sailors lost on a voyage far from the rolling coastal plains of Texas. But the song had a plaintiff refrain that Adeline Harper put to memory upon first hearing.

The fate of Franklin,

No tongue can tell

It was a tune that her Aunt Maggie heard her humming, notes she hummed dolefully herself on their way back up the trail—to who knew where.

The melody was what Yarico heard in her own mind, whenever they came to a ferry crossing with a raft meant to transport just a few at a time.

Adeline was humming to herself when bluebonnets spilled into the hills north of the spot once called The Place at the Bend, now only ashes. She would hum when they passed the charred ruins that had been San Felipe, and up to wherever the Brazos trail took them. The refrain haunted her when so many blue flowers looked to her like the silken curtains of heaven. The fields—like quivering banners of color— were just too pretty to bear, and the thought of Goliad's bluebonnets were just too sorrowful to imagine.

The Dove Shall Fly to Thee

Chapter 16   Sweet Pine Remembered

"Why wouldn't there be nightmares?"

That's the kind of thing Yarico said softly to Adeline mornings after her fretting and tossing in the night woke all three of the women stretched out on the soft dirt floor of the cabin. When Maggie's sudden crying ripped through their slumber, Yarico would bring her a sip of lukewarm leftover tea and tell her the bad dreams needed to leak out like dark flavor that finally quits oozing from a tea leaf. One day the nightmares would all be leaked out and gone. And it was like Yarico to cry only within the borders of semi-conscious imagination. In this world, however, in the realm of changing seasons and tactile reality, she would only turn over once roughly in her sleep, never bothering the other two.

The pine forests around Bastrop, Texas, were a good place for the three women from Macon, Georgia to purge much of the nightmare pain they'd seen the first few months of 1836. They had seen the smoldering remains of The Bend encampment and San Felipe. When big Abel Wainwright and Ned had finally met up with the Harper group in the ruined ghost-town of Washington on the Brazos, Annabel wanted the three women to stay with her family and go on up to Nacogdoches, where there was still a town and some good Southern people.

But Adeline exhibited a stubborn dedication to the worn trail as it curved up northwest. Her Aunt Maggie, whose need to flee had brought them to Texas in the first place, was relieved about no backtracking toward Louisiana, or any parts so accessible to American law. And Yarico understood she would find herself in slave territory, whether they turned east or west. At least in the west, the plantations thinned out, and people of every skin color were somewhat more likely to note and value an individual's toughness. Adeline had her own quiet reasons for staying on the trail up to Bastrop. They had been told there was a pocket of pine trees farther north along the Colorado.

The Harper women had been inhabitants of the growing Colorado River town since June after the revolution. As new residents they took in stride the changing of the settlement's name from Mina back to Bastrop. A few hundred long-term citizens there, however, were of a hundred opinions on the matter.

"Texas? Wouldn't even exist! Not if ole Baron von Bastrop hadn't been so wily about permits for colonization!"

"You say 'wily'—I heard other descriptions—I don't reckon a town should be named for a man whose pedigree gets called into question—"

"Why do we gotta switch away from Mina? Stephen F. Austin was proud to be called *Estevan*—I'll draw a sword on anyone says our Señor Mina wasn't a hero as good as any!"

"Now that you bring up the honorable, deceased Mr. Austin—that's the real hero of it all, poor man died before Texas even had her first birthday as a republic—his steady friend was Bastrop! So let's give the baron a namesake, fer Pete's sake!"

Debate in the lost pines hardly counted as political upheaval. The name of their settlement had shifted back and forth just once. Who could count how many times the Texas capital changed since the spring of '36? After Washington-on-the-Brazos was abandoned in favor of Harrisburg, the Harper women could hardly keep up. With Harrisburg burned to the ground by Santa Anna himself just before his capture, the capital had been hastily switched to Galveston, but was just as quickly moved on over to Velasco where a fort was already secure.

The Macon family grew incensed—along with many other Texans—that General Santa Anna was kept prisoner there—kept alive—though he had ignored the humanitarian appeals of many of his own generals and had demanded the execution of Goliad's unarmed prisoners. What was said about the vengeful intent of Minerva Fannin, still living in Velasco at the time, made Adeline harbor a private wish that the widow would indeed find an opportunity to break past the dictator's guards. She hoped Mrs. Fannin succeeded in strangling the villain with her own hands!

But these were the kinds of sentiments that fomented terrible dreams. Adeline, Maggie, and Yarico tried to stay abreast of changes and events without dwelling on any that caused them personal anguish. They didn't mind, after the long spring—Alamo, Goliad, and San Jacinto—that the provisional president Burnet changed the capital for the next full year to Columbia. Or that the republic's first elected president, Sam Houston, then moved Texas government to the city named after him. The republic called Texas—let its capital be Houston—aged three years in a blur of relative peace to all who had survived the revolution.

With the election of Mirabeau Lamar as the second President of the Republic, however, spirited discussion bubbled. Bastrop inhabitants speculated about where the capital might move in 1839. Lamar wouldn't tolerate its Houston location! And if rumors were true, the river town lying in the midst of picturesque loblolly pines would witness enough bright change to sweep out nightmares for good. The republic's entire government might soon travel Bastrop's road. If their own town weren't chosen as the new capital, then word was legislators would pass through on their way to Waterloo, the settlement thirty miles farther up the Colorado.

In the days after Christmas, though, the Harper women found time only for thimbles and thread. Adeline and Maggie finished piecing together two pairs of silk dancing slippers for Mrs. Eloise Moore's two daughters, while Yarico set fancy lace on the third fawn colored pair for their mother. No different from other rebuilt communities, structures in Bastrop could be counted on to have dirt floors. In one evening of Virginia reel and a two-step shuffle, any woman's prized shoes would be ruined. At least the Harper women could make sure ladies' feet would look elegant at the beginning of the evening, and their slippers would wear longer than the dancers who wore them.

"You all kin jest thank me," Eloise said about her brother Otis. She brought her own sewing with her when she sat to watch the slippers coming along.

"I'm surprised he never married."

"I'll brag on his fiddlin'—not what type husband he might make!"

"Don't you go tellin' him I spoke any interest," Maggie laughed.

"He's a bachelor—confirmed—don't listen to squat a female says anyways." Mrs. Moore jiggled when she was amused. "Just glad I made him promise last year in Alum Creek—'I know this here's yer hometown, Otis,' I told 'im, 'but you kin ride two hours to give us in Bastrop a taste of yer fiddle come New Years!'"

Though last year harmonicas and singing were all that accompanied clapping and stepping on the dusty floors, plenty of Bastrop wives had vouched for the Harper women's handiwork. For this year's celebration, they were swamped with work but cheerful about the income. Mrs. Moore hemmed flounced dresses for her eligible daughters, a year younger and a year older than Adeline—fifteen and seventeen. But she had no patience for painstaking work on silk shoes. It made a pleasant visit, to drive a cart along the mat of pine needles and knock at the tiny cabin that the men had cut and set for the school teacher. The Harper women were likely to come out after greeting any of the town ladies and sit on the campfire logs to measure and pin. There was no need to convince any Bastrop people of the soothing pleasure a pine forest gave.

Adept now at piecing slippers, Adeline worked inside on the basic seams of a dark rose pair the next afternoon, her seventh pair this season. She fingered the smooth borders and sensed that life, too, was piecing itself together. A roof of fragrant pine, family safe and close by, a kettle of beans cooling outside, new reading lessons for the children after the holidays, strips of cloth as soft as angel skin—a mortal needed nothing more to lift bright hope up again, out from a dark chasm. The three newcomers had not lost what some original Bastrop settlers had—the ones who had drifted back to their beloved pines after the dreadful April three years ago to find their town utterly destroyed by Santa Anna's northern general. But the Harper girl, Margaret Linder, and their Yarico had survived *the scrape*, same as the rest. The last of the nightmare's potency was slowly oozing away.

"Miss Adeline," said Tabitha Ellinger. "I surely am glad I put my name somewhere near the top of your list." She was the first to pick up her finished slippers for the dance just days away. "Look how much can change in a year. Some months ago I would not have pictured myself paying one whole dollar for slippers that can't last longer than a night—but you never know when this life will turn out to be worth less than two rocks—" She broke into a hearty laugh. "I say you'd best dance while you can!"

"You didn't go to the dance last year?" Maggie wanted to know.

"I certainly did, and I put the heels and toes out of my good stockings, too!

"Are your boys coming?"

"Don't you worry about if they'll be asking their teacher to dance!" She laughed again.

"I hope they do! I'm going to write down any boy under ten on my dance card!" Adeline teased back.

"Well, darlin', they're all in love with you by the end of the school day, but I imagine some young man'll beat them to it by the time any of mine are grown enough for serious asking."

"My Matthew would be into his teens by now," Maggie said suddenly. Mrs. Ellinger quieted down and gave Adeline a kindly look. It had not taken the women of Bastrop long to understand what topics among them were best listened to with sympathy and guided to other thoughts as quickly as possible.

"It's going to be a new year now," Tabitha stated. "It's been weeks since any worry over Comanche raids—you can always take that as the blessing coming along with an end to hunting season. Little game, but less fight over who gets it." She sighed. "And that Otis plays a fine fiddle. You didn't hear him some years back, but I remember—and we're all going to be wearing the prettiest dancing slippers this side of the Sabine!"

"We'd better see to it we have our own slippers, Maggie."

"If you see me tapping my toes, Addy, that'll be a high credit to Mrs. Moore's brother. My knees aren't what they used to be, but I do love to listen to good fiddling. When I was young, there was some in Kentucky that could make your hair dance out of its bonnet."

Four women visited in the Harper's cramped cabin, but Mrs. Ellinger was about to leave. She flattened out an American dollar bill and observed Adeline hand the money to Yarico, who put it in a plain latch tobacco tin. Most traders along the trails going east accepted any cash that was good on the Mississippi. Tabitha Ellinger hesitated. She was an especially amiable woman, and she wanted to say something friendly to Yarico, who had the rarest gift with lace and design. It pained her to think of the seamstress alone on the upcoming evening, when her needlework would be put to such a festive test.

"If it's a nice New Years night, and not too much chill, Yarico might want to come with you two ladies and set a spell outside the courthouse where she can hear the music. The boys and I are bringing the big wagon, and I don't mind one bit if she wants to bundle up, watch the reins, and tap her own feet a little."

"That's as nice a thing as I've heard in Texas or any other country I've lived in," Adeline said. She had seen Yarico look up from her needle, unsure who or what to answer.

"Well, all the town is proud you come to pick us as your stopping place, I know that. All three of you!"

Adeline saw her out the front door to the little square of split logs that made a stoop. They walked together over matted pine needles and onto the shady path that had been worn to the Harper door.

"I didn't want to speak more of relatives, with your aunt gone to talkin' on her lost nephew just then—"

"I appreciate that."

"But I was wantin' to just mention about my own cousin Robert— went off and lived with some Caddo Indians up past Nacogdoches. That was long ago. Some would say it showed his weak mentality, but that man's thinking wasn't any more flimsy than Sam Houston's! I say it shows there's plenty of Indians just as good as the Lord made 'em, no better nor worse than you or me—"

"I think you're right—"

"I know my husband tells me to just hush on the subject, but all I wanted to say is— if it takes all kinds, then some of us just ain't from anyone's regular mold."

"No—"

"That Yarico of yours," Tabitha said, as she gave a little wave. "She's from out any mold I know of, that's the holy truth. I never saw fingers work more beauty into a patch of cloth!"

Adeline stood out among the thicket of pines for several minutes after Mrs. Ellinger went on down the path in her rig. The fragrance of pine trees soothed her in ways she could not articulate to any other person. It had been so, since her earliest days of scampering up Sweet Pine Hill. She had not realized then that the little patch of evergreens was not as characteristic of Macon as were mixtures of deciduous woods. Georgia did not typically turn to great stretches of pine forest until farther north. But the distinctive, pungent smell was what she identified with home, and that early attachment solidified her love of such scenery. The whoosh of those symmetrical branches in every season, the bronze carpet of needles, the serenity the blanket lent the view in every direction, where only ferns and bright seedlings poked up—all these attributes, Adeline loved with a deep sense of belonging.

What a gift—in this setting—to hear especially kind words spoken about the human being she loved as well as she had her own mother. Adeline needed to stay in the woods outside their little cabin for a few minutes. She had not felt so happy since the morning just over three years ago that she'd run down her hill to give Yarico an ancient prize from Sweet Pine. But in recalling childhood rapture, she reflected as well on the good-hearted men lost from home, lost from Texas and all earthly terrain.

Low talk emerged occasionally during the past three years that some in Lieutenant Colonel William Ward's captured battalion had been detained in Victoria to build ships. Some Southern physicians, they said, were spared because of their usefulness to injured Mexican troops. A few wounded Americans were fortunate enough to be sent by General Urrea as prisoners to Matamoros before Santa Anna began brutally enforcing his extermination edict.

References surfaced, even more hushed, to a very few who had madly run with the others as shooting began at Goliad, who somehow had survived to reach a creek, and beyond. So many tales flourished after the decisive Texas win at San Jacinto, when Santa Anna's stupefied soldiers were overtaken, then half of them killed by Houston's outraged army. Who could believe that the Mexican general had needed to flee in his shirt and breeches before capture the next day? Who did not want to believe that among the Texans at San Jacinto was at least one survivor of Goliad, recounting the harrowing details of escape three weeks earlier?

Adeline felt suddenly ashamed of herself for indulging in selfish fantasy. How must the older brother feel now with duties of the grown son resting solely on his shoulders? The pair in the tobacco field had spoken fondly of a father, who had since lost perhaps his most tender child. Where had such tenderness in the family come from? If anyone deserved to cultivate a meager seed of hope, it would be Francis Marion's mother. And what, then, of all the others, who knew beyond doubt that their sons were slain?

Who was Adeline Harper to cradle memories—of a man picking up a baby, of a farewell gift at the wharf in New Orleans, a farewell kiss on the cheek, the brotherly smiles of friends, the pleasant duty of mailing letters from Francis to his parents, to his aunt, and to his older brother Thomas? And yet Adeline handled these recollections as some must finger rosary beads, lightly and with reverence.

"You gone into a trance again, Addy?"

"I fear I have, Aunt Maggie. I'm coming back in just now—I know the good light won't last much longer."

"We're finished up with Mrs. Moore's, and now we have just two more before we start on our own." Maggie watched Adeline turn around slowly and step back toward the cabin. "You do look a young lady about to turn sixteen. I think your mama would be proud what you turned out to be in the nine years since she's gone."

"She'd be proud you stayed all this time to be my aunt," Adeline said. "Most surely."

The courthouse was the logical setting for the new year's start. It was the only public structure surrounded by a stockade, unless one were to consider the small fort on the edge of the settlement. But the courthouse was merrier, not being where inhabitants scrambled if a cry went up about warriors with arrows, banding together for attack. People stayed together, their numbers usually a deterrent to threats. The log courthouse was among the first structure resurrected from ashes. Bastrop had then rebuilt its general store and hotel, and Tabitha's Ellinger's husband Ernest had just finished a new gunsmith shop, better than the original, he claimed. He was glad to get his metals and oils out from his children's reach at the family cabin.

It was Mr. Ellinger who greeted Adeline and Maggie at the courthouse door the first day of 1839. His reddish beard with flecks of gray fell to the same length as his mane of hair. He spent the morning dragging benches and the long judge's table from the center of the room to the sides, where his wife and other ladies arranged sweet potatoes, corn casseroles, and berry cobblers.

"Miss Adeline, Mrs. Linder—I know the talk will turn to cooking as soon as you set that covered dish down—that or dance slippers—but I want to know how you women like your cabin over east?

"If I get us a house built every time I set twenty children straight about their letters and arithmetic," Adeline answered, "Texas might suspect me of having royal ambition—might banish me from these parts!"

"A satisfactory house, then? Lumber hereabouts is for the taking—"

"It's perfect how it sleeps and dry inside as any July. Not a drop came in with that rain in November, and we all moved our cooking rocks to make a pretty little hearth—out in the clearing like you warned, Mr. Ellinger."

"Don't know how many times I thought about that—"

"We sweep the needles away, and no one leaves the fire, not for a second. Put it out twice before turning in."

"When the families came back that May, after running ragged nearly all the way to Louisiana..." The man in front of Adeline was someone she might have chosen for the good-hearted Tabitha. He was as likely to speak with emotion as his thoughtful wife. "On the trail back here, I'd been steadying for the worst—to find every building in Bastrop burned to the ground like so many were all along the trail." He had to look away while he was shaking his head. "But you know, the second after we saw the pile of ashes and cindered houses, we seen the glory of what had not come to pass—"

"All that rain," Adeline nodded.

"They couldn't burn the forest down!" Ernest said gleefully. "If they'd been fit to bust on takin' our forest that particular spring, they would have torched their own fingers tryin'!"

"We still have the pines—"

"And what I hear is, we might all stumble into something of a fortune from these long, straight timbers."

"Not an uneven chink in any wall of ours," Adeline said.

"Well, you can testify on our building credentials, because President Lamar has let out word—unofficial—that the new capitol of Texas is going to be built just up the road in Waterloo. It'll take a new town layout, is what we're hearing. And a new name, to give the republic a capital of proper stature! I guess you know how tickled folks here feel about renaming Waterloo for the republic's founder—they're gonna call the town *Austin*! Anyway, no hard feelings our town wasn't chosen. Texas is going to get its lone star town built with pine lumber from right here in our sandy Bastrop hills!"

Like everything in the adult world, Adeline was learning, the news about Austin provided a mixture of joy and regret. With more people coming through Bastrop to Austin, and more people moving to Bastrop to join in the work of lumbering, there would be more children who needed her tutoring, and more sewing of all kinds for the Harper women to take on. The first two years they'd lived among the families returning to Bastrop, they had contributed their even stitches to canvas covers for temporary tents, mattress ticking, hems on curtains, tablecloths, and towels, and to altering clothing that had to wait to be replaced, and to mending of all kinds. Finding out about a new boom for Bastrop and its neighbors was an answer to everyone's prayer for livelihood.

But the teacher from Macon couldn't help thinking with some dread of streams of people and the swaths of felled trees. It seemed to her that deep peace and brimming joy were made to be ephemeral. She ordered herself to enjoy the New Years dance, as Tabitha Ellinger had suggested, "While you can!"

Otto Gilcrest's fiddling galvanized a hundred of Bastrop's citizens into a dance to forget all woes. Those who weren't lined up or paired up to lock arms with a particular person shuffled and stepped rhythmically on their own. Adeline had seen individuals joined for action, and she had seen a crowd moved to appreciation, but she had never witnessed more purely expressed joy in congregation. Among Mr. Gilcrest's tunes were reels and jigs, and Alum's jolly preacher squeezed polkas from his accordion. But Adeline grew partial to the waltzes, even though Tabitha Ellinger's two boys mashed the edges of her slippers.

From the Harper cabin, Yarico caught some strains of music. She was not comfortable, though, to think of a stranger suddenly approaching the wagon where she'd been invited to sit in town. She recognized kindness as an Ellinger trait, but single men, too, in so animated an evening, were likely to slip in and out of the courthouse to light up a pipe or sip from a whiskey flask.

In her earliest days in Savannah with the Pagnols, Yarico comprehended the ultimate control men had over family possessions—wagons, horses, pianofortes, slaves. She was fortunate about Delphine's father, because he had wanted the solitary Pagnol daughter to have company that the older parents were at a loss to provide. And then Delphine had found a husband just as accommodating. What peril Yarico had managed to avoid in life—April of 1836 notwithstanding—she wanted to keep at bay. No fiddle strings could entice her to sit out on even the friendly Bastrop streets, where drunkards might swagger by.

Besides, with Maggie and Adeline away, Yarico enjoyed an opportunity to finish Adeline's birthday present. Miss Harper would turn sixteen in February. The gift was something she'd swapped for a bonnet. A lady coming up the trading road from San Antonio, on her way to Nacogdoches in the fall, had heard of Yarico's flair. The single woman had fallen in love with the bonnet of light blue silk. She had wheat colored hair and blue eyes that were set off so well by the fancy hat, the widow Bedeford might have claimed a premonition about incarnations the original cloth would know. Yarico meant to delicately refuse the traveler's Mexican currency, though there was still plenty of trade across that border, too, but the woman had thought of a swap instead.

"I think this was meant for you anyway," the lady said, taking out what first looked to Yarico like an elaborate broach. "Some pieces came off, but as clever as you are, I imagine you'll have it fixed and pinned to your pocket better than it was first made." Fine chains hung down from the central decorative piece.

"A little pair of scissors on one chain, a pin cushion—and what's in here? This chain holds the pins, and a tiny bucket for a thimble?"

"The thimble bucket needs some repair, but if you're as adept at working with metal filigree as you are lace filigree, you'll set it to rights."

"This looks like silver and ivory, m'am. I'm sure my bonnets won't trade that high in a fair market—"

"Miss Yarico—Harper, is it? Yarico Harper?" There were kind eyes everywhere on earth, from Macon, Georgia to New Orleans to Bastrop, Texas, Yarico was thinking, and they were as likely to be blue as any color. "You can call me Lila, and here's what I know. This world is hardly fair to any female on her own." She smiled as she looked at herself in a mirror. The silk bonnet pleased her so. "If I was a woman in your shoes, I'd be looking at maps and the cost of steamboat tickets—and *fair* would be the last word on my mind."

"I think I'll be glad to have this broach—these fine sewing notions—"

"Just don't land yourself short in a place like Missouri, Miss Yarico!" The lady traveler had kept her eye on the window that day to see that Maggie was still outside by the cooking hearth. "When you see your chance to go, get on all the way up to Louisville or Cincinnati before you ever turn to look what's behind you!"

The exchange, words and possessions, left Yarico thinking about what all can't be assessed from looks. Had she been asked to render an opinion based on appearance, she could have judged the blond woman in the rich jersey dress to be a haughty woman of means, self-involved and possibly—without a man—up to no modest good in her travels.

But she'd been the first person since Walk Far to address her as an individual. Or maybe this Lila had seen the same thing that Madame Genet and then the Tonkawa man discerned. She had not thought of the name *Stand-Like-Free* for a while—three years, if she were honest with herself. In Georgia, Macon would have claimed among its inhabitants a dozen free black men, fewer females, and the next town would claim twenty or thirty or two. How, she had sometimes asked herself, how did it feel to set a destination for a day or a year, and proceed to fulfill that course of action without asking permission, without the apprehension of admitting an idea and an ambition had come to mind in the first place?

Conversation with the blond lady had brought a response from Yarico just as she might have spoken with Adeline and Maggie. So simple and free an exchange of words was itself a liberation. Staying at home during the dance was her own decision. During the new year celebration, Yarico sat working a straight pin and a thimble to reset the tiniest chain links. She would give Adeline the unique broach for her sixteenth birthday.

An air of anticipation continued after the courthouse dance, and by February, the Harper women and neighbors studied calendars to see when President Lamar might start the lot sales for building in Austin, his formal selection. And at least one foreign country—if not the United States— was preparing to recognize Texas as an independent republic. The thought of a French dignitary passing through their town on his way to the capital added to Adeline's elation on her birthday.

Wrapped up in her cloak and a blanket, the young woman danced a pine needle jig in front of the Harper cabin to Aunt Maggie's rare fling with their harmonica. Yarico's clapping helped shape the music, and the gold and ivory sewing broach, a gift seemingly brought about by magic, jingled at Adeline's waist.

"Listen!" She went to fling her arms around Yarico again. "If snowflakes were to make music—not that I remember any—listen, hush a minute, Maggie, did you here the tinkling charms?"

"You're our music and our sunshine!" Maggie said, tapping the harmonica.

Adeline stepped out onto the cold pine needle carpet, where she lifted her skirt to the tops of her boots and danced from the doorway to the hearth.

"I didn't miss a thing not seeing you at the ball," laughed Yarico, shaking her head.

Adeline Harper was permitting herself one more childlike skip back to the doorway, when all three women stopped in stony silence and disbelief.

The bell at the courthouse was being rung continuously. Everyone in Bastrop knew it meant some calamity to be unfolding. February was not the season when central Texas people expected Comanche incursions, yet the warning bell would not stop ringing. In the echoing loblolly thicket, cries of alarm and shouts rose up.

Maggie didn't look as if she could walk back into the cabin without Yarico's aid, so Adeline understood the need to ride a Harper horse to the center of town as fast as possible. She had retained the reflexive skill of holding the middle of her skirt hems together front and back, in order to mount a saddle the way a man would. When she trotted up Main Street, the Ellingers were fussing at each other in front of the gunsmith shop.

"Let the captain see what can be done, Ernest—you don't know how many there might be—"

"They've killed a woman and her children not four miles from here, Tabby! I don't reckon I can let some other men see to it that you and our boys aren't the next who get slaughtered!"

"Just wait and see if they want us to stay in the fort—"

"There's more'n a dozen of us." He freed Tabitha's clutch from his arm. "We can at least let 'em know we retaliate, plain and simple!" She threw her arms around him again. "Lemme go, Mrs. Ellinger—You wouldn't want me if I couldn't show myself to be a man!"

"Oh, Adeline!" Tabitha called up to her, as her husband rode off. "He's goin' with Captain John—I can't make him stay—no telling how many Comanche are up around the creeks to the north! We got two cut pretty bad from where another band up the riverbank got to skirmishing with farmers. Doc Robertson is over in Alum Creek seeing to a sick baby, so—" Her husband was gone from sight, and she turned her full attention to the young woman. "You can't sew up people, too, can you?"

Adeline hadn't thought about the needle tucks Dr. Judkins showed her since their boat trip down the Alabama.

"You got some whiskey?"

"Some hard cider, peach brandy—"

"Go get your boys, and tell them to bring me the longest hog hairs they can pluck!"

"You done this before?"

"Just tell them to be careful." Her mind raced. "I don't want to stitch up bite marks, too—"

Two wounded men were stretched out in the Bastrop hotel. The one with a gash on his forehead moaned in a leather chair, where the mayor held a towel to the victim's brow. Another man writhed on a red carpet near the stairs. An arrow had gone into the fleshy part of his lower left thigh and the shaft had already been shoved clear through. Mrs. Moore's graying husband wrapped strips of sheet around the bleeding leg. When Adeline asked for three glasses of brandy, the onlookers didn't ask if the third one was to steel her own nerves. From her waist band, Adeline removed the silver needle holder and plunked the entire little cylinder down in one filled glass.

"Show me the wounds," she demanded. She had never seen a bleeding injury before, but what she had seen of other horrors steadied her from any lightheadedness.

The mayor needed to run outside, when Adeline dabbed at the torn and exposed flesh.

"The leg wound," she said. "His name is Horace?" He was the more dangerously injured of the two. "Boil me a half dozen towels. Set the pot out in the street where they can cool fast." The two Ellinger boys tore in from the street.

"We got ten hairs!"

"There's more, but the hog was none too happy—"

Adeline asked their mother to go wash the fibers in the hotel kitchen. She dipped her own hands in a basin the innkeeper brought out, then lifted the needle caddy out with the tiny silver scissors. Although Horace was close to passing out, he drank a glass of brandy, and when Mrs. Ellinger came back with the stitching strands, Adeline dropped them into the equipment glass, as well.

The hairs grew supple in the brandy, but not too limp for Adeline to thread a needle easily. When she began taking tucks in the side of Horace's knee, the little Ellinger boy was the first to pass out, but his mother went pale immediately after. The older son was determined to follow his teacher's directions.

"When I pull the needle and get it taut—you dab with a towel—"

"I could do that," Mr. Moore said.

"No, I need you to push the gash together. Just easy, so the edges touch."

When Adeline ran out of thread, she did as she would have with a strand of silk. She tied off one end neatly, only to run yet another hog hair through the needle eye. By the time the man's thigh was sewn up, Tabitha Ellinger was recovered enough to bring in cold towels. Adeline wrapped his leg before people covered him with blankets to settle his shivers.

"Just let him get warm and comfortable before you move him anywhere. Is there a bedroom downstairs?"

"I got a little chaise in the office down here—"

"If it's long enough to hold him, it would be better if he didn't try any stairs for several days."

"We can fix it up, Miss Adeline," he said. "Go on and see to Mr. Sullivan's brother, if you're done with Horace—"

Adeline was relieved her hand had become entirely steady, because she could tell that the second man would be living with whatever she did to his face. The scar would be a lasting testament to her nerves as well her flair with a needle. He might have caught the edge of a tomahawk, since the cut went deep at the top and came out like a shallow graze.

"Can you sew me up?"

"You'll be fine," Adeline said. "Not nearly as much sewing as Horace needed."

"I'll take another brandy anyhow."

The wound was less threatening, but it required the finest needle. Her tucks took almost longer than the man had patience to endure. The second glass of brandy made him more cooperative, but Adeline worried that a third might have the opposite effect.

With Mr. Moore's help and her student's, she tied off the last stitch an hour later. More chilly towels were hauled in from outside, and Tabitha pressed one to the wounded man's head. He let his friends prop up his feet so that he could doze off after the ordeal.

"You must have done that a lot for your soldier friends," said Tabitha where the two rested later. "I guess those Georgia boys had pretty good care while they were around you."

"We did more work on feet than heads or legs," Adeline said. She felt no need to explain how it was only socks and shoes the Harper women had mended while in company of the Georgia Battalion, not flesh.

"I'm going to pray God we don't need any more stitching when our own men get back with Captain John Grumbles," she said. Still, she needed reassurance from the sixteen-year-old. "But you'll come on back down if you hear the bell, won't you?"

"Of course, I'd best get back and let Maggie and Yarico know what's—"

"Go on, darlin', it'll be getting dark." Then Tabitha smiled. "Here I thought our men had built a little ole house for the town's teacher—and now it turns out to be where the doctor lives."

"Just stitches. If anyone goes to fainting or stomach ailments, I don't know but what Maggie is the one to consult."

Outside, the young woman got up on her horse, and Tabitha Ellinger broke into her usual hearty laugh about the mounting style Adeline had resorted to, when she had no time to hitch the cart in the emergency.

"Lord knows what I'll see you do next!"

"I'll come back in the morning to find out what the swelling does. The thread can't come out for ten days, so it might get to looking pretty bad."

"Adeline," the woman said. She was looking off in the direction her husband had ridden with thirteen other men. "If my Ernest doesn't come back—I don't know what—"

"I expect he'll be back here before I look in on my patients, Tabitha. The captain knows how to size up a fight." Both women had thoughts of what the Gonzales wives and children must have faced, watching their men folk ride off toward the Alamo.

"I know you're right," Tabitha said, giving Adeline's horse a little pat on the rump. "I know you're right."

In the next week, terrible hostilities came to a boil in the creeks just northwest of Bastrop, not far from settlement Texas had determined to make its capital. A group of Lipan Apache did their best to warn settlers about Comanche attacks. Some farmers and town men never returned from a battle around Brushy Creek, where no small raiding party, but a gathering of three hundred warriors answered a previous skirmish with settlers.

But Mrs. Ellinger's husband was not among those lost. And yet, the bearded family man was changed when he returned home. Maybe being in the thick of rifle fire and seeing a neighbor shot in the back of the head, Adeline concluded soberly, is one of those scenes that lose nightmare potency only after many, many seasons. Ernest Ellinger had seen a friend die in such a way. A Mr.Gilleland had been mortally wounded in the Brushy Creek battle while helping a youth no older than Adeline get back onto his horse.

It couldn't be easy to live with a sense that death had skipped over you, while taking someone so clearly engaged in selflessness and generosity.

The tempering of elation late in February was a prelude to what all Texans expected of March. A day of jubilation on the 2nd for the anniversary of Independence was followed in four days by memorials for those who had died to the last man in the Alamo. A sense of unspeakable outrage and inconsolable grief marked the 27th, the date of the Goliad executions. March left Texans with the need again to settle in their minds what life there could be after death.

When Bastrop had been called Mina, people were remembering, it was Mr.Gilleland who started up the town's first Methodist services. The Harper women read the Bible for him that Easter Sunday, as well as for souls they knew best and missed most. Aunt Maggie relapsed some into distracted worries over Matthew Linder, but April blooms eventually cheered the Harpers and their community. The anniversary of the San Jacinto victory brought tolling bells to Texas, everywhere, including the Bastrop courthouse.

By May, invigorating activity was all that residents witnessed on the old Brenham road winding through Bastrop to Austin. In the past, one traveler per month rode through the pines on the trail to Waterloo. Now ten each week rumbled in that direction. Few dressed in the rugged buckskin hotel guests wore prior to President Lamar's election. These new Bastrop visitors dressed in fine cotton coats, pleated shirts and leather breeches with tailor made fittings, more often than in home-spun clothing, and they traveled often by hired stagecoach. Gentlemen frequently sat at the hotel table to discuss their surveyor charts and the new capital's layout.

Dr. Joseph Robertson, newly elected to represent Bastrop County in the Texas Congress, found Austin accommodations a compelling topic. Since he was called away now on government duties as often as with medical emergencies, he took on Miss Adeline Harper as his assistant, when her teaching hours permitted.

One summer day Adeline sorted through a box of surgical supplies in the Bastrop Hotel. When a frequent hotel guest came in on his way back from Austin, the doctor asked her to complete the inventory. Other guests, too, recognized the late afternoon coach as official transportation of the republic. Whatever people had been reading or discussing in the lobby, they paused so that they could hear what Edwin Waller was planning for the capital.

"It'll be a beauty," the surveyor said, rolling out a map and sketch. He had to stop for another drink of cool water, since the June heat had made the thirty mile coach ride a trial for humans and horses. "We've got a long avenue coming up from the Colorado on the north bank—" Mr. Moore and Dr. Robertson leaned over the oak table where he'd stretched out his drawings. "Straight up this-a-way goes to where you have a nice rise. It's perfect for the capitol building if we can ever get out of debt to build one—"

There was general laughter at the thought of Texas getting herself in secure financial status of any kind. The republic had still not been able to pay its army and revolution volunteers, much less invest in the niceties or formalities of government structures.

"Don't laugh too hard," Waller said, "Santa Anna was laughing before all hell broke loose on him in San Jacinto, don't forget. Anyhow, could be the French will hand over some cash if their recognition and settlement swap goes through."

Adeline set the doctor's instrument tray carefully inside a roll-top desk, which amounted to his office in town. She was accustomed to being the only lady in view at the hotel. If Horace, the turnkey at the stockade, ever heard anyone question her age or maturity, however, he would roll up his pants leg and show them the scars where she had stitched four inches from his knee to his thigh.

"There are already some cabins going along up this avenue—that'll be Congress—and up from the river to the capitol. We'll number the streets for eleven or twelve blocks.

"How many acres is this thing fixin' to be?"

"Nearly seven hundred—I guess we're counting on some revenue at that!"

"Are the lots going up for sale soon?" the doctor wanted to know.

"Not until later in August, but look what I wanted to show you next," Mr. Waller went on. "We'll have the streets going east and west off Congress named after all our big rivers. Over to the east—Brazos, Trinity, Neches. Going in the other direction, it'll be Colorado, Lavaca, Guadalupe, Nueces, Rio Grande—"

"Did you ever think you'd get the chance to lay out a country's capital, Edwin? Do you know now how the feller that sketched out Paris felt?"

"Hell—excuse me, Miss—I've got this pictured so fine in my mind, I figure I'll be running for mayor—on a ticket of municipal pride!"

"You ought to!" people were chuckling, but they also looked at Mr. Waller with serious admiration.

"That's not all, if you're in a mind to daydream about the future. We got permission to put hold on forty acres just north of where the capitol building will be some day. Before you know it, we'll all be sending our sons to a fine Texas college on land set aside."

The room grew quiet in awe. If there could be a university in the town where, at the moment, only a dozen or so log cabins existed, surely a reasonable hotel, an office for a doctor, an inn with more than one table, a general store, a post office, blacksmith, livery, even a barber establishment would soon be set in motion. A spasm of building—at last!

"Just point me on the map where you noticed an untended cabin gone up for lease or purchase," Dr. Robertson said.

"Right here on what'll be Congress." He slapped his friend's shoulder. "The sign was still out this morning— a ways down from where a Mr.

Bullock has already got himself a hotel going up. You won't believe what's been framed since you were there three weeks ago, Joseph. If you want it, you'd best put some cash down. Bullock is handling bank transactions temporarily, since he's owner of the only safe—"

"Adeline, can you be here for any stitching or quinine drops for the next two days?" She was nodding, but she thought she should take the Harper cart back to the cabin to let Maggie and Yarico know.

"I'm going on in to Austin first thing tomorrow," the doctor said, as much to himself as anyone. When he saw Adeline putting on her bonnet, he followed her out to Main Street. She was gathering the cart reins.

"I need to see what my family—"

"I know—me too—this year has sent me spinning—maybe a little too fast," he said. "You have your nice cabin here and you three women are all settled in, but this picture of Austin I have in my mind now—a real city in the middle of Texas!"

"There could be a female academy before it's over," Adeline said shyly.

"My wife would approve of that, and it's along the lines of what I'm wondering. Would you consider moving to Austin—where you could be on hand in a medical office I aim to start up? If I get there in time tomorrow!" Her expression told him she too had caught some new spark about Austin. "You've got the gift for several medical procedures, and you or your Yarico could fetch me if there were anything grievous while I was tending a patient elsewhere."

"Waller has told me before about this cabin on Congress. Has two rooms, dog-trot style, so you and your aunt and all could live on the one side. I'll be back and forth between here and Austin, while I'm in Congress for two years." He had to stop himself from rambling on with excitement. "But I haven't had my appetite whetted so for a permanent move, since I first came to Texas in '36!"

Half bewildered and half elated, Adeline listened to the physician. She too had been sent dreaming about the future, shortly after Edwin Waller rolled out his maps of the new Texas capital.

"I don't know whether my aunt could tolerate leaving these woods—hard enough for me—"

"I know, they're what made me put down roots and bring my family to Texas the very next year—"

"There'd be more books in Austin, though, wouldn't you think? Once things get organized—"

"All kinds of books—you could take any of mine off the shelf for an evening—"

"I suppose there'd be ladies in town with their husbands, and fancy work for my Aunt Maggie. And Yarico—"

"You wouldn't have to sell your cabin here—I'm sure the hotel will be needing cabin space to let often enough while Austin is getting built and the lumber wagons start taking off from here—"

"Do you think the French are really coming to Texas?"

"Who knows about their settlement plans—maybe several thousand—but it's almost sure they'll be sending a delegate after recognition—You don't speak French, do you?"

"Not as good as—Yes sir, pretty well. I suppose my reading is better than my conversation—"

"Between your needlework, your teaching experience, your medical gifts, and your French literacy—you'll be in keen demand, Miss Harper. What do you say?"

"If you'd asked me just six months ago—six days ago!—I'd have said nothing could entice me to leave these peaceful pines—"

"Nothing—except the calling to help birth a country could budge me," Dr. Robertson responded.

When Adeline returned to the Harper cabin, Maggie and Yarico were sitting by the outdoor hearth minding a kettle of chickpea soup. Linens were drying on a rope line, and the women touched short needles to their embroidery hoops. They listened to the sixteen-year-old physician's assistant without glancing at each other, so absorbed were they by her message and her dear, earnest request for consultation. The two, who had very little else to adore in life other than this bright young figure before them, were more absorbed by her intensity than her words.

"I think we should ask the Reverend Haynie what he thinks this Sunday," Adeline said finally. "I don't want to be the kind of person who can't be thankful for blessings that are present, who always has to satisfy a shallow curiosity about what's just over the hill—when you're already living in near heavenly peace."

The preacher John Haynie had been in Texas only since the beginning of 1839, and in May he preached the first Methodist sermon in Bastrop. His circuit took in both Bastrop and Austin, so he, too, was among people traveling the riverbank path between towns. He was different from most church men Adeline knew of, not so stiff even on the Sabbath, and unique in his adamant refusal to carry a rifle.

"I used to run uphill in the dark, when I was a child, Reverend Haynie," she admitted, "and even then I warned myself about swollen pride and failings." The gray-haired man preached that Sunday about *callings,* and she wanted his critical view. "If you think this chance to go to Austin and learn what more I can about medicine, use some of my French, and latch on to any library I find—if you think I'm following a vain pride—"

"Miss Harper—" His chuckle was enough to disarm anyone, she thought. "It's my opinion that the Lord and his angels are smiling about you. He surely knows good energy when he sees it, and your plans have got him very pleased is what I'd say."

"You think so? You do?"

"I most surely do," he said. "And I think you ought to know, by the way, that I've been called and pulled myself with a similarly uplifting sense of purpose."

"—Reverend?"

"I'll be serving as House Chaplain in Austin come November when Austin's first Congress convenes!"

Chapter 17   Moving Heaven and Earth

Few comparisons could be drawn by the Harpers between the autumn month they had spent at Macon in 1835 and the October they watched unfold in Austin four years later. Five thousand people inhabited their Georgia hometown. Five hundred lived in the new capital of the Republic of Texas. Nearly two hundred were carpenters, builders, and men busy hauling loads of lumber from Bastrop. Only a dozen log buildings squatted in what had been Waterloo when Dr. Robertson first requested that Adeline and her family come to Austin by coach. Locals assured them it would take more than a decree by a politician to get them to refer to their main crossroad *Pecan* as "6th Street," as set out in the new plan.

The same number of buildings were erected almost overnight along Congress, the main street running perpendicular to and up from the flat banks of the Colorado River. Unlike Macon, shopping in the Harper's new home proved meager—no choice of pewter or porcelain candle holders, no mercantile company advertising fall fashion coats. But the first newspaper was starting up, a hotel across the way at the corner of 6th and Congress was already in regular use, and the temporary capital building was getting its finishing touches. One side of the single room log structure would be for the Senate and the larger end would accommodate the House.

A citizen needed imagination to conjure a majestic stone capitol upon the hill rising up past Fifteenth, though the surveyor Mr. Waller carried sketches with him of a grand dome. Meanwhile the Harper women enjoyed watching as a pastime. The temporary government headquarters was built just two blocks up Congress from Dr. Robertson's practice. As often as they heard tales about outsider attacks on the town, Adeline, her aunt, and Yarico breathed easier figuring how fast—if a Comanche alarm went up—they could convey themselves to the stockade entrance of that log structure.

Some evenings, as the Harper women sat out on the doctor's porch, they felt they'd moved to parade stands, where there was more to gawk at on the street each day than three people could possibly testify to before bed time.

Though Dr. Robertson's practice drew notice slowly, he was elated to secure the dog-trot structure, and his office easily served as a living quarters for the upcoming legislative session. The women missed their forest cabin, but in Austin they enjoyed a rock cooking hearth on the south wall of their large room, a duplicate of the doctor's quarters across the adjoining walkway. That sheltered space, as well as a covered porch, gave them a home more protected from nature's brutality than they'd enjoyed since leaving the widow Bedeford's pale house.

The scarcity of female company in the new capital shocked them. But as long as the street commotion kept up, and as long as the doctor scurried back and forth to Bastrop where new shops sprang up each week, the Harpers thrived. Dr. Robertson was so happy to have an assistant maintaining his accounts while he was away, that he never grumbled about bringing back thread and yards of calico. Adeline embroidered, between ordering bandages and dispensing headache powders, but she was often reading medical books when her aunt or Yarico reminded her not to burn too many candles in the solitary pursuit.

The hotel owner across the way, Mr. Bullock, was no relation to the Georgia soldier who had gone cheerfully down the Alabama with them, only to meet, they supposed, the cruelest fate. The Austin businessman hired the Harpers to hem twenty linen napkins, and all three were invited across the dusty avenue one afternoon to see how his dining room had been set up.

"We love the good smell of pines!" was the first comment Aunt Maggie made to the hotel owner.

"These logs weren't cut but three months ago."

"We'll come over just for the reminder of forest—"

"It'll quit by next year." He wasn't chewing on a stick, but Adeline thought his disposition might be similar to the father, Sean O'Brien, who'd spoken so little on the trail to Gonzales.

"Well, there's your handiwork. That's what I was aimin' to show you."

The dining tables and chairs had been rough hewn from the same lumber as the hotel's exterior. Yet on the tables were fine tablecloths that must have been imported from Galveston, if not all the way from New Orleans. The Harper's napkins, made of darker tan linen, were folded elegantly underneath shining utensils. A framed painting hung behind the hotel counter—a herd of buffalo grazing in hills just before a violet sunset. Stair railings chiseled from thinner logs led to the second tier of rooms, with doors barely scraped of their bark. The startling mixture of the rugged and the stylish made Maggie clap her hands and her companions laugh.

242

"What's funny?" Bullock asked.

"We're so pleased, we're tickled," Maggie said.

"It's been a long time since we've seen table linens set out for use."

"You ladies did a fine job on the napkins. My helper, Angelina, says I'd have saved some gold dust if the three of you'd hemmed up the bed sheets too." He didn't seem to want any laughing about that. "But I'll know to call on you if we get in a fix with more guests than we're ready to handle."

"We saw you take in a number of gentlemen last week—"

"Shoot, we're already full up on the second floor—legislature won't even move in officially until next week."

"Not in town yet? I thought everybody in Texas must be!" Maggie went on. "The street's a snarl with coaches and wagons all hours of the day."

"Not hardly!" Now Mr. Bullock was sounding the way Dr. Robertson had, Adeline thought—barely able to contain his anticipation. "That last coach driver? He's got word from Houston where things took pretty nearly all last month to get boxed. He swore there's a caravan of fifty oxcarts on their way here now with the republic's archives! I don't know what all they plan to fit in the sovereign structure up the road."

"Well, I declare!"

"And since we just got us a formal recognition from France last month—there'll be other foreign countries visiting before long—we're fixin' to get some kind of French official assigned right here to Austin, too!"

"C'est incroyable!" When several people idling in Bullock's lobby turned to stare at Adeline, she regretted having given in to her own enthusiasm.

"Well, now I know who to come to if I can't explain the menu to our French customers—" the surprised hotel owner said.

"We'll be sitting right *over yonder*—" Maggie was pointing in the direction of the doctor's porch.

"All right then, Mrs. Linder. I'll wave to you from my own upstairs lookout, because that's where I aim to be when those four dozen wagons come rolling in next week." Now he was clapping his hands. "I'll bet you all the silverware on these tables that you'll be able to hear those ox carts creaking by the time they roll into Bastrop thirty miles away!"

Six days later, when the government of Texas entered from the Bastrop road and went up Congress toward old Pecan Street, the Harper women recalled their exit from Macon as the only scene they could compare. They would never forget the drum-roll departure of their own wagon behind the Georgia Battalion, the cheering throng of townspeople as the formation moved out.

For Austin's grand occasion Adeline, Maggie, and Yarico sat on the benches of their comfortable porch. The thick planks they rested on began gradually to vibrate, and the sound coming from a distance was a groan sustained by a grinding shudder. What the country Texas had managed to accumulate in just three and a half years of self-governance, the three women could not imagine. But the number of ox carts grinding their way slowly up the avenue from the direction of Bastrop to the intersection at Bullock's Hotel had not been exaggerated.

"You count 'em now, Mrs. Linder!" he hollered across the way.

"Don't you cause a stampede!" Adeline's aunt called back.

The first ten carts rolled along as far as the stockade perimeter of the government building. And the next ten went past that line, on up Congress to where a domed building was only fantasy. The next twenty-five carts had to pull up alongside in the middle of the street, and the last half dozen didn't make it up from the river until close to sundown. Wagon drivers laughed and cursed and bragged. Bellowing oxen contributed to the tumult, as officials from the capitol building came out and checked off what was being carried, and argued with one another over what should be hauled past the stockade first.

The pungent smell of oxen dung wafting through the streets did not deter Mr. Bullock's smelly pigs from investigating the scene. Squealing with excitement, they angled back and forth through the bizarre assembly of visitors and buzzing horse flies. There were so many extra men in town that the hotel bulged six to a room, even in their overflow cabins behind the main building. Many drivers went on down toward the river bank where they camped in the cool fall air.

It was another week before the last of the carts from Houston was unloaded. Most crates found a place in the log government building, but some of the republic's more precious documents were secured in Bullock's safe until the country could afford superior locks. Dr. Robertson, caught up in unpacking and organization, dashed in and out of the capitol. Because he was preoccupied, Adeline dabbed salt water on a man's puffy thumb where a splinter from a rough storage crate was deeply embedded.

Life in Texas appeared to Miss Harper to pass that way—in waves of excitement or terror almost more than the mind could take in and bear, followed by a stretch of calm that challenged a person's ability to cope with tedium. The city of Austin had just two weeks to recuperate from the convulsion caused by the oxcarts, before newly elected delegates from all over Texas descended upon President Mirabeau Lamar's chosen capital.

The scene generated identical frenzy among the hotel owner's pigs, but the arrival of government people struck the Harper women as distinct and unforgettable. Since the three knew seams the way they knew breathing, variety in clothing consumed their interest.

"That's fourteen—I'm counting stovetop hats," Aunt Maggie said. "And coonskin caps if I don't get the two counts mixed up—That makes eleven."

"I'm counting Indian blankets," said Adeline. The women were squeezed together at the small window pane that looked out upon Congress Avenue. The sun was bright, but the temperature had dipped into the forties overnight. During the day, it warmed up considerably, but a wind whistled down from the north that cut too deeply for porch sitting. "Well, I think I already lost accurate numbers. Look at the man with a beaver hat and two blankets, one wrapped front to back and a second going the other way."

"You think that fellow in the discolored buckskin is warm with nothing on but the rawhides? Or you figure he's just too proud to ask his neighbors where they got their wraps?" Yarico believed he might smell a little like the hotel pigs, but she admitted there were worse qualities than the stench of sweat.

"What part of the country do you think those fine gentlemen are riding in from? See?" Adeline pointed to three men whose horses appeared to prance even after their long journey. "That's tailor-made wool from the east coast. Look how his lapels go to the waist button. They're the only ones with overcoats, so you know they had to order such things from a city that imports from the North."

"Do you see their boots? Are they all wearing boots like that in Houston?" Maggie was marveling at the shine on the upper parts. "Maybe they're representing Nacogdoches, where they can get their orders in from the Mississippi trade across the border."

"Wouldn't I just love to go over with Dr. Robertson as his clerk, or some excuse!" Adeline said. "Can you imagine what these men will be talking about in the next few days?"

"Angelina said the other day that they're not doing much except to get sworn in. That's why a few wives went ahead and made the trip," Maggie said shaking her head. "The ladies wanted to come along in case the issues were too dry to keep their husbands interested in sober discussion."

"This town is either fireworks or fizzle."

"Well, you two better get your French lit up, according to Miss Angelina—that new ambassador, or whatever his title is, will be arriving in Austin not long after the New Year."

In the first few days of 1840, a new census was taken in Austin, and its earlier residents were astounded to learn that their settlement of a puny two hundred had grown to over eight hundred in a matter of months. Word was out that a Frenchman, Alphonse Dubois de Saligny, who didn't mind just going by *The Count,* had arrived to considerable fanfare in Galveston, and would be making the muddy trip to Austin by the first of March to make contact while Congress was still in session.

Roads from Houston and Galveston were no less hazardous than they had been the spring of the revolution, so Dubois impressed Austin officials when he insisted on traveling to the capital at the end of February. Texas dignitaries rode out Pecan Street toward Bastrop to escort the count's entourage into town. They had taken the alternate route, away from the swollen banks of the Colorado.

Mayor Waller, as well as President Lamar's representatives, rode their best mounts out to meet the count's sleek black carriage. His staff looked out from two varnished carts with awnings, and a wagon with trunks and boxes jostled behind. The first country to recognize Texas as an independent republic deserved a special welcome!

"He's not god-all-powerful, Angelina!" Bullock reminded his helper as they fussed inside the hotel.

"Did you unpack that crate—the quilted bedspreads?"

"Hell, I thought, Clay did—What's that boy good for?"

The inkeeper and his workers waited in a dither. One moment, they arranged beds and tables as if there were no reason to take any greater pains than they had for Sam Houston or David Burnet. Then, they panicked that some lapse in their preparations would shame their country with the wide world looking on. Mr. Bullock begged Adeline and any other Harpers, to wander on over when Dubois showed up, in case the newcomer's English was as bad as his own French.

The three women perched on oak stools near the stairwell, an inconspicuous if uncomfortable place to hear.

"We shall be pleased to dine and then to retire," the count Dubois stated when Bullock registered his company.

"How many rooms in all?"

"Neuf? Ou quatre. Les femmes vont partager?" A slender woman discussed numbers with the count's head man. Three dark-haired servants, their brown, pretty faces registering fatigue, shrugged and stared at the furnishings.

The count's staff appeared to speak only their native French, but he easily made himself understood in English. His accent, however, was British rather than American, and the Harpers smiled at his pronunciation. They nodded when they caught a French phrase exchanged between the coachman and domestics.

"Ah! Bon!" said the count, as venison and corn bread were brought to his table. "Parfait! We thank you," he said about the sherry. No doubt beds were all the travelers really yearned for.

"Angelina will show you the rooms," Bullock announced nervously in the evening. He indicated the buildings behind the main hotel as well as upstairs. "You all let me know how it sleeps."

The Harpers hadn't needed to translate, and they slipped out when the biggest trunks were carried upstairs. At home they discussed how many flounced layers appeared in the French servants' skirts. How were the sleeves on the ladies' velveteen coats set in? Were all the bonnets in Paris now tied with long satin bows? Was the count's elegant topcoat made of the smooth, heavy silk they'd read about—peau de soie?

The women never spoke about the hardships of travel. In the spring, especially, the topic was abhorrent. They could not speculate on the difficulty in March of the count's trek from the coast.

For an entire month, the elegant Alphonse Dubois de Saligny strolled among individuals Adeline noticed coming or going from the Bullock Hotel. His pastel, embossed clothing threw a contrasting sparkle into the street scene, no matter which political faction courted his opinion. The steady throb of debate stole attention from the season's somber dates. When raucous rivalry between the Lamar supporters and Sam

Houston's devotees faded away during the Easter recess, quiet settled in Austin and its avenues cleared. For pleasure, full-time residents drove their carriages to the Colorado.

Bluebonnets and verbena began to carpet the river banks, and the town's original families wondered at how their town, too, sprouted and flourished. Two newspapers now came out daily, private homes took in overflow lodgers, and a mercantile across from the capitol posted handbills saying summer parasols were on the way! Even Reverend Haynie's preaching duties expanded. It was the Presbyterians who met regularly in one of the Bullock buildings, but Haynie proudly officiated in the county's first wedding.

"Travis County —May 7, 1840!" Haynie exclaimed to Adeline. "I don't suppose our Alamo hero William Travis was ever as happy as that young couple."

"It's good the country remembers some of its lost patriots—"

"If I don't ever get lost on my circuit to and from Bastrop, the Lord will make me as content as he's been keeping me busy!"

Any chat with Reverend Haynie made other conversations muted by contrast. But Adeline was noticing how subdued talk was with Yarico these days, in particular. Her reserved demeanor was different from the quiet satisfaction of other Austin folks. After the Dubois entourage left, she withdrew interest in any of the town's diversions. The presence of smartly dressed, brown-skinned French speakers had transfixed Yarico's attention, but their swift departure by April sharpened her sense of isolation.

Adeline had her medical books and occasional medical stitches to keep her occupied, but Yarico had run out of the hem work that busied them all prior to the swearing in of Lamar. Aunt Maggie could keep herself from searching every knot of passersby for a certain Linder profile, if she wandered over to the Bullock Hotel daily to chat with Angelina or the housekeeper.

Loneliness in Austin, Yarico consoled herself, was partly the encroaching emptiness any mother feels, coming to terms with a maturing daughter. Adeline was growing to love interests beyond her childhood habits. She moved with grace in an adult world ordered to be her world in every way.

In Bastrop Yarico had leaned on the companionship of the forest, though the Ellingers were friendly, with a startling disregard for who owned whom. But ever since the loblolly pines, since crossing small plantations and coming up the new Congress Avenue, Yarico felt a sorrow she'd never known before. She recognized a new layer of sadness at the outer edges of inhabited Texas. When all the attendants left with Count Dubois de Saligny, the finely laid out city of Austin was home to only one other black skinned soul.

A ten-year-old girl was the live-in maid for one prominent family, and they often came down Congress to the mercantile. Yarico was tempted to walk out onto the Harper porch and wave, but good sense kept her inside where she peeked near the window frame. If her grasp on reality had been fragile, like Aunt Maggie's, she might have run out to greet the pretty little thing—"Ma nièce—c'est toi?" But, let the darling enjoy her unique loveliness for a while. The girl likely believed herself the only person in the world fortunate enough to have lovely dark skin, along with lovely dark eyes. Let the beautiful creature of God rejoice! Let the child carry her *joie de vivre*, for as long as she could.

Somber contemplations were only made worse that year by blistering temperatures and unremitting drought in June and into July. The atmosphere at the Bullock Hotel prior to the return of Monsieur Dubois was much less charged with friendly anticipation. In the worst heat of central Texas summers, often a succession of temperatures lingering over one hundred, no one had patience for accommodating the needs of others. Summer meant boiling afternoons and the incessant crackle of cicadas. Summer meant every man for himself, regardless of political designation, linguistic preference, or fashion sense.

When the Dubois carriage at last rumbled down Pecan Street toward the hotel, there had already been suffering on the trail from Galveston. No solicitous concern over the travelers' welfare would make amends for the Frenchman's condition. His attendants were decidedly worse off. Dubois himself was too drained to speak for his servants, so Bullock sent across the street for Adeline to make sure he grasped their complex lodging needs. So many staggering in—or being carried—suggested medical needs as well.

But in Dr. Roberston's absence, Adeline was busy setting the broken arm of a carpenter. She pleaded with Yarico to go, despite the woman's dread of public scrutiny.

Yarico had been inside the split-log hotel once before, but then she had sat in the cool of a stairwell. She didn't think she could tolerate the furnace atmosphere this time, or the unrelenting glare of strangers.

"There is one woman, ill from the heat." Yarico said in the lobby. She had conferred with a lady in the count's staff and a man. She lowered her eyes to tell Mr. Bullock the rest. "The young woman has been in and out of consciousness since before Bastrop."

"I saw when they carried her in—limp as river weed— but I don't remember her from last March—I'd have recollected that near-yellow hair."

"The valet explains…that Monsieur…bought her in New Orleans," Yarico said. Apparently the count had heard some of the French and English exchanges, because he raised himself up from the chaise where another servant waved a paper fan.

"If the girl does not recover, I have no way to recoup the three hundred I spent for her purchase. And I lost two horses as well—one from this cursed heat and one that hadn't the strength to make it across the Brazos!"

"What does Monsieur say the sick woman needs," Bullock asked Yarico.

"Let the physician say—if there *are* any in this wilderness," Dubois said. "I hope my own faculties can repair themselves after the thrashing this journey has given them, though I doubt I can find adequate rest— just let us repair to our rooms, and we will see what any doctor might advise—"

"Tell the count we have his bed linens turned down already," Bullock said. "The same buildings in back." He was speaking to Yarico, less in recognition of her language flexibility than of his growing disapproval of the Frenchman's manner in handling business. It was trouble enough to house an entourage as opposed to a single hotel guest. The additional demands for doctors and critical medicines put a burden on the hotel staff that the deadly heat made them slow to undertake.

Dr. Robertson remained out of town, and it was not another doctor who came a few days later to see about the delicate New Orleans slave, but the undertaker. The coffin maker usually hammered nails into horse shoes, but had discovered he was just as apt at finishing the edges of pine boxes when the need arose. His carpentry for such orders was only second rate, but in this case no one was overly engaged in what manner of funeral might be held for the French female—stolen from the Antilles, perhaps?—who had not survived the Texas weather long enough to be able to say how friendly she found the people.

Reverend Haynie rode in from the Bastrop length of his preaching circuit, and he was the kind of man who believed in saying proper words over any departing soul. Adeline went with Yarico to stand with the count's servants at a little clearing among live oaks on the far western edge of Austin. A man named Henri was the leader of the Dubois household staff, and he asked Yarico to tell the preacher "Merci bien." A footman spoke something to Yarico that Adeline could not hear, and when the short service was over, the two Harper women went back to their dwelling on Congress without talking much.

"Your mama's the one who reminded me, when we read the history of France," Yarico said softly. "She said to me 'wasn't it wonderful' that France abolished slavery, at the same time they took to heart American rights, and started their own revolution."

"It looks as if Dubois forgot." Adeline said, without looking at her. It was the most speech she'd heard from Yarico since the woman had taken charge during the frantic weeks of Texas revolution.

Aunt Maggie greeted them at their door with apologies for not having gone.

"I find I can't spring back from funerals like I could in my younger days," she said. "If they don't bend me into thinking about—well, if I don't snap in that direction, then I start to dwell on my own service one day soon—"

"You're tougher than Texas heat—"

"I do hate it when I hear of a young person being taken by the afternoon temperatures…such a daily thing—"

There was little visiting between the hotel and the Harpers for a while, although the women learned that the Frenchman had moved into a house farther down Pecan Street. A Dubois acquaintance, one of Austin's wealthier landowners offered the dwelling. But there was still a pall hanging in the town's main intersection, and a growing animosity toward the representative from France over the manner in which he and his attendants had come to Austin the second time. When the issue of unpaid bills began to mix with whisperings, a sharp tendency grew among residents to badmouth French of any kind.

Mr. Bullock claimed he was stuck with medical costs, as well as the lodging bill for the month of August. Dubois countered that he'd lodged elsewhere for the entire month of August and was only too ill to get out of bed and settle his accounts at the hotel. Besides complaining to authorities, Bullock used insulting speech whenever he met up with the count, referring to him anywhere as "Count No-Count." Bullock refused an arbitration that reduced the count's bill by nearly half, and hostilities between the Dubois household and the Bullock camp developed into a full-fledged feud.

Few Austin inhabitants cared to take up sides in the unsavory matter, but the count's outsider status made him an easy target for ridicule, especially those given to belligerence when drunk. One evening Adeline and Yarico were sitting on their own porch when a sandy-haired man they had never seen before staggered from the hotel and accosted them.

"Who d'you think you are—" he drawled, "—with all your French goin's on?"

"We're going inside our house," Adeline responded, calmly standing up.

"Too good for us Texans…" He was trying to complete his thought. "But not too good for some French…royalty!" He closed in on their porch and started to step up into the breezeway where Adeline had turned.

"Don't you come up here," Yarico said. The man stopped swaying and took a long still look at the older woman.

"And who almighty do you reckon *you* are?"

"We both live in Dr. Robertson's house here," Adeline went on, "and we're telling you to go on away from here."

"French who don't pay their money—" he said spitting, "We make 'em pay other ways!"

Friendly discourse with the hotel staff across the street ended. Without occasional chats, Aunt Maggie slid into a melancholy spell. Dr. Robertson gave her a thorough examination and warned Adeline that her aunt might have suffered some mild conniption or dropsy. Her left side functioned less well than her right arm and hands. Her walking could not recover from a stiffness, and when her fingers wouldn't do what she wanted them to do with a needle, her depression worsened.

Adeline and Yarico took turns watching to make sure she wouldn't fall. In early October, one night after the three women turned in, Maggie suddenly tried to stand at the side of her bed. She sank, without saying a word, to the floor. Adeline dispatched Yarico across the street to the hotel where the doctor often continued discussions with congressional colleagues late into the evening.

In about an hour, Dr. Robertson rushed down the dark street to the Harper's room. Yarico had needed to check with two different households before finding him, and the doctor couldn't stop apologizing. All over town discussions about tariffs were spilling into lengthy debates about a Santa Fe expedition. Some said the journey would help Texans secure their western frontier—others said inroads there might just stir up old troubles.

"Anyway," Dr. Robertson said, still perspiring from the sprint home, "I'm just sorry you couldn't get hold of me sooner—" Maggie's color was good, but she couldn't be brought to an alert state.

"She's been like this for an hour—I didn't know what to do, except tilt her back, so she wouldn't pass out. I've been keeping a cool rag to her forehead and trying to talk to her," Adeline rushed on.

"Fifty isn't all that old in some ladies," the doctor said. "Come on now, Mrs. Linder—Can you open your eyes and follow this match I'm holding?"

"She doesn't seem to have a fever—"

"No, you're right to check for any signs of something contagious," he said, trying to reassure his assistant.

"Maggie was there with me...ever since my mother died. She's been right here with us for goin' on ten years," Adeline said.

"Your aunt's been through a lot since you all came to Texas."

"We couldn't have made it without her...without all of us staying together—"

"What is it?"

"I didn't see Yarico."

"She was right with me coming down the street," the doctor said. "She was coming along behind. I ran in the dark, the last block or so..." He had lost track. Stepping away from the bed where Mrs. Linder had been resettled, he reached for the door latch. "There's Yarico. She's just outside on my end of the porch. I imagine she just didn't want to make it a crowd in here. Looks like she's breathing pretty hard from the worry."

Yarico sat slumped against one of the doctor's porch posts. Her shoulders were shaking and her hands covered her head. By the time Adeline thought of her again—after Maggie could be roused more easily and had taken some water—Yarico had already slipped inside unnoticed and taken her usual position, lying on her side on her corner pallet.

For the next weeks, most attention at the doctor's log structure was on Adeline's aunt, since her condition required both able women to feed and bathe her, as well as spend time talking to her so that her speech would improve. Lowering her into warm water at least once a week for sponging off was difficult, and both Adeline and Yarico had bruises from resting their arms on the unforgiving edges of the metal tub. The cough that Adeline took in early November, she was able to fend off, and whatever stomach ailment Yarico caught, gradually wore away, and she was more herself by the beginning of December.

A change in season was finally pronounced. With the passing of an unpleasant fall, the women anticipated Christmas and the New Year as they always had. The bitter exchange between the hotel owner across the way and the French dignitary farther down the street subsided into a flurry of letter writing behind the scene. The unreimbursed hotel keeper only infrequently blurted insults.

The Harpers were all feeling enough themselves one morning that they sighed together at their fireplace about how trivial municipal warfare seemed. Small-minded people forgot grand ideals rather quickly. Human nature was mighty poor to forget the grim sacrifices it had taken for this territory to become a country in the first place.

"What was...any of this...before?" Maggie had managed to say.

"Before better men took bullets—" Adeline had stopped herself. "Took care just to make this place safe for free, self-government—"

Yarico was saying something low about *better men.*

"To think those two," Maggie stopped to form her words, "nearly declared war over a hotel bill—" Adeline went to the window and looked absently across the street at the inn they referred to.

A soldier in a dark blue uniform stood before the Bullock hotel, arranging the straps on his horse. He paused before mounting. Soldiers, as well as congressmen, traveled often enough in the streets of Austin, and there were changes in their military colors according to division and rank. But there was nothing surprising about this soldier, with his blue wool pants tucked into shiny black boots. Three others similarly dressed mounted their horses, but this soldier had a red sash, and Adeline thought he must have some higher rank. A twinge of recognition struck her when he turned to pick something up from the hard dirt street where he had dropped it. She had seen this man before, but she couldn't think, because her head began to throb, and her mouth went dry in a way that made her believe she might be having a seizure like the one her aunt barely survived.

And then the soldier lifted up the back flap of his coat and reached into a rear pocket. When he took out the light blue handkerchief,

Adeline thought her legs had disappeared below her knees. She thought the rough wood planks of the Harper room could do some serious damage to her head if she were to fall in a heap full force, so she willed herself to keep breathing. She realized that Maggie and Yarico were shouting to her, but she got hold of her breathing well enough to race for the door and run down the open walkway out onto the porch. Adeline was calling a name when she dashed out into the street, though she hadn't even put on a cloak—she had only grabbed a blanket— but she was running, and when she reached up at the stirrups where the soldier had just hoisted himself up, she was laughing and crying at the same time, but her brain made a last connection before she could stop herself from saying, "Mr. Gideon!"

The face was so familiar. It was a good face from Georgia. It was the face of someone from those Macon days, that never-forgotten candlelight meeting, that beautiful collision of words and action.

"Miss?"

"I'm sorry," Adeline said, flustered. "I saw a Georgia soldier, and I had to—"

"I'm Colonel McLeod," he said. "Hugh McLeod. Are you from Georgia?"

He was so kind about telling his men to come back for him in a few minutes. He went back into the hotel, and he sat with Adeline at one of Mr. Bullock's tables. Either there was no one else in the lobby, or other people were thoughtful enough to seek errands elsewhere.

"I was there at the speech you gave, November of '35," Adeline said. "Everyone in Macon was holding candles. I was there."

The two sat at the table for several minutes without talking. There were some common experiences that deserved something more and something less than talk.

"I asked for a leave from Fort Jessup in April that same year," the colonel responded at last. There was no need to explain what March of 1836 would always mean. "I came over to Nacogdoches to see what I could do." Adeline waited before she thought her voice would be of any use.

"My family and I traveled across to Montgomery with the Georgia boys—we went down the Alabama together and on to New Orleans—"

"I remember when we started off—there was a wagon with women." The street outside was clear, except for a blond boy walking fast to beat the chill. "I resigned my commission that summer," he went on. "I'm in the Texas Army now. Looks as if we'll be making a trek to Santa Fe."

His voice as he sat at the hotel dining table was different from how it sounded up in front of all those Macon people. He had sincere eyes, and Adeline thought he must have family back home, still terribly proud of him, even if he'd ended up doing something unexpected with his West Point degree. Nothing ended up like what was counted on. She could have talked to him the entire morning. She wanted to ask what course of action in life creates an inner peace. What are the signs, of absolute certainty about purpose? But soldiers probably weren't interested in talking to young women about the meaning of *mission*. Adeline supposed they were helped to understand those concepts by their superior officers, and she thought she would have to pester Reverend Haynie again about her nagging questions.

They were outside the hotel minutes later, and McLeod was getting back up on his horse.

"I think we'll be collecting some of our medical supplies for the expedition from your Dr. Robertson, so we may cross paths once or twice before the regiment heads out."

"Wait!" Adeline almost forgot. "It was a blue handkerchief that made me run over here in the first place—I know that material—at least it looked so much like—"

"Here," he said, reaching back into his pocket again. "It's a Georgia keepsake—now it's yours. A Mexican rancher gave it to me when our troop was patrolling not far from Victoria. He heard me talking about home…about Georgia, and he said he'd been keeping it for someone like me—"

"It's faded, but I—"

"It has a stain. There was a little star in one corner, but it came off from wear," the colonel said. Adeline couldn't look back at the soldier just then. She could only touch the spot where the star had been.

"It wasn't sewn on very well. A little girl made it."

"Well, you keep it now," he said, and then he remembered what he had picked up from the street, "Keep this too, it was wrapped up inside when I got it."

"A gold cross? I don't know—"

"Neither do I," he said shaking his head. "The friendly rancher—the nice fellow said they came together—now they're yours." McLeod tipped his hat. "Got to head out now, Miss Harper. Pleasure meeting you."

Adeline took some time watching the soldiers ride on down toward the Colorado. She wanted to watch the sharply prancing horses, and to give Maggie and Yarico time to step away from the window across the street where they had been watching. She needed to draw a curtain over her own emotions before she could go on with today, or behave as if tomorrow had not shifted again from reach.

Chapter 18   No Tongue Can Tell

Adeline doubted the Christmas card she found at the Austin Mercantile had a chance of arriving in Macon, Georgia by December 25, but she wanted to send something to Mrs. Bedeford after five years. After so much loss and change, she wanted the generous woman—if she were still living—to know that the gift of blue, Sunday dress material meant a great deal to her. After meeting Colonel Hugh McLeod, now of the Texas Army, she wanted to let someone in her hometown know their beginnings had not been forgotten. Adeline Harper needed to send a message of cheerful remembrance to someone in the town that sacrificed so much in the name of Texas liberty.

The card she purchased for seven cents had a picture of a young girl on an iced- over pond. The skater's red cloak felt velvety, and the white fur muff that she held, as well as the ice, glistened. Simpler cards in brown pencil cost two pennies, but Adeline felt if the greeting were destined to be late for Christmas, she wanted the envelope to hold something special whenever it arrived.

The impossibility of getting mail through in the winter of 1840 caused a different kind of anxiety to Austin's main hotel owner and the French diplomat, still sparring with words at one another. Bullock succeeded in getting some Texas officials to act on his behalf—among them Acting President David Burnet, who stepped up when illness forced Lamar to take a leave of absence. Requests were drawn up and mailed to France. The suggestion was made, respectfully, that time had come for the European ally to replace its delegate to the new country, Texas, before international relations worsened beyond repair.

On his side, Dubois quite unexpectedly won the good will of Sam Houston, with whom he had traveled to New Orleans and who was expected to be the next Texas President. The mail that winter, however, was stupendously slow. Many of the count's letters of assurance to King Louis Phillipe, as well as a pile of Bullock documents, stalled short of Galveston. The republic's muddied postal routes put the Austin dispute at a standstill.

Monsieur Dubois de Saligny kept busy visualizing an official home somewhat removed from the city limits. He pictured himself in circumstances superior to anywhere he would have to endure Bullock's insults in the Austin streets below. Before the holidays, he purchased for France over twenty acres on a lovely hilltop at the far eastern end of

Pecan Street. He was less interested in the plans and furnishings, which he left to his staff and architect, than he was in deliverance from the atmosphere of mockery he'd suffered since early fall.

The count slept better for a while even in his temporary home some blocks west of the Congress hotel, just knowing that lumber for the French Legation would soon wind its way from Bastrop to the knoll overlooking town. He felt he could put up with threats from the innkeeper and incursions by the hotel pigs. Sometime in the next year, he reasoned, he would rise above the petty fray over unpaid lodging bills.

The Harper women were no more likely than any other peace-loving residents to guess that pigs would bring the conflict to culmination. Though, as close as they were to the Bullock Hotel, they were hardly strangers to frustration over the innkeeper's un-penned livestock.

"I'm going to make dancing slippers this New Years out of sows' ears," Adeline threatened several days after Christmas. She stepped into their Congress avenue home in her stocking feet, because pig dung needed to be scraped from the heels of her boots before they were fit to be brought inside. She couldn't guess how so many people living in tents avoided the filth.

"Before all this started," Yarico said, shaking her head, "one of you two might have taken a hammer on over and politely asked Mr. Bullock, did he need help securing the pig pen."

"Well, I'm not the one...speaking French and...getting on people's bad side," Maggie laughed.

"Whatever made the hotel folks think we're so friendly with the count."

"We went to that poor girl's funeral—"

"We did, Yarico, and I don't recall Dubois was in attendance." Adeline didn't think her own mother would have found much to admire about the French count. But he and the hotel owner were equal contenders, in her view, for best at holding the worst grudge. She knew Yarico's dislike for the dignitary ran deeper.

"I don't care to have people thinking every Frenchman must be like that—showing so little regard for the pitiful way that New Orleans girl ended up."

Adeline and Maggie both reached for an embroidery hoop, something to look at instead of Yarico's expression, because it was so unusual for her to express hostility. The two women had worried over Yarico's uncharacteristic moodiness during their second year in Austin.

They understood how her adjustment to a new setting took more time. It was not so easy for her to discover townspeople willing to exchange amicable greetings. Fewer females of any type—sociable or aloof— resided in Austin than had called Bastrop home. When the count's attendants stayed in town, however, the Harper home brightened. Among his domestics, there certainly were people who loved to exchange greetings and thread with Yarico, who loved saying her French was *à la perfection!*

This *Count-No- Count*, for causing strained relations all along the main streets, was hard for the town to tolerate. On some days Austin citizens, and even inconsequential passersby, spoke against anyone seeming to take up for Dubois. All three Harper women shuddered to remember the drunk who had staggered across the street to threaten them, and over nothing but their friendliness to the French household. It was ridiculous!

"I'm afraid...it's my illness—" Maggie couldn't easily endure Yarico's unhappy moods—"that's put a strain on both of you this year."

"No, Miss Maggie," Yarico stood up and pulled the shawl around the older woman's shoulders. "I'm surely not faulting you for a thing."

"Well we know—plenty of folks see the difference—that the count's staff are fine people—especially Rosanne and Pluyette, and that Bernard is as pleasant a coachman as you'll find from any country. He's a gentleman, if you ask me," Adeline said, smiling at Maggie.

"We've noticed him walking you home...after you visit with Rosanne...and the other housekeepers," Maggie said, winking at her niece.

"He doesn't want any pigs running me down," Yarico said bruskly. Then she seemed to reconsider her tone of voice. "Yes, he's a gentleman. And it's ladies' bonnets I work on while I'm over there—it's not just for visiting. Madame Rosanne let me take one apart from last year, sketch out the pieces and make a pattern."

"Paris bonnets—like the ones they wore when they arrived—with the long bows?"

"Anyway," Yarico said, being somewhat coy again. "That's what I work on over there when I visit. I don't even look at the hotel when I go down to the corner, and I watch for any sign of *le grand monsieur* when I go on up Pecan. If the count is at his residence, I don't set one foot inside."

At New Years, the three women spent a quiet day and evening. It was their second winter away from Bastrop, and they couldn't help thinking about the neighborly dining and dancing that ended December among the pine trees. While there had been some glitter and moving of carriages to mark the holidays in Austin, most of the legislators had gone back for the month to be with their families in the far-flung parts of the republic.

Dr. Roberston's congressional term was drawing to a close, but he still had not decided on an adequate home site in town for his family, even though his medical supply business and practice were finally growing. With him gone to Bastrop at least through January, Adeline, Maggie, and Yarico experienced a stretch of tranquil winter days, except for interference from the Bullock pigs.

It may have been the relative quiet of the city streets tempting the hotel owner into even shoddier livestock oversight. Whatever the cause, an increase in the pig nuisance was noticed by all residents along Congress and Pecan. Not only had the animals gained in numbers, but they had also demonstrated an appetite for damage as they had never shown before—to various gardens, fences, laundry lines, bench legs, handbills, and feed bags in stables belonging to others.

One could not be sure in late January whether the rumors were true, but the story traveling from Bullock's hotel to both lengths of Pecan was that a number of hotel pigs had run directly into the Count Dubois' open door and chewed on some of the Frenchman's important documents, as well as his bed linens. There was no doubting that a majority in town chuckled about such a scene. But there was also dread that another shoe would drop before this stage of the contest was over. Other people on the count's end of Pecan had used gunfire to scatter the pigs away from their property. Dubois apparently put the order differently to his secretary, Monsieur Pluyette.

In February, when several of Bullock's pigs came marauding again on the property where the count resided, his head employee did as he was told, picked up a rifle, and shot several of the animals dead. For days, people along the cross-streets peered from behind window curtains or peeked from their tent flaps, expecting to see Bullock and the count marking off the paces for a duel. Adeline and her family hoped they would not spot that sandy-haired drunkard bellowing in the street that French speakers needed to be shot. There was no countdown in the main avenue. What did occur within the week, though, put a halt to any jest used previously in describing the town's feud.

One night in the packed dirt street, Mr. Bullock himself accosted Monsieur Pluyette "for killing my pigs!" The two came to such blows that the French fellow's life was in danger for several days, and the other doctor had to be called from his office near the Colorado, since Dr. Robertson had not yet come back to town. The thrashing not only incensed Dubois enough to start legal action against the hotel owner, it also created a new level of fear among the count's servants.

Rosanne refused to walk along the street unless accompanied by the footman, and Bernard escorted the kitchen help whenever they needed to walk to the small grocery around the corner. The ridiculous feud escalated beyond any laughing matter. The very idea, many inhabitants agreed, that the capital of this new republic should become a nest of vigilante retribution, unseemly threats in the dark—such uncivilized *repartee* was infuriating!

"I have a mind to talk to President Lamar himself next time I see him walk down the street, or beg Mr. Houston to put an end to all this!" Adeline said to her aunt. "I've heard there's taunting endured by all Dubois' people, not that the count hasn't been insufferable—"

"I don't think that poor man should have met up with a beating... for following what the master of the house says to do..." Maggie's hand had quivered as she spoke. Any additional stress worsened the woman's condition, and Adeline was sorry she had let her own anger show.

"It'll be all right," she said. "But it does seem such a waste of energy. And poor Pluyette won't recover completely until spring. It'll be all right, though," she said again. "Maybe Mr. Bullock's pigs will take to gnawing on their owner's toes while he sleeps—"

"Oh, Adeline!"

"I'll be glad when Yarico doesn't have to fear walking occasionally without an escort."

"I don't think she went to the Dubois house this afternoon."

"Of course, she did," Adeline said. "She's been gone since three, I'm sure. She's over with Rosanne, doing something with a new bonnet."

"I thought... maybe you sent her on a longer...errand."

"What do you mean?"

"She pulled up my shawl," Maggie said, working to remember, "... and she kissed me on the forehead—"

"What do you mean?"

"When she left…she had that handbag with her…the big tapestry one…I thought you sent her to get—"

"She'll be back shortly, I expect," Adeline said, "but I think I'll go knock at the Dubois house, just to let her know it's getting late."

Adeline had the kind of funny feeling that she'd felt five years ago in the widow Bedeford's dining room, when Aunt Maggie had told her she was not her kin, after all. She had the odd feeling of watching her own motions from a distance, of walking and of standing frozen, at the same time. It was only a short distance across Congress to the hotel corner, but her head was throbbing as if she'd run in the dark on a hill she didn't know, and when she turned along the cold dirt beyond the Bullock establishment, she found that end of Pecan looked oddly unfamiliar. She thought she might get sick when she reached the block where Dubois had stationed himself, his stables, and his staff. She hadn't liked to go anywhere near the somewhat larger log structure, ever since the death of the young woman in the sweltering summer.

It surprised her that Yarico could make herself knock even at the back door of the residence, where the domestics and delivery people entered and left. Adeline suffered that same nauseated twinge she fought off five years ago, and she was telling herself again that there was something she should have guessed all along, that there was something she should have known, that she might have been able to prevent. Something was terribly wrong, and she couldn't help feeling she would have herself to blame for a shift to the unthinkable.

When she reached the count's front gate, she refused to walk in toward the main entrance. She went around to the back door, where no pigs rooted, fortunately, but where Yarico must have knocked time after time for a chat with her French friends.

"Mademoiselle" said Rosanne, finally answering. "You should come to the front, *non?*"

"Bonsoir, Madame, I'm looking for Yarico—"

"Yarico? Non. She has not been here today—"

"*Non?* Not here?" Adeline hadn't planned what she might say next. "Did anyone else—did Bernard talk to her today?"

"*Mais non*—Bernard is driving the coach of Monsieur Dubois today. He should be back *tout de suite*—it will be dark soon, I think."

"She hasn't been here?"

"Bernard is driving monsieur. Poor Pluyette cannot drive this month. We are alone working in the *cuisine,*" she said. "Today has been very dull, Mademoiselle. Tell Mademoiselle Yarico to come visit tomorrow, *d'accord?*"

"I will."

"Her sewing is *a la perfection, non?*"

"Yes. It is."

"Come to the front door next time, Mademoiselle Adeline, *s'il vous plait.* Monsieur would not like this way."

Adeline shivered as she headed back down Pecan Street to Congress. The sun dropped down quickly behind the western hills in the late afternoon, and it was easy to find oneself in the plunging temperatures in early evening, and without enough wraps. By the time she turned the corner at the hotel, she was cold to the bone. And when Adeline made it to the walkway between the connected cabins, she looked back again, out onto the covered porch where the north wind was gusting down toward the river.

She wanted to see Yarico sitting—for some silly reason that she would laugh to explain—out in the cold. But the doctor's side of the porch was empty, too, and there was no one on the other end of the walkway either. The last colors of the sunset turned red and purple, and when Adeline made herself open the door on the women's side, there was only Maggie in the candlelight, who had managed to get herself into bed and had already drifted off. Hours later, when her aunt had reached the deep sleep that permits steady snoring, Adeline still could not make her own shivering stop.

She was shaking before dawn the next morning and wondering if, when the gray room took on some sunlight, she would be able to climb out of bed and face the day. The next twenty-four hours and the next weeks were no easier for Adeline Harper. In March, she felt no difference between the festive Day of Independence and the somber memorial days later in the month. She vacillated between self-recrimination and anger. Why had she made the Harper family move from the protection and serenity of the Bastrop pines? Why had Yarico deserted her, after having traveled with her and Margaret Linder this far, to this strange, unpredictable territory?

Adeline possessed enough cautious judgment, and a wealth of protectiveness toward Yarico, not to send out any hired hands in search of a run-away slave. She banished any grim imaginings that *Belle-Mère* was stolen or attacked. Inquiries came from the Dubois household. Rosanne called one morning and to ask if poor Yarico could have been a victim of Bullock, *le villain!* But Adeline didn't believe the feud between the count and the hotel keeper to have any direct connection to Yarico's disappearance. Yet, the vanished woman could very well have felt threatened. After Pluyette's shocking injuries, she could very well have feared for her life. And with only a girl under twenty for protection? With no count, no man of any kind to stand up to dangers in the street? Still, no—Adeline did not think Yarico could have been abducted from the streets of Austin.

She would not permit herself to think the worst might have happened. As distraught as she was to conclude her confidante had abandoned her, Adeline taught herself to take some comfort in the final recollection Aunt Maggie shared. Yarico had taken her tapestry bag, her traveling bag. She was gone on her own volition.

But not too many years ago, Adeline had watched a friendly neighbor sail away. He and his cousins sailed off to the horizon on what all believed would be a short parting from their home country. And all were lost. None of the kind men—none ever seen again.

Sometimes after Aunt Maggie fell asleep, Adeline took out the sketch Madame Genet had given them. The sheet of drawing paper was kept within the only Pagnol book to make it across the Brazos in the run-away scrape. A paper miracle, it remained unbent and without smudges. One night Adeline looked so long at the image of Yarico, she thought the quiet figure in the background, in the shadows of Avignon, would surely look up from her needlework and explain herself or speak some reassuring farewell. She listened for Yarico's familiar, comforting voice.

"Just tell me where you are," Adeline wept to herself. She couldn't remember when she had said to her, as a daughter does, *I love you.* Was it somewhere on their journey, before reaching New Orleans? Before the artist had come to sketch? Was it on the trail after the three crossed into Texas on their own? "Just tell me you know how much I love you!"

"Addy?...Are you...Addy dear?" Aunt Maggie had struggled out of bed and was standing behind her.

"I was just—" Before she rose, Adeline slipped the picture back in the book and fumbled for a different paper. "I just get to reading this fond letter from Zeke sometimes," she lied.

"First love...is hard to...lose," her aunt nodded. "Seems like the end of...the world." She was already turning back to her bed. "But don't get to carrying on so...Addy dear." Aunt Maggie rested her hand on the rosebud quilt. "Let's be a little quiet. We don't want...to wake Yarico."

Her aunt had said such wrenching things many times in the last weeks, but Adeline's hands still drifted up to her own lips. Maggie was not quite in this world. "Let dear Yarico sleep. She...gets up so early...to go off where she sews..."

If anything provided distraction in the spring, besides the explosion of red and blue flowers in the hills and meadows around Austin, it was the equally spectacular estate rising up for Monsieur Dubois on the hill beyond east Pecan Street. Adeline sometimes walked the distance, especially if her aunt was having a good morning and looked well enough to sit on the porch or inside with some easy knitting.

In twenty minutes, the young woman could reach the end of Pecan. It might take twenty years before people could call it *Sixth*. Then after crossing over to the narrow Bastrop path, she followed it a short distance before circling north. The hill on which the French Legation rose up was too steep to be approached directly by horses, and the trail winding up proved more pleasant for travelers on foot as well. Since Count de Saligny rather suddenly himself disappeared from the scene in April—it was said to be another New Orleans vacation—a steady trickle of curious onlookers helped wear a trail to the sumptuous property.

That spring the basic structure was complete, and in spite of Monsieur Dubois' exit from legal entanglements in Austin, he left most of his servants behind to furnish and maintain the quarters. There was nothing like it nearby, and it rivaled any Texas architecture claiming elegance beyond the central vicinity. Log dwellings and abundant tent domiciles in Austin proper compared to it like kennels to castles.

A few plantation homes that Adeline remembered on the coast and riverbanks in Louisiana boasted pillars, as the main house did. Six columns lined the edge of a broad covered porch, which stretched across the entire façade. Double doors opened from the dog-trot hallway, suggesting the same style in which Dr. Robertson's cabins in town adjoined. But the exterior of the house was fashioned of perfectly smoothed planks, painted white. Dark louvered doors from each identical half opened separately to the front. Behind the main house, was the kitchen —at least twice the size of settlement cabins the Harper women had lived in—with its massive cooking hearth. And located farther to the north on the property were stables, grand enough to accommodate Monsieur's coach and smaller carriage as well as several horses. Servants' quarters stood just down the north edge of the hill, and from the south side, the Colorado River could be glimpsed off through the trees.

A visitor could admire all these features from the outside, and Adeline often loitered at some distance from other townspeople, who curved up into the edge of the legation property, only to gawk briefly and then depart as if they had made a wrong turn. The excursion was a favorite Sunday afternoon pastime among Austin inhabitants. Adeline, therefore preferred any other time. Solitude consoled her. On a day when no other town individual peered from the edge of Legation grounds, she felt no qualms about walking around to the back of the property and knocking at the kitchen door. It was predictably open that late in May.

"Ah, bonjour, Mademoiselle Adeline—Everyone is at the springs, you know. Would you like to take a water jug and go surprise Rosanne?"

"Bonjour, Giselle," she said reaching for the porcelain jug.

"You have not the sad look this morning, mademoiselle—"

"*Non*, the flowers are making me happy!"

"Don't pick the ones on your way to the spring—" The kitchen maid laughed. "That Bernard, he will be a man crying if you pick his *belles fleurs!*"

"Moi aussi—I leave them where they grow."

"I never see a man more in love with *zee* beautiful!"

Adeline knew where the small grove of oaks and pecans was at the east side of the property. She knew the architects reserved that part of the hilltop and left it uncleared. The springs ran there, and it was an easy place for the cows Dubois kept to find shade in the hottest months. The white flowers that sprang up along the path to the water source proved to be daisies—*marguerites*. Yarico could have told her if that was what the French called them.

Adeline hoped she might surprise Bernard down by the legation springs that morning, as well as Rosanne, because the few times she had suddenly appeared before Monsieur's coachman, she felt he was about to say something to her. She felt when she asked, as nonchalantly as possible whether he had heard anything from or about Yarico, that he'd had a difficult time containing himself. But that morning she found only Rosanne and another maid, too shy to speak.

"Ah bon! Now I do not have to come down here again in one morning," she said smiling, and taking the jug to dip into the fresh pool. "But what have I to complain, look what a day—merveilleux!" When their employer—owner, as it was the case for at least three—was not in town nor likely to be, these French were some of the happiest people Adeline had ever met.

268

"I came to see if you needed any help pleating the draperies, or anything hemmed," she said. "My aunt would be able to work on any straight seam, I'm sure."

"Come and look! We will go to the main house," Rosanne said. "Then you must stay for *déjeuner!*"

"I can't stay too long—our *très petit* porch will be too warm before long, and I must—"

"Yes, yes, you take very good care of your aunt, and we hear all the time what a good niece you are." Rosanne stopped herself and blushed from chatting too much. "Well, let us hurry back with the water, and I show you the big house, how it looks!"

The front and back doors of the dog-trot hallway had been opened and a lovely breeze found its way through from south off the river. Coming in the back entrance, a room opened immediately on the right for monsieur's grand office. A fireplace defined the inner wall—"a fireplace in every room!"—and against an inner wall stood an elegant desk, where Adeline could imagine Pluyette taking up a fine pen and making artwork of whatever the count dictated. The high ceilings were smooth grooved boards, and it seemed fantasy to see a room finished overhead with building material less rustic than peeled or split logs. What Mrs. Bedeford's ceilings had looked like, or her own square house at Macon, Adeline had gradually forgotten.

The other room on that west end of the dogtrot was a formal salon, with a red velvet settee and matching velvet chairs that made the young woman doubt anyone accustomed to such seating luxury could handle the rough plank arrangement behind a team of oxen. Across the breezy hallway was another formal room for dining or entertaining—for sophisticated banter. Would she know how to even sit in delicately curving chairs? The embellishments on cabinets and decorative tables reminded Adeline how far such pieces must have traveled before finding a home in central Texas. Hatchets and crude saws were incapable of these flourishes. She wondered who had time to shape raw elements into marvelous artwork. Well, she thought, clothes were different and could be played with discreetly by candlelight after the work of a day was done.

"But now, you must see where it is Monsieur retires—if ever he is to spend a night in his estate—what do you think, Mademoiselle Adeline?"

"I think—the dreams in this room…belong to someone I have never known."

"Ah—poètique!"

"This kind of bed might be against the law in Texas!"

"Oh no—do not tell, we beg you, we have enough of the trouble about Texas law!"

"Je plaisante—I'm only playing!"

"Ah ça," Rosanne said, shaking her head. "But it is a bed worthy of New Orleans, non?"

Yes, Adeline agreed silently, and what must have been the cost for shipping the count's furnishings! She could not imagine the fee for hauling a canopy bed, delicate settees, fine cherry desks and sideboards across the impossible trails of inner Texas, and then for bringing them in wagons along the last skimpy path from Bastrop. How could one afford to vacation in the jewel of the Mississippi after spending enough to create such luxury in this rough territory?

"But, I'm staying too long," she told Rosanne. "Dr. Robertson is making new arrangements in town, though. This summer, my aunt and I will move into a nice little cabin of our own down closer here on Pecan, since the doctor wants to enlarge his office and house there on Congress."

"You will visit more often?"

"*Bien sûr!* And he still wants me to manage his medical supply books, and—"

"Your head for being a doctor—this I have heard too!"

"He's lending us his smaller rig, so—"

"Bring your Tante Maggie! But of course, she must see this view!"

They were standing on the front porch of the Legation. In only one setting, as a child, had Adeline enjoyed the sensation of looking at creation from the top of the world. This hill on the edge of Austin was not Sweet Pine, but it would be difficult to stand looking out on the green hills mounding up behind the western edge of town, to look directly out onto the curving world, without sensing colorful life in bloom below. Adeline could never leave the expansive front porch lookout without feeling that Yarico was alive and well somewhere in some world, looking back upon her with tender admiration.

Dr. Robertson made the move as easy as he could on Adeline and her aunt, and in many ways the relocation of their home, to an end of

270

Pecan least affected by the Dubois tumult, was like a new start for the two remaining Harpers. Adeline and Maggie both enjoyed the gentle stream of families, more than they had the previous year's political ebb and flow. German settlers camped on the outskirts of town, getting their bearings and accumulating last supplies before planning a final leg across the Colorado.

Other cheerful newcomers rolled through Bastrop to Austin, hoping to settle somewhere in the area where attacks against homesteaders were infrequent, but where hunting would be a sure enterprise if farming proved too difficult.

Without Monsieur de Saligny in residence, the Legation staff grew relaxed enough to test the waters of enterprise themselves, and one morning Madame Rosanne stopped by Adeline's and Maggie's cabin to give them each a cinnamon stick from the candy shop she and Giselle just opened.

"After today, one penny!" she called back, on her way up to Legation Hill. "And we may be selling bonnets and fashion shawls if we start the mercantile we have in mind!"

They were sitting in their chairs—with rockers and spindle backs that Dr. Robertson and his wife insisted they have. It had been a perfect summer, only two days in July too hot to seem bearable, and then a burst of rain in August broke the worst of impossible temperatures. Maggie had just finished telling a neighbor from Ireland to come over the next morning and they would look at pillow case edging. The neighbor knew how to tat lace, and Maggie wanted to watch, even if her own fingers didn't do what she ordered them to do so much any more.

"Straight hems…are all I'm good for," she had said to Adeline, before unwrapping the cinnamon stick that Rosanne had given her. The orange-pink sky down the street was so beautiful in the early evening that she and Adeline forgot entirely to worry about whether Mr. Bullock was going to be arguing with anyone out in front of his hotel, several blocks away. Any such frays, though, seemed over. In fact, in the last months, he had taken to tipping his hat when Adeline passed by either walking or in their fast rig on her way to Dr. Robertson's Medical Supply.

It was a softly changing sunset, where a water color artist might reach for pale blue and rose and the fairest purple all at the same time. And Adeline and Maggie were just rocking in their chairs, because they were adjusting finally to what life turned out to be—moving and resting and changing and stopping and resting again.

And Maggie did not say anything for a while. Her chair had stopped rocking or moving. It was silent for a spell as the sky melted to its deepest shades. And Adeline understood that life's colors would never stop changing. She knew that she would just sit for another hour. She would sit until the sun disappeared altogether, and then she would go over quietly to talk with the people next door, after the Irish woman had taken the time to put her children to bed. And then the lady and her husband would come and help Adeline carry Maggie back into the cabin to lay her down in her bed for the last time.

For a while, Adeline Harper just sat on the porch in the rocker, and wondered at how much kindness this woman Margaret Linder had shown her these last years. And she wished she could take Yarico's hand and feel a little less alone in the world.

The burial was attended by the same group who had seen merciful words said over the New Orleans slave. Reverend Haynie was soon moving on from the Austin-Bastrop circuit, but he halted his packing to preside at the service. Shadows rippled through the woods northeast of Austin, and sparrows hopped along the cemetery wall.

Dr. Robertson was there, though his wife was too ill herself to attend, and their newer neighbors along Pecan came along in their wagons, the Irish people and a German couple whose oldest daughter stayed back to care for the younger ones in their tent. Rosanne brought some daisies, and Bernard had not seemed to mind because he was there, nodding while the Lord's Prayer was said in English.

"A preacher is supposed to have a sermon ready," Reverend Haynie started, "about the Good Book lines—'What ye sow, so shall ye reap.' But I'll tell you what—" He wiped his forehead and eyes with a handkerchief. "For the short time I've been in Texas, I have yet to meet a human mean enough to deserve the worst hardship this dang wilderness can throw down." He laughed softly. "Well that's not how the sermon is supposed to go."

He took Adeline's hand and Dr. Robertson's hand and the others took hold of whoever was standing near.

"Here's what I want to say about our Mrs. Margaret Linder." He bowed his head. "She was put on this earth to sew. But Miss Adeline and Miss Yarico, the two who knew her best, came to find out it was people she poured her soul into stitching together—their happiness. Her family and friends made her happy in return. I don't know a one of us here in doubt she had a happiness she deserved."

It was summer, not December, but the German man started humming "Silent Night," and everybody knew the carol. So the music, and the two languages, added a lovely layer to bird song in the woods. It made Adeline think of dance slippers and of how cheerful Maggie had been to just let her toes tap at the Bastrop dance two and a half years ago.

In the fall, a certain stoicism settled into Adeline's demeanor as she adjusted to Maggie's absence too, to being alone. She kept herself busy with teaching again, when she was not keeping the doctor's records or reading his medical books. She had rounds to make with her reading primers and headache powders. She kept busy.

Even though residents of Austin grew increasingly worried about attacks from disgruntled Comanche off the western edge of the city, and the republic had grown more wary of new attacks from Mexican generals still seething—including their new President Santa Anna!—Adeline had reached a certain unflappable state of mind. Either she had achieved an immutable level of serenity, or she was reaching for self-possession in a way that only the most fragile do. Rosanne was worried about her.

"Let me put your hair into something," she said one afternoon on her way back from the fashion mercantile. "You will be going to dances in the holidays, *non?*"

"I really don't think—"

"But, of course—a young thing like you. How old are you, Mademoiselle?"

"Next February, I'll turn nineteen—"

"Mon dieu! Quelle belle âge!"

"Rosanne—Do you think the count will keep his house?"

"What are you asking?"

"It looks as if Sam Houston is going to be President again—that's probably a good thing, but I'm wondering about the capital—"

"He does not so much like Austin," Rosanne said nodding. "Yes, I have heard Bernard and the others talking about what Monsieur will do—."

"I just don't know whether to stay...what I'll do if you...and the others leave—"

"Mais non, Mademoiselle—you are worry too much," she said. "Look at your hair now, just a comb here and...here—voilà!"

The Robertsons insisted on taking Adeline along with them to Bastrop for the winter ball. It was the end of the term, and the President

Lamar himself was well enough to be there. She stayed with the Ellingers, who had added an upstairs over their gunsmith shop. Mr. Ellinger was far cheerier than when Adeline had seen him last, and Tabitha prattled so about the decorations and her dress that Adeline could hardly get in a question about the boys and their studies.

"Well, it's not like they were ever to look at a book the same way after you left!"

"They've both grown a foot, if not two—"

"Let's hope they don't call a shootout over you, looking so pretty the way you do—"

"We'll remind them I specialize in stitches, not bullet holes—"

"Ole Horace'll be there, and I don't doubt but he'll be raising up his pants leg to show off what you did," Tabitha laughed.

"I don't much feel like dancing or bragging. Maybe, I should just stay close to a hearth here in town and tend someone's babies, while all this is going on." Her friend had gone suddenly quiet, so Adeline looked at her quizzically. It was best not to ask women, but to let them offer information about such topics.

"No, no you're going to be at this dance," Tabitha went on in a rush, "and—well I was just hoping Horace doesn't get hold of enough brandy that his britches go down instead of up!"

The evening of the winter ball was cold and bright, and even though worries about attacks on every edge of the Texas frontier had citizens of the republic rightly worried, the Bastrop inhabitants—those wise enough to stay put in the beautiful pines— exuded a level of merriment beyond what daily news might prescribe. Mirabeau Lamar had recovered enough from his ailments to dance with several ladies in the community, and the music inside the courthouse where the festivities were held reminded Adeline of the jolly New Years she had celebrated there. The fiddler was not Mrs. Moore's brother. Instead, three had come all the way from La Grange to play for the gathering of Texas dignitaries and the friendly people of the Lost Pines!

But, Adeline couldn't help thinking of Maggie and Yarico. And when she looked at the silk dancing slippers scooting across the new wooden planks in the courthouse floor, she had to take her cloak and heavy shawl and go outside to the walkway on Bastrop's main street. A flood of townspeople enjoyed the street as if it were a second dance floor, and while most folks were stepping to the rhythmic sounds they heard from inside, a solitary street fiddler first swung his instrument into the mood of more somber Christmas carols, and then steered on to other solemn folk tunes in his repertoire.

It had been some months since Colonel Mc Leod's men came by Dr. Robertson's office for supplies to be taken on the Santa Fe expedition. News back from Santa Fe was not good. In keeping with her stoic response to Maggie's death, though, Adeline had refused to consider what suffering another Georgia fellow might be going through on the long march to a Mexican prison.

But someone in the crowd around the fiddler, thinking of those unable to celebrate, made a request in remembrance. The song the musician took up was not about the ruinous Santa Fe effort, nor about spellbound shepherds at a nativity scene. It was a melody Adeline remembered hearing first out on the open Texas plains not far from the Trinity River. One line had plaited itself in her memory, even when victory at San Jacinto was all that most fleeing settlers would let themselves comprehend.

She had heard that melody more frequently in the last years. The ballad was composed after the loss of a British sea captain who sailed away up north looking for a passage across frigid arctic waters to the west coast. But like any powerful song, the words had become her own. She knew what the lyrics were going to be as soon as she heard the fiddle strains, but she was drawn along on silk shoes she had hastily sewn for herself, to the edge of a group listening for the singer's words on that cold December night.

> *The fate of Franklin, no tongue can tell.*

Adeline knew it was just that she hadn't been able to cry for Maggie yet. And she knew it was just that she had never really let herself believe that Yarico could be gone from her life.

> *Ten thousand pounds would I freely give,*
> *To learn that Franklin on this earth lives!*

When she started crying, it felt as if she would never stop in this life. She carried the light blue handkerchief in her deepest pocket, always, but she wouldn't let herself bring it out, for fear she might reach too far off a swell of emotion, lose her balance, and not make it back to shore.

It was one of Tabitha's sons who came and half-carried her back to his father's shop, and then he sent the other brother for Mrs. Ellinger. She had always been so kind to the Harper women, and mostly she just let Adeline cry herself out, though what she said was comforting, the way mothers can sometimes provide a reassurance that's lacking from even a good friend.

"You never know, darlin', when everything in this poor world will brighten up." She just let Adeline cry like a little girl, probably for the last time in the young woman's life. "If sorrow comes to a point where 'no tongue can tell,' well I'm of a mind that joy springs up in an equal way, and you'll be hard pressed for words when that side of living comes along, too."

Chapter 19   Belle-Mère

During the year of Monsieur Dubois de Saligny's unofficial leave of absence, nothing was gained or lost about rapport between France and the Republic of Texas. Though Austin politicians had hoped recognition of sovereignty would be followed by financial aid, France offered Texas no significant loans. And though the cash poor republic was pleased to win international goodwill, Texans did not welcome extensive French settlements to buffer them from Mexican aggression. Loans being contingent on settlement rights, no partnership was made. The count could at least relax about the feud. Unpaid bills and renegade pigs were neither country's headline news.

In the spring of 1842, talk shifted again to statehood and, in the meantime, how best to fend off bothersome raids from across the border into west Texas. Incredibly, troops from south of the Rio Grande slipped in as far as Goliad and San Antonio once again. Meeting no resistance, they raised the Mexican flag and immediately retreated back across the wide river. Their pesky movements wrung belligerent talk from Texans, but the calmest leaders prevailed, and diplomatic solutions were given preference. President Sam Houston, in office again after sitting out one term, decided to move the capital back to the safety of his namesake city.

Except for the small group of French colonists that Henri Castro arranged to bring across the ocean to settle between the Colorado River and San Antonio, people began trickling not *to* but *away* from the Austin area. Newcomers seeking the western edge of the established republic went no farther than Bastrop. It was an opportune time for Count Dubois to pause briefly in the vicinity of his estate one last time, collect whatever items deserved rounding up, and retreat to New Orleans where he could serve as a permanently removed chargé d'affaires to Texas.

When a late norther threatened the peach buds in the first week of April, Adeline saw smoke from three chimneys at the Legation. She wanted to take the rig, which the Robertsons insisted she keep as her own at Christmas, on up the lovely hill. She assumed the extra activity to mean her French friends would be leaving soon with their employer. But she had no desire to cross paths with Dubois. She waited a few days until only the usual curl of gray rose from the great stone chimney of the kitchen behind the main house.

As she rounded the lower curve of the path leading up, she was not surprised to see four wagons being loaded, and Rosanne giving directions to the count's attendants. Adeline had grown used to scenes of departure. In town, hardly any tents now flapped in the breeze along Pecan Street or Congress. While many of the cabins were still inhabited, the frenzy involved in packing and testing out the weight of wagons had replayed many times in Austin since the republic's capital reversed itself to Houston.

"Non, Giselle! Pas comme ça!" The lady in charge placed her hands on her hips and disdainfully shook her head about the way the count's Provençal platters were being wrapped. "Ah—Bonjour, Mademoiselle! We are glad it is you and not Monsieur again! Non, he has departed. He is only too happy to leave this place for the last time, but us—non, we are more than a little sad."

"I was afraid I might miss you," Adeline said, wrapping the reins of her horse on a post not far from the kitchen. Her friend came to give her a hug and a kiss on each cheek.

"Yes, we will be gone soon—tomorrow morning, at the latest. Monsieur says there is a ship in Galveston, if we can be there in two weeks—That seems so much time, but oh là là, these roads of Texas in a spring. So, if we have only the chill and no rain, we must move quickly to make the port." She stopped to look again at Adeline, and she still shook her head. "Look at how I am talking too much. I will miss you, Mademoiselle. We have a friendly hill, a beautiful hill here for this year, non?"

"I don't know what I'm going to do without you."

"You must come visit New Orleans—" Adeline could see she was distracted, and she thought it best to just say goodbye and let them finish their work.

"I made you and Giselle a little silk pouch of wildflower seeds—some from last spring—I don't know—"

"Merci—Oh, mon dieu—I was going to send Bernard down the hill if we did not see you—letters for you, Miss Adeline! All pieces of mail for you with your name! Monsieur Pluyette brought along a large valise of mail from Velasco and Brazoria—who knows where else!— all the way to this place it should have gone, but he says here the mail has always been so slow—and now it may never get down *zee* hill to Austin as it should—"

"Some letters for me?"

"Two and one paquet!" Rosanne fetched the keys to the main house, and was motioning for Adeline to follow her. "Mon dieu—I almost forgot! In here, Mademoiselle—you can sit at Monsieur Pluyette's desk and read. They are gone for good—it is only us here."

One large envelope was addressed from Macon, Georgia, and the other was from Bastrop, in a hand she didn't recognize. Rosanne had left Adeline in the count's study, and she could not quite dismiss the sensation that she had broken into a room at Versailles and was handling documents of worldly import.

The letter script was in an unsteady hand, but she recognized the voice to be the widow Bedeford's. Harper women still had a friend in Macon!

My dear Adeline,

Praise God! I am so happy to receive the Christmas card from you and am very surprised, since June is not when one expects such greetings. Mr. Collins, our new postmaster, brought it to me himself on his way home, as they are still so very thoughtful about any mail that comes from Texas.

We have seen a flood of grief here, and I fear our lively town will never be the same. Time, it may be, is no salve for some wounds. Mr. George Tidwell has taken up the cause to see that Texas delivers to the surviving families what poor payment our boys were promised for their valiant action.

Of spare comfort will worldly paper be to their mothers and sisters.

I must write but little more, lest my own sorrow rob me of strength. I cannot say how the families greet each new year, except by faith.

I am so cheered, nonetheless, that you and your Aunt Margaret and Yarico are well and flourishing in your adopted country. Most surely I am happy that our purchase of blue silk brought you some measure of joy.

In the envelope is a page of the Telegraph from May, 1836. You undoubtedly know how the article reports the outcome at Goliad. May the poem printed on the same page give you some comfort, as it did many in Macon.

Fondly,

Louisa Bedeford

Adeline looked only momentarily at the folded newspaper page that the Macon woman had included. She did know what news the report would contain. She felt she would need to take those passages slowly, and that whatever the poem might say would be something to look over on Sunday mornings in May or later in summer.

The smaller envelope from Bastrop was making her wonder whether Mrs. Ellinger might be reporting news about her boys or her husband, but when she opened the seal, she found there was yet another worn envelope inside, and a little note that had been set in alongside slipped out and fluttered to the count's splendid pine floor. There were only two sentences written on the scrap paper, and when she saw the name signed at the bottom, she turned around quickly to see if the man Bernard might be standing right there, playing some silly game about the mail. But Adeline's memory had been given a faint nudge, and she looked again intently at the second envelope resting inside.

The message from Bernard said,

> *There is more, Mademoiselle Adeline. It will be for me to explain, and it will be for you to not be angry. Bernard*

The envelope inside was one she had seen before. In reading Mrs. Bedeford's letter, all her recollections of Macon had come to the surface. Even though the Harper women's stay in town had lasted only a month, there was so much to remember about the vibrant streets, and the academy lessons, the two-story pale house, the candlelight ceremony, and Yarico's odd little shed in the back yard. The older envelope was the one she had seen Yarico secretly take from her boot late one evening. Adeline had seen her read, or recite, the contents of a yellow piece of paper before folding it again and hiding it away from all eyes. Adeline opened Yarico's envelope, and read, as one might be struck witnessing a resurrection.

The document was dated the year Adeline had turned five, and when it started off :

"*I, Delphine Pagnol Harper,*" the content that followed took on momentous importance. This was a declaration in her mother's handwriting, something that Yarico had kept all these years. It was, as she found reading on, precisely for Miss Yarico Harper—

> *"to be given her legal and complete freedom from all Harper ownership and legal obligations forever, to pursue her own happiness on the date of my death. She expressly is invited to remain in the company of my only child Adeline Therese Harper and to provide care, if she so wishes, until my daughter reaches her sixteenth birthday, at which time the trust for Adeline's education*

will be dispensed by Macon attorney, Joshua Gibbs. What sewing implements Yarico Harper possesses are her own, and what monetary support she or Adeline's legal guardian, my sister Margaret Linder, might require from my estate, I trust my daughter Adeline to dispense justly, with gratitude."

Adeline was unable to move. She tried to take in the implications and the dates, and at the same time it seemed impossible that she should be the person holding the precious sheet of paper proving Yarico's emancipation—unless Yarico were still alive and entrusting her with it! Unless, her *belle-mère* had indeed perished or been stolen, and the document was worthless, except as a poignant memorial.

Absently, almost numbly, Adeline took Monsieur Pluyette's letter opener and cut the strings on the small package that also bore her name and Margaret Linder's as equal recipients. On top of folded tissue was another letter to them both, in Mr. Gibbs' handwriting—an apology for the means of delivery, but a short testament to the necessity of closing all accounts in their name. He said something about a small sum being enough to convince the uncle to sign a severance agreement. The rest was theirs, to be shared as Delphine Harper had wished. Under the tissue was a velveteen box with three thick sections of American bank notes that Adeline had no faculties to assess.

Footsteps approached from the kitchen walkway to the main house, and Adeline rose next to the chair where she'd been reading the mail. She thought she might have to be taken to the spring and revived by supernatural powers if it were Yarico, but it was, as the note on the scrap had suggested, Bernard who had come to see mademoiselle's state of mind and temperament.

"Is she alive? Tell me!"

"Yes, Mademoiselle Adeline."

"Oh, my darling Yarico!" She put her arms around Bernard and began to cry and laugh at the same time."

"You are not so angry?"

"Thank God!"

"She is in Bastrop, Mademoiselle." He had stepped back in wonderment at Adeline's response. "She said you would be happy, but it was too difficult for her to come today."

"Why didn't she— just leave? She could have left—long ago!"

"She wants you to see the yellow paper, the letter your *chère maman* gave to her."

"My mother—"

"There is another paper, Mademoiselle." He hesitated, and Adeline thought she might need some of the count's sherry still in a bottle on the desk. "I would not let her send it along, in case you would be angry, but I see—"

"What more? What more?" He was taking something folded, another small document from his vest pocket.

"I and Miss lovely Yarico—we are married since one year." That was when Adeline sat down again at the Dubois desk and put her head down, so that it would not roll off her shoulders as she laughed and cried. Bernard stepped back out of the house again and came back with Rosanne, who looked relieved but was shaking her head about the state of their friend.

"Oh-là-là, Mademoiselle. Look what I have here—three glasses. We will toast to the happiness of Bernard and our Yarico, but we will also say *au revoir* to each other. You know, this husband and wife do not come to Galveston with us— *non*. These two will travel later to the Mississippi, and where do you say, Bernard? Cincinnati? Wherever the fashion mercantile can grow. Ah—Monsieur Dubois, he is not so bad—I think he feels remorse, you know, over the girl from New Orleans. He will release Bernard from his work and see to it—there is safe journey up the river to—you say the north is for free only, *n'est-ce pas?*"

"You must be patient, mademoiselle," was Bernard's final advice. And then they had helped Adeline back into her small carriage, asking if she needed Bernard or someone from the kitchen to drive. But she had recovered enough from her exhilaration to bid farewell one last time to Rosanne, to gather herself and her bundle of mail into the rig and take herself home to the cabin on Pecan.

Adeline spent the summer of 1842 being patient. She spent part of her days as a traveling tutor, since there were fewer children in Austin—the population down to just two hundred from a peak only the year before of nearly one thousand. The candy shop and the fashion mercantile were boarded, as were three fourths of the other shops that had bubbled up and flourished briefly.

Still, it was a more cheerful enterprise for Adeline to walk to the homes of families that had young children, and stay long enough those mornings to see faces brighten at the ability to read a chapter without stumbling, or to come out with the same long division answer that Adeline had on her own piece of slate. She thought the older Irish girl next door might make herself a teacher one day. In the afternoons, she kept busy in Dr. Robertson's Medical Supply, where she had a standing invitation to pore over his volumes on anatomy and diagnosis.

Sometimes, if the early mornings provided any respite from the heat, she would drive her open carriage all the way down to the riverbank, and look out upon the wide glistening curve of water. The rivers of Texas each had their own stories, but she would always think of her first Colorado crossing as the last juncture where she'd enjoyed a child's expectation of fulfillment—for those who dare travel to the farther shore. She wondered what had become of the helpful Tonkawa man, and she wondered whether those two galloping soldiers, in dusty jackets and red pants, had delivered their message north to Sam Houston so quickly that they'd had time to get back to Gonzales and follow Matthew Linder on his ride into the Alamo. Maybe they had been sent next to keep Colonel James Fannin informed and were among the battalion soldiers pinned down in the grassy fields between Goliad and Victoria.

When she stopped in at the stone works shop, she thought it was one of the enterprises abandoned, until a man with a black, gritty apron came out from a ramshackle cabin behind the storefront. He smiled and said that no matter how puny a town might become, there would always be a need for undertakers and engravers. It wasn't so unusual for a family member to ask for a gravestone for someone already buried.

"The burying has to get done, whether you're ready in your heart or in the bank," he said. "Just show me what words you want, and I can have a nice marker chiseled by the middle of the month."

Adeline had been reading and reading again the *Macon Telegraph* article and the poem Louisa Bedeford had sent her. The last line of the first stanza planted itself in her thoughts like a seed. It was from a poem entitled, "Texas and Liberty," and she believed her Aunt Maggie would appreciate resting under words that spoke to the place she'd come to so hopefully, and under words that suggested the ideal for which her beloved nephew had offered his life.

The stone engraver was so pleased with his work that when Adeline arrived with two students to collect the granite headstone, he asked if he and his helper could come along with the group to make sure it was set right.

"Them six words was just right in their meaning, but I had fits trying to figure how they would get theirselves chiseled without too much squeeze or uneven spacing." He couldn't help reading the carved words aloud—

"The Dove Shall Fly to Thee."

"It's beautiful, and the stone is lovely, like the pink that's either sunrise or sunset, it's perfect," Adeline had said. "If I had enough money, I'd ask you to carve about four hundred more just like it."

"Yes'm." He looked around the Eastwood Cemetery, as if wondering how such a tribute could be arranged. "I reckon if someone was to bring the stones on up here, I'd carve this message and every name for free."

For the last two weeks of August and the entire month of September, Adeline practiced patience. She thought several times of driving the rig down to the Colorado and just taking a sharp turn toward Bastrop, following the riverbank and making it to the lost pines in a few hours. *Inexplicable* was the word that came to her mind—that she should have visited in the friendly town for the winter ball less than a year ago and not thought of walking out to the small, simple cabin that had been built for the Harpers on the east side of town.

She had not wanted to be alone, facing memories of where the three once enjoyed relative peace in the sublime setting. But had she gone, Yarico would have been there! It seemed certain to her that the Ellingers must have allowed her and Bernard to use the cabin as their secret dwelling. There had been signs that Rosanne and Bernard, the kitchen helpers, and Tabitha Ellinger were hiding something from Adeline, but there was no point in harboring hurt feelings over the lonely stretch she'd survived.

Several hundred stories in these parts could be told about what was worse than loneliness. Adeline decided she would wait patiently for whatever timing Bernard and Yarico had in mind.

In October, there was talk at the Medical Supply and talk coming from across the street at the Bullock Hotel that the French Legation—untended entirely for a half year—was going to be visited by its new owner, a Father Jean-Marie Odin from Galveston who planned to start a Catholic school on the property. One Sunday afternoon, when the sky and temperature collaborated to make the dirt street where Adeline lived look as charming as an artist's sketch, two coaches came rumbling along Pecan in tandem. They slowed down in front of the Harper cabin and came to a stop. Then one went on to the east end of the street and out of sight toward the path winding up to the Legation.

Adeline had just come in from her porch, and the turning of coach wheels made her stop to look back out through her window. The driver was a man she'd never seen, but the gentleman getting out of the coach was unmistakably Bernard. He was not wearing his usual uniform of plain brown pants and matching tailored jacket. He had on gray trousers and a coat with longer tails and, when he turned to set the carriage door more widely open, she saw that his shirt was white silk, and he was smiling at whoever sat inside. Adeline knew it would be Yarico stepping out, but it was going on two years since she had seen her, and having thought during some of that time that the woman could be dead, Adeline found her hands trembling and her breathing uncertain.

The next person emerging from the coach was not Yarico. It was a sturdy little girl of about a year and a half. It was Yarico's shawl, and then Yarico's familar arms holding the child out, so that the little girl could be taken up by Bernard's strong brown hands and held to his side.

Adeline's hands rose slowly to her cheeks. Her mouth opened. The child had sandy braids and sandy curls and skin the color of a doe. Her face was a duplicate of Yarico's, only no laughter in Texas had ever been so lacking in restraint. The tiny girl was giggling to be in Bernard's arms, but she could not have been his child. Adeline dabbed at her eyes with the edge of her sleeve. She felt rage, but also jubilation. There was only one sandy-haired man that could have fathered such a child, and the shocked woman comprehended instantly that the subject would have been rejected long ago as anything Yarico would ever speak of.

When they came up on the porch, Adeline already held open the door, and after a long embrace, it was not so easy for the two women to speak to each other as both might have hoped. Bernard excused himself to go talk to the coachman about their travel plans, and Adeline listened to Yarico explain what they had packed up for, why they had left Bastrop, and come down this way before saying goodbye. They watched the little girl—Adelphine—toddle on the dirt floor of her cabin and reach immediately for a book lying out on the edge of her bed. Adeline went to get a wooden spoon and a bright cup for the girl to play with, and she listened to Yarico—now Madame Giroux—talk about the family's intentions.

"The New Orleans papers have ads about Cincinatti, and Bernard knows some people who moved up there. There are places where clothes are designed like Paris fashions and made to order or sent out to mercantiles all up and down the Mississippi, and Bernard's father was a tailor, so he's been around patterns and measuring tape as much as I have, and we think—the cold will be new to both of us—but—"

Adeline and she were both watching the little girl dip the wooden spoon into the cup and then put it to her lips. She was utterly preoccupied in her play, and she didn't seem to mind whether the conversation grew animated or fell away altogether. Adeline pulled up a stool close to the child and held out her hand, so that Adelphine dipped into the cup again and ladled some air into her open palm. What a bright angel Yarico must have been, Adeline was thinking, to come into her own mother's life at this exuberant age. But she knew that Bernard and Yarico were caught up in the swirl of their plans, and she didn't want parting to make her forget any of the essential exchanges bound to mark the day.

"You need this, I'm sure," she said, going to a box on her shelf, where she'd kept the freedom letter. "I was glad to hear Bernard say the count would be some help seeing you off at New Orleans. In some parts of the city, there could be trouble without anyone to vouch for you."

"I only half believe it will work out anyway," Yarico admitted. She took the envelope from Adeline, but it was hard for the two to look directly at each other. So much had happened to each woman in the interval of separation.

"Will she chew on a tortilla? There's a lady who comes by Bullock's twice a week, and I just bought some yesterday."

"It won't make the mess cornbread would. She's just now eating anything you give her." There was something else Yarico was about to say, but she seemed to hesitate. "The innkeeper allows you to shop at the bakery in his lobby?"

"Hard feelings drift away after a while."

"Sometimes they do," Yarico agreed. "And nothing you ever did—or our darling Maggie— was in the wrong anyhow—"

"Yarico—" She knew there was no time to grieve together for Aunt Maggie. "There's something else I have that's yours." Behind Adeline's bed was a deeper compartment, and from it she took a bundle of the bank notes Mr. Gibbs had sent. "It was kept for us all in the Macon Bank, and it finally reached me the same day I got your envelope and Bernard's little note." Yarico gazed at the stack of bills, and she shook her head.

"This should be for your academy—or female college by now—"

"It's your part—what my mama wanted—"

"Adeline, I don't even know if I'll be drawing a breath by this time next month. Bernard says it's easy to travel, but he's talking about in the company of a French count, and he's only known routes from the Antilles and New Orleans to here. He doesn't know what can happen to people moving along on their own. Even this envelope won't mean a thing to certain folks, even a book full of documents proving you are who you say— that you're free—People chained to wagons were once free. We're all free until someone sends you down a river in the wrong direction—"

"I think Bernard can—"

"Men are like that—even the good ones—They think they can see what's right and make it happen according an idea of what should be—"

"Sometimes it does work out—"

"And sometimes a crazy woman with a gun will load a dozen chained people together on a raft, watch them go down into the Brazos to drown in the muddy current—"

"That's not going to—"

"Adeline, I can't let that happen, I couldn't live with it." Then Yarico stopped and she looked to the floor where Adelphine was playing cheerfully and shredding a tortilla. "That's why I want you to keep this good money that was your mama's. That's why I'm begging you—to keep Adelphine for a year or two. Bernard loves her—he'll be a good father, but not if we never make it to Cincinnati, not if somebody with a gun sells us away in three different directions—I'm begging you, if you can take her for—just until we get there, get settled and let you know—"

"Yarico—"

"Look at her, Adeline— how my precious baby looks. With Bernard and me three towns away from New Orleans, up the Mississippi, well before we get to the free states, there could be men along those parts with nothing but profit scales for souls—"

The little girl stood up and was walking to Adeline to hand her the spoon or the piece of flat bread, whichever she wanted.

"Father Odin will let us travel with his people back down to Galveston. We'll be safe to that point, and then he'll send Brother Beaulieu out to see us off at the dock. He says it's all in God's hands, but I can't abide my little girl suffering some of what this world twists into—"

"Of course I'll keep her, Yarico. I'll move on back into Bastrop for a while, if need be, where there's better safety from the raids, or go stay with the Robertsons for a spell or the Ellingers—There are good folks here. And I don't know why, but this wild place has grown inside me—not like a child, I don't know how you—but this place is turning into my home, and look what a beautiful girl you have, born right here in Texas!"

"You keep this money for her until we send word we made it and have somewhere to live—"

"Here—"Adeline gave her half of the bills back.

"Only what I can fit in my bonnet," she said. "No one will bother a lady like you, when you come with the rest—and our beautiful daughter!" Yarico's breath caught then as if she had forgotten something, and she reached into a bundle of the child's blankets and clothes. "I had all the time in the world to work on it. I'm keeping the other half with me." The embroidered pillow cover was sky blue with a white star in the middle. Along the wide edges were every color for wildflowers and pines, redbuds and rocky trails. "You tell her the words that go with it all. We'll sew the sides together next time."

She stooped down to give Adelphine a little kiss on the forehead. Bernard had come to the door, his eyes glistening as if he'd knew how the talk had gone and how it needed to end, or the temporary separation could never take place.

"I love you, most wonderful daughters—I don't care what color the world declares itself to prefer or what borders it chops itself into!" Yarico was talking to Adlephine, and she was talking to Adeline at the same time.

"We'll see you in Cincinnati in another autumn or two—"

"Maybe Louisville—the cities up north are all so much closer together! The Ellingers and the doctor are fixtures in these parts. Just don't you two move around any farther than that!"

"You and Bernard will be fine—you'll make it just fine—"Adeline gave Bernard a hug and a kiss on the cheek, and she didn't think she could hug Yarico again without breaking into sobs, and little Adelphine was intently watching the departure, so it was a moment when all the adults maintained their composure.

After the coach rolled away, Adeline took the little girl for a walk down Pecan Street. She carried her part way and sometimes let her walk to chase and pick up red bud leaves that were tumbling noisily at their feet. When they visited a while with the Robertsons, Yarico's two daughters returned to the cabin, and Adeline found a key with a note. It was from Brother Beaulieu, saying that though the big house would be locked, the two should come up to the Legation kitchen whenever they wanted to enjoy the view and give the cooking hearth some use.

For weeks after the departure of Yarico and Bernard, Adeline went up to the legation grounds regularly, even though the chores of motherhood left no time for other diversions. Regardless of the calendar, whenever the sky turned bright blue and a cool sun seemed to shine from both below and overhead, she and the child rode up. The two watched the last strands of geese fly south in November from the French hill, and they spent a day there in December after the hotel cannon went off—when it had only been some of President Houston's men attempting unsuccessfully to carry away from Austin the country's archives. Adeline and the child went to the hill on Christmas Day to enjoy the bright windows on either side of the *cuisine* and to try some Dutch oven crumb cake that Adeline felt was not nearly as tasty as what she had once enjoyed on the Brazos trail.

But Adelphine was speaking a few words, and by the end of winter, the nineteen-year-old guardian felt her birthday could be merrily celebrated with the syllables and two word sentences the little girl was giving out freely. And spring, solemn as so many of its days were, would never be as somber as it had been in the past.

There were doves gurgling in the eaves of the Legation stables in late March, and at first Adeline did not hear the rumble of a single carriage winding its way up the hill. She and Adelphine had just finished a late breakfast of biscuits and molasses, and the two were walking around to the front of the main house to the broad porch, where Yarico's little girl liked to slide in her stocking feet. It was Brother Beaulieu, coming to make some plans for the school Father Odin would soon start. He was with his assistants who measured for bench space and did their figuring for tables and looked for the best spots for an herb garden and vegetable rows. They finished their note-taking by midday and were going to try to make it back to Bastrop before dusk. Adeline listened to their discussions with remembrance of the gardens at Sweet Pine.

"My mother's family was from France," Adeline said to the jovial young priest. "She would always insist on having herbs."

"We travel far in this world," he sighed. "And do you dream to go home?"

"My own home was Georgia," Adeline explained, "but everybody I ever loved came here to Texas to live—" She stopped for a moment. "Or to become immortal—"

"*Non, c'est vrai,* we cannot always see what is in God's eyes for our destiny—"

"I'm here to stay, it turns out." They had come around to the front of the house, where Brother Beaulieu was locking up, and Adeline looked from the western end of the sprawling porch out to the edge of the perfect hill.

"You have the gift of motherhood, I see," the man went on, "The child of your friend is as cheerful as a bird—you will have your own some day—"

"I'm already Adelphine's *belle-mère,*" said Adeline, and she laughed when the girl came to her saying *Maman.* "Belle-Mère," she repeated gently. "Next fall or the next, we will go take you to your *Maman* in the north. And your Papa." And then she said suddenly to the robed man who was about to bid adieu, "I'm going to be a doctor!"

"Ah!" he laughed with her, "So much imagination—"

"I'm going to cure positively everything ill in this world for as far as I can see!"

"Well, God's peace be with you, Mademoiselle Adeline—you are talking of divine dreams." They were moving off toward their wagon. "Such dreams, no mortal will be seeing on earth—"

"Then, I'll live trying!" she called out as much to the sky as to the fellows packed up and about to go. "I know some perfectly beautiful people who lived trying!"

Adelphine ran in delight at the sight of her belle-mère's sudden dance, and when the startled doves in the eaves of the main house began to flap their wings and warble, the young woman scooped up the little girl and kissed her fingers. They waved to the kindly travelers on their way down the hill, on their way off to the trail along the banks of the Colorado. She would think about them later on in the evening, wondering about how much closer they might be by the next day or the next to the turn for Gonzalez, and about how many doves a divine imagination would send to mark the souls who had lived trying in the meadows of Goliad.

Afterword

At Goliad in 1961, I stood next to my grandfather at the Texas monument to Colonel Fannin's volunteers. After honorable surrender during the revolution, they had expected deportation, but the unarmed hundreds were instead marched out on Palm Sunday in 1836 and shot. A newcomer to Houston, I had only a fourth-grader's grasp of the tangle leading to Texas independence—glorious death at the Alamo, glorious victory at San Jacinto. Little explanation accompanied the textbook's bleak illustration of Goliad. My grandfather visiting from Georgia, Joseph Huddleston Hunt, wanted to see the less visited memorial—"Papa had an uncle."

So my mother drove the station wagon southwest one hot summer day.

In my memory, Grandpa Hunt is standing before the engraved granite panels. The list is long. He finds the letters he is looking for—*Francis M. Hunt.* That great-uncle's cousin must be there, too, but the name doesn't come to mind. I still remember my grandfather's expression.

I would want him to know what has since been discovered:

That our family's uncle was only twenty-one when he stepped forward at a candlelight rally in Macon, Georgia; that joining Francis on the thousand mile trek to Goliad, Texas in 1835 was his first cousin Joseph A. Stovall. A hundred other young men from nearby Georgia towns also joined up, as well as scores along the way from Alabama to New Orleans. Thomas G. Weeks—a *lad from Mississippi* as accounts refer to him— joined the same company, probably in New Orleans, and was surely treated as kin, the *Weeks* surname being tied in family records to Hunts as well as Stovalls.

I want my grandfather to know what I learned from muster rolls, first-hand narratives, and military accounts— that through a string of improbable shifts in rank our Uncle Francis "commanded the company in the fight," and that before their capture the entire Georgia Battalion made a valiant effort to rescue families at a church in Refugio.

All this is true.

The fictional characters *Francis* and *Joseph* appear only as I visualize them, since no family records shed light on individual traits. My early shift of the name Thomas to *Malacai*, his Macon ties, special bond with Francis, and Irish heritage all arose from my imagination. I stayed steadfast, though, to facts I could gather about events of the Texas

Revolution in which Georgia's Francis M. Hunt and Joseph A. Stovall, and in which young Thomas G. Weeks played a role.

The undisputed Fannin scholar Harbert Davenport notes that First Sergeant Hunt "almost certainly died at Goliad," along with Stovall and 340 other men. In the slow accounting for losses, the death of Weeks at the Battle of Refugio was eventually verified. Joseph's father, George Stovall, spent many years making sure his son, nephew, and others lost in the battalion were compensated as promised for their service to Texas. There can be no doubting the grief of so many families—from Macon, Georgia to the Mississippi River— who never saw their loved ones again.

Also factual in this novel are changes portrayed as unfolding in 1839, when the log cabin town Waterloo was rechristened Austin to be the republic's capital. The French Legation would be under construction soon to house a grand foreign dignitary. Grand Texas men stood ready to govern.

How women of the early 1800's survived such upheaval can only be imagined, their struggles often traced solely through documents drawn up by fathers and husbands. The stories of the oppressed were seldom noted at all.

My mother's passion for history helped drive me back over one hundred and seventy-five years to speak for some of Goliad's forgotten. And she has forgiven me for plucking family names as I wrote, without regard for their true genealogical placement—the names *Harper*, *Phinazee*, *Judkins*, and *Mulholland*. There was an *Adeline* Weeks who married into the Hunt family, and a younger sister of Francis also named *Adeline*.

I want my mother, Josephine Hunt Mills, to know that I wish I had inherited her greater patience for unearthing detail. But her distress, at finding the words…*slave girl named Yarrico*…among our earlier ancestral records, was never lost on me.

I hope two lines from Thomas Gray's "Elegy Written in a Country Churchyard" will stay etched in my memory—

Perhaps in this neglected spot is laid
Some heart once pregnant with celestial fire.

Sources

Books and Periodicals

Barker, Nancy Nichols (translated and edited). *The French Legation in Texas, Volume 1: Recognition, Rupture, and Reconciliation*. Austin: Texas State Historical Association 1971.

Bradle, William R. *Goliad, the Other Alamo*. Gretna, Louisiana: Pelican Publishing Company, 2007.

Crawford, Ann Fears, and Crystal Sasse Ragsdale. *Texas Women: Frontier to Future*. Austin, Texas: State House Press, 1998.

Elrod, Frary. *Historical Notes on Jackson County, Georgia*. Jefferson, GA: Frary Elrod, 1967.

Fehrenbach, T.R. *Lone Star: A History of Texas and the Texans*. New York: MacMillan Publishing Co., Inc., 1968.

Lamar, Howard R. *Texas Crossings: The Lone Star State and the American Far West, 1836—1986*. Austin: The University of Texas Press, 1991.

Mills, Betty J. *Calico Chronicle: Texas Women and Their Fashions, 1830-1910*. Lubbock, Texas: Texas Tech Press, 1985.

Monroe County Historical Society. *Monroe County, Georgia: A History*. Forsyth, GA: Monroe County Historical Society, Inc., 1979.

Roell, Craig H. *Remember Goliad! A History of La Bahia*. Austin: Texas State Historical Association, 1994.

Scarborough, Jewel Davis. "The Georgia Battalion in the Texas Revolution: A Critical Study." *The Southwestern Historical Quarterly*, Vol. 63, No.4 (Apr., 1960). Austin: Texas State Historical Association, pp.511-532.

White, Rev. George, M.A. *Historical Collectibles of Georgia*. New York: Pudney & Russell, Publishers, 1854. (Reprinted in Danielsville, Georgia: Heritage Papers, 1968.)

Online Sources

Davenport, Harbert. Notes from an Unfinished Study of Fannin and His Men, 1936. H. David Maxey, Editor. Online. http://tsaonline.207.200.58.4/supsites/fannin

Handbook of Texas Online. http://www.tsha.utexas.edu/handbook/online/articles

Index to Military Rolls of the Republic of Texas 1835-1845. http://tshaonline.org/supsites/military

Lively, Garland. Colonel James Walker Fannin's Regiment at Goliad. http://militaryhistoryonline.com

Macon Telegraph Archive (Georgia Historical newspapers: Macon Telegraph). Online. http://www.galileo.usg.edu

Presidio La Bahia. Online. http://presidiolabahia.org

Sons of Dewitt Colony. Online. http://tamu.edu/ccbn/dewitt/dewitt.htm

About the Author

Judith Austin Mills characterizes her fiction as "stories about coming of age in the most macho state in the union—not any easy undertaking for any young woman or man." Having moved from up north to Texas when she was ten, she still misses the catharsis of distinct seasonal change.

In 1989 at the University of Texas, the author earned her M.A. in English with a concentration in creative writing. Stories from her collection *Lost Autumn Blues* and poems from *Accidental Joy* have appeared in literary magazines. *Tripping Home* won the Writers' League of Texas mainstream novel competition in 2001.

Judith Austin Mills is an Adjunct Associate Professor of English for Austin Community College, and takes on French students when the opportunity arises. She has been teaching and writing in central Texas for over thirty years.

She says that her wonderful sons and their families do not seem to mind that she is "still, always, coming of age."

CPSIA information can be obtained at www.ICGtesting.com
Printed in the USA
244614LV00002B/3/P